Y0-CRV-405

Reel Men at War

Masculinity and the American War Film

Ralph Donald and Karen MacDonald

THE SCARECROW PRESS, INC.
Lanham • Toronto • Plymouth, UK
2011

Published by Scarecrow Press, Inc.
A wholly owned subsidiary of The Rowman & Littlefield Publishing Group, Inc.
4501 Forbes Boulevard, Suite 200, Lanham, Maryland 20706
http://www.scarecrowpress.com

Estover Road, Plymouth PL6 7PY, United Kingdom

British Library Cataloguing in Publication Information Available

Library of Congress Cataloging-in-Publication Data

Donald, Ralph.
Reel men at war : masculinity and the American war film / Ralph Donald and Karen MacDonald.
p. cm.
Includes bibliographical references and index.
ISBN 978-0-8108-8114-3 (hardback : alk. paper) — ISBN 978-0-8108-8115-0 (ebook)
1. Men in motion pictures. 2. Masculinity in motion pictures. 3. War films—United States—History and criticism. 4. Men—Socialization. I. MacDonald, Karen, 1947- II. Title.
PN1995.9.M46D64 2011
791.43'6521—dc22 2010049137

∞™ The paper used in this publication meets the minimum requirements of American National Standard for Information Sciences—Permanence of Paper for Printed Library Materials, ANSI/NISO Z39.48-1992.

Printed in the United States of America

Contents

Introduction

Reel Men at War: Masculinity and the American War Film considers the influence that war films may have on the socialization of young males in American society. Boys and young men in the United States spend a considerable amount of time watching and learning codes of manly behaviors, values, and taboos from war films, other genres of action films, and television. These impressions of manhood are later reinforced when they play video games on their laptops or handheld devices. And since Hollywood never wastes a popular story on a single medium, these scenarios are often repurposed in other media as remakes or sequels of earlier war films, graphic novels, comic books, television series, and even earlier video games. Sadly, American boys often spend more time exposed to fictional media models of manliness on the screen and television than they spend with their fathers. In prior generations, fathers and father-figure relatives were the most influential examples to imitate as boys transitioned from the nurturing world of women to the often insensitive, taciturn, and stoic world of rough, tough, manly men. So, if media have become the principal teacher of socialization, what are boys learning? What Hollywood-created manly behaviors, values, and taboos do war films reinforce? Conversely, what unmanly behaviors do war films clearly prohibit?

The scope of this book cannot hope to cover the waterfront of multimedia impressions from which the modern youngster can choose. Instead, it concentrates on the eldest and most established of these influential media—the motion picture—viewed today on the big screen as well as on television and portable personal media. As previously stated, since successful stories are routinely recycled among various contemporary media, studying a historically great source of initial stories is as good a place as any to begin an investigation. *Reel Men at War* presents an analysis and critique of screenplay texts, acting, directing emphasis, and visual communication of this phenomenon as found in 143 representative American war films and other motion pictures made for television.

Also, in notes found at the end of each chapter, coauthor Dr. Karen MacDonald comments on these films' treatment of the psychology of war and warriors, as displayed in the behaviors and statements of the characters that American war film writers and producers have chosen as principal and supporting actors. It is our hope that these psychological perspectives will put fictional movie characters and their behaviors into a more realistic human perspective. This is especially relevant today, as reports estimate that between 20 and 35 percent of the men and women returning home from combat in Iraq and Afghanistan are burdened with some form of post-traumatic stress disorder (PTSD). In her clinical psychology practice outside St. Louis, Missouri, Dr. MacDonald herself has had many such returning warriors as patients. Does such a high incidence of PTSD among returning soldiers have anything to do with the huge disparity between the romantic, tidier versions of wartime killing and dying these men learned from movies they viewed growing up? Establishing cause and effect relationships is far beyond the scope of this or any single book, but it is hoped that the many myths about manhood and manly behaviors discussed here—how a real man should act when dropped into the middle of a war, or afterward—contribute to the body of knowledge of lasting impressions on young people created by modern media, and, in particular, the American motion picture.

Chapter 1 discusses the process boys experience when they leave behind their childhood world of women and enter the male milieu and how this is mirrored in films depicting military training. Chapter 2 considers the controlling influence of sports on males—as a peacetime alternate to manly combat—and the widespread use of sports metaphors in the rhetoric of both war *and* sports (war is not a game, remember?). Chapter 3 outlines male stereotypes in war films, both the positive, as specific, mediated models to emulate, and negative ones, as examples to avoid. Since the pecking order for manly men begins at the top, we have included chapter 4, which considers how men in war either learn to be leaders (a manly virtue), or fail to lead, providing yet another negative, unmanly, "mamby-pamby" example for young audiences to avoid. In chapter 5, we inquire among various war film notions of courage and bravery and their reality in fact. Finally, in chapter 6, we examine why some men admire and even love war and revisit the sporting concept of winning. In this chapter, we consider how these films reinforce the value of winning so highly that characters wantonly sacrifice themselves and other soldiers' lives to obtain it and avoid at all costs donning the mantle of "loser."

This book is dedicated to young American soldiers, who, under the influence of all these impressions, confidently march off to fame, glory, and "the win" but never return.

> If you are able,
> save for them a place
> inside of you
> and save one backward glance
> when you are leaving
> for the places they
> no longer go.
> Be not ashamed to say
> you loved them,
> though you may
> or may not have always.
> Take what they have left
> and what they have taught you
> with their dying
> and keep it with your own.
> And in that time
> when men decide and feel safe
> to call the war insane,
> take one moment to embrace
> those gentle heroes
> you left behind.
> —Maj. Michael Davis O'Donnell
> 1 January 1970
> Dak To, Vietnam
> Shown onscreen at the end of the film *Hamburger Hill*, 1987

1

Men and War

In *Sands of Iwo Jima* (1949), sensitive, intellectual Pfc. Peter Conway (John Agar) bitterly recalls his marine colonel father's constant disapproval, revealing his jealousy over the colonel's admiration of macho Sgt. Stryker (John Wayne), by saying the following:

> I embarrassed my father. I wasn't tough enough for him—too soft. "No guts" was the phrase he used. Now Stryker: He's the type of man my father wanted me to be . . . yeah. I bet [his father and Stryker] got along just fine together. Both of them with ramrods strapped on their backs. (*Sands of Iwo Jima*, 1949)

During the process in which American boys become socialized, parents, relatives, and peers present them with hundreds of admonitions describing what they must *not* become. Unfortunately, most of these caveats, delivered by well-meaning family and friends, amount to simplistic, anxiety-arousing prohibitions against any behavior deemed vaguely stereotypical of the female or homosexual male (Hacker, 1957; Hartley, 1976; Sabo and Runfola, 1980). In addition, because maleness is sometimes a difficult concept to define in positive terms, and because men themselves are often closedmouthed about it, youngsters are mostly left to their own devices to sort out manly from unmanly behaviors to imitate or avoid.

Increasingly in our television-centered culture, boys find that male heroes they view in popular media are among the most accessible, frequently encountered, and publicly approved models for manly socialization. It is a sad but true commentary on our society that these youngsters often spend more time per week observing these mediated men than with their own fathers (Barcus, 1983).[1]

Stryker (John Wayne) arguing with Conway (John Agar) in *Sands of Iwo Jima. Republic / Photofest © Republic*

Besides what they find in other forms of electronic media, there are many kinds of simplistic examples of stereotypical manhood readily available to children and young adults in films and television series. They range from such older, basic types, as the heroes found in westerns and war pictures, to newer permutations of the warrior, as found in *Superman*, *Batman*, *G.I. Joe*, *Teenage Mutant Ninja Turtles*, and *Mighty Morphin Power Rangers* series. Regardless of which heroes and eras are viewed by young boys, it is in portrayals of the warrior that the aggressive qualities of the male of the species are the least inhibited by the moderating influences of civilization.

COWBOY HEROES

For males over the age of fifty, the cowboy was one of their earliest media models: "The rugged 'he-man,' strong, resilient, resourceful, capable of coping with overwhelming odds" (Balswick and Peek, 1976, 55). Thus, many of these boys' first adult male role-play simulations consisted of imitating some six-gun-toting symbol of tall, tanned, squint-eyed, understated masculinity. It's no wonder, then, that this first generation of young men to display the results of television's power to create such models (those raised on Hopalong Cassidy, the Lone Ranger, and the Cisco Kid) would dream dreams of frontier life similar to Philip Caputo in his book and subsequent television miniseries *A Rumor of War* (1980):

> (voice-over) I would dream of that savage, heroic time [the old west] and wish I had lived then, before America became a land of salesmen and shopping centers. This is what I wanted, to find in a commonplace world a chance to live heroically. Having known nothing but security, comfort, and peace, I hungered for danger, challenges, and violence. (*A Rumor of War*, 1980)

As both Ronald Carpenter (1990) and Julian Smith (1975) suggest, war films are really just westerns taking place in locations other than the west. After all, in addition to their many similarities, both are essentially melodramatic portrayals of men performing virile, courageous deeds designed to protect helpless civilians from some variety of aggressor. Whether these villains are land-hungry cattle barons, rampaging Indians, rapacious Nazis, sly Japanese, stealthy Viet Cong, or religious fanatics on a jihad, the positive outcomes (good triumphs over evil) are mostly the same. Thus, regardless of the passage of time and the popularity of genres, sooner or later, most young boys' playacting evolves in sophistication into their twentieth-century equivalent—the soldier in modern warfare.

WAR IS A GENDERING ACTIVITY

Susan Jeffords (1989), Eric Leed (1989), and others maintain that war itself is a gendering activity—one of the few remaining true male experiences in our society. Even the increasingly androgynous U.S. armed forces' liberalizing of regulations regarding sexual equality still stops short of complete parity in many combat assignments. Female casualty lists in Iraq and Afghanistan notwithstanding, American paternalistic culture seems to stop short of equality when deciding whether to order women into harm's way. When women do fight in American war pictures, Hollywood often shows it to be an aberration. For example, in *A Guy Named Joe* (1943), Irene Dunne flies a dangerous bombing mission, but she does so without permission, and only with guardian angel pilot Spencer Tracy to assist her with the manlier, tactical aspects of the attack.

In *This Land Is Mine* (1943) and *Edge of Darkness* (1943), Ann Sheridan and Maureen O'Hara end up fighting back against the Nazis, but only as civilians attempting to resist an occupying force, not as soldiers. In more recent years, such heroines as Meg Ryan in *Courage under Fire* (1996) and Demi Moore in *G.I. Jane* (1997) have pushed the envelope in war films, but the plots of these films center on their femininity, gender discrimination in the military, and their fellow male soldiers' disdain for women accompanying them into (ironically) no man's land: the battlefield. Although science fiction often manages to equally place women in harm's way and even promotes them to positions of command, it is in a future that has yet to arrive. Assisting with the notion that women can fight was the Vietnam War allegory *Aliens* (1986), in which "civilian" Sigourney Weaver finds herself propelled into deadly personal combat with an army of monsters, but only after most of the platoon of mostly male marines sent for that purpose have been killed.

In the majority of American war films, the purpose of including women in screenplays has historically been to provide men with love interests and add a little sex appeal to the film. In short, whenever the men who decide which screenplays get the "green light" for production can help it, war is reserved—or at least preferred—for males, for whom the quality of belligerent performance is also clearly prescribed:

> Be a man. Conceptions of masculinity vary among different American groups, but there is a core that is common to most: courage, endurance, and toughness; lack of squeamishness when confronted with shocking or distasteful stimuli; avoidance of display of weakness in general; reticence about emotional or idealistic matters; and sexual competency. (Stouffer, 1976)

INITIATION RITES

In most human cultures, there exists some rite of passage from the relatively sexless existence of a child into the adult community of their gender. In this transition, each has its own set of rituals. In Homo sapiens' history, becoming a male adult in the tribe usually meant achieving the status of a warrior, since most of that same skill set was also needed for the hunt to provide meat for their families.

In examining the ceremonial rubrics of several native cultures, Arnold van Gennep (1960) describes a process that bears close resemblance to the basic training regimen practiced by the U.S. armed forces: As occurs today in military basic training, candidates for male adulthood in the tribe are first separated from their families, most specifically from the world of women, which has been their childhood milieu. More often than not, initiates are also stripped of the clothing they previously wore in favor of whatever is the male "uniform." Their hair is shaved and/or rearranged in the fashion of adult males. They then undergo a period of instruction in the behaviors and responsibilities of adult males/warriors. Suzanne Frayser (1985) notes that in these rituals, initiates must passively and submissively obey all orders given to them by their male elders, as befits their status as neophytes. Lionel Tiger (1970) adds that like the rigors of basic training, this process often includes ordeals and tests of manly endurance. Finally, having successfully completed their tribal version of basic training, the initiates "graduate" and take their places as full-fledged adult males.

BASIC TRAINING AS AN INITIATION RITE

We can view this ancient ritual of becoming a man/warrior in such films featuring U.S. armed forces basic training as *Jarhead* (2005), *Full Metal Jacket* (1987), *The Boys in Company C* (1978), *Take the High Ground* (1953), *Tribes* (1970), and *The D.I.* (1959). Recruits are separated from their families and local subcultures and removed to training depots that are usually located in some other part of the country. For the majority of their training, recruits are deprived of female interaction, and they have no direct contact with their families. In *Full Metal Jacket*, the marine drill instructor sometimes refers to the girls the recruits left behind in less-than-complimentary terms (e.g., "Mary Jane Rotten-Crotch") or insists that in bed in the barracks each night, recruits sleep beside their rifles, their *new* sweethearts, replacing their high school girlfriends in their beds, if not in their minds.

In the six aforementioned films, recruits are deprived of their former hairstyles and given the standard GI butch haircut, the military equivalent of primitive head-shaving. Then, recruits' clothes are exchanged for uniforms and standard issue marine/army gear. Finally, some recruits, when on their first leave, add to military training's similarity with primitive male initiations by getting their first tattoos ("USMC," or a likeness of the mascot [eagle, etc.] or symbol of their unit, or a slogan, such as "Semper Fi" [always faithful, the U.S. Marine motto]), further identifying themselves as new members of the warrior class.

THE "OTHER": WOMEN OR HOMOSEXUALS

At the outset of training, recruits are not automatically given the status of soldiers. That they must earn. Initially, they are labeled everything from "maggots" to "boots," "trainees," or "young people"—never full-fledged marines or soldiers. Sometimes recruits are not initially permitted the status of males. Often derisively called "girls" or "ladies" by their drill instructors (D.I.s), recruits must earn their manhood by successfully completing their training. Failure to achieve the benchmarks of their training is labeled as a weakness, associated with the female, asserting the importance of measuring up to the standards that society demands of a male. In *The D.I.*, when Sgt. Moore (Jack Webb) reports to his company commander that a certain recruit continuously "fouls up" in his training, the captain insists on harsh treatment. Webb is hesitant to push the youngster too far too fast, but the commander orders immediate action. Otherwise, he threatens to personally assist Webb in "cutting the lace off his panties."

When D.I.s tire of using the female as the designated undesired mode of living and behaving, another way to denigrate a recruit's manhood is to implicitly or explicitly imply that the soldier is homosexual. In *Full Metal Jacket*, when a recruit says that he hails from Texas, the D.I., Gunnery Sgt. Hartman (R. Lee Ermey), retorts with the following verbal assault:

> HARTMAN: Holy dog shit! Texas! Only steers and queers come from Texas, Private "Cowboy," and you don't much look like a steer to me, so that kinda narrows it down. Do you suck dicks?
>
> COWBOY: Sir, no sir!
>
> HARTMAN: Are you a peter pumper?
>
> COWBOY: Sir, no sir!
>
> HARTMAN: I bet you're the kinda guy who would fuck a person in the ass and not even have the goddamn common courtesy to give him a reach-around! I'll be watchin' you.

Sgt. Hartman (Lee Ermey) yells at Pvt. Pyle (Vincent D'Onofrio), while Pvt. Joker (Matthew Modine) stands stiffly behind them at attention in Kubrick's *Full Metal Jacket*. *Warner Bros. / Photofest © Warner Bros.*

Of course, in air force basic training, one of your authors heard the same speech from a training instructor, directed at a basic trainee from California. Instead of "steers and queers," he used "fruits and nuts."

Similarly, in *Jarhead*, an equally odious D.I., Sgt. Fitch (Scott MacDonald), insultingly introduces himself to Pvt. Anthony Swofford (Jake Gyllenhaal):

> FITCH: Are you eyeballin' me with those baby blues? (then he shouts) Are you?
>
> SWOFFORD: (also shouting) Sir, no sir!
>
> FITCH: Are you in love with me, Swofford?
>
> SWOFFORD: Sir, no sir!
>
> FITCH: Oh, you don't think I look good in my uniform, Swofford?
>
> SWOFFORD: Sir, the drill instructor looks fabulous in his uniform, sir!
>
> FITCH: So you're gay then, and you love me, huh?
>
> SWOFFORD: Sir, I'm not gay, sir!
>
> FITCH: Do you have a girlfriend, Swofford?
>
> SWOFFORD: Sir, yes sir!
>
> FITCH: Guess again, motherfucker. Jody's bangin' her right now ["Jody" is a nickname for men who do not serve in the military, but instead stay home and poach GI's wives and girlfriends]. Get on your face and give me twenty-five for every time she gets fucked this month. Down on your face!
>
> SWOFFORD: (in a voice-over, as he does push-ups on the floor) It was shortly after meeting Drill Instructor Fitch that I realized that joining the U.S. Marine Corps might have been a bad decision.

Later, after Swofford fouls up a blackboard assignment for Sgt. Fitch, the exasperated D.I. asks him what he's doing in the Marine Corps. Swofford replies, "I got lost on the way to college, sir!" Fitch responds by pushing Swofford's face into the blackboard. (See chapter 3 for a more detailed discussion of the gay soldier.)

Despite all these indignities, like their tribal forefathers, recruits are required to passively submit to all orders, no matter how disgusting, demeaning, or physically taxing they may be. For example, in *Full Metal Jacket*, a feebleminded recruit, whom the D.I. has used as the platoon scapegoat, is punished for failure to properly respond to drill commands. He must march behind the others with his thumb in his mouth, his trousers around his ankles, his hat turned backward (long before the time when askew hats became cool), and his rifle carried on his shoulder upside down.

Finally, suitably reconditioned and instructed in proper soldierly (read manly) behavior, the initiates, now full-fledged marines or soldiers, graduate and are transferred to advanced training.

A RELATIONAL CONSTRUCT

Of all of these initiatory customs and practices, probably the most significant is the physical and symbolic separation of neophyte soldiers from the world of women. But unlike Tiger's description of native tribesmen, Americans begin to establish this separation long before boys reach puberty. Michael Kimmel (1987) writes that gender is a relational construct, providing males with the opposite sex as a basis of negative comparison and a clearly drawn, inferior role model. Practically from the time an American boy-child is old enough to understand English, he hears that "Big boys don't cry—only girls do," or other such behavioral prohibitions as "Don't play with dolls, dolls are for girls" and "That scraped knee doesn't really hurt a little man like you, does it?"

In various ways, boys are shown multiple examples of the so-called inferior, flawed, incomplete variety of human being they must avoid becoming at all costs: a female. By the time most boys reach manhood, having experienced so much negative comparison with girls, it's not surprising that they have become convinced that females must be grossly inferior to males—at least with respect to traditionally male activities and behaviors. And by systematically excluding females from their sports teams, clubs, the "old boy" network in business, top government positions, and combat roles in the military (at least until quite recently), a self-fulfilling set of male role definitions has become firmly imbedded in American history and culture. And needless to say, in Hollywood, a patriarchy if there ever was one, nearly every film is written and produced from the paternalistic perspective, as if there is no other possible point of view on the planet.

THE QUIET MAN

There are many subtle and not-so-subtle characteristics that lead to the construction of war films' stereotype of the male American warrior: Chief among them is that he should be a man of few words but mighty deeds, capable of stoically enduring privations and pain and able to pass the constant "stress test" that war imposes on them.

In *Marine Raiders* (1944), one's branch of service imposes even more emotional and personal restraint than other services. Marines, apparently, are expected to be unsentimental killing machines, at least to hear them tell it. When Lt. Ellen Foster (Ruth Hussey) confides in Maj. Steve Lockhart (Pat

O'Brien) that she admires him as a close friend, Lockhart reminds her that he shouldn't really react in a sentimental manner, because marines don't get sentimental. But then, he lowers his guard just a little and tells her that he considers her and her new husband, Lockhart's best friend, Capt. Dan Craig (Robert Ryan), his family. Later, when Craig asks his wife if he looks okay in his uniform, Craig maintains his manly marine esprit de corps:

> CRAIG: How do I look?
>
> ELLEN: Beautiful.
>
> CRAIG: (embarrassed) A marine can't look beautiful.

Warren Farrell (1976) explains that since showing emotion is considered a feminine characteristic (and therefore should be avoided), men must cultivate the image of quiet, strong dignity. In this stereotype, in contrast with the much more verbose female, the fewer words said by a man the better. John Wayne typifies the foolish extremes to which this philosophy can be extended in *She Wore a Yellow Ribbon* (1949), when he gives this admonition to young second lieutenant Pennell (Harry Carey Jr.): "Never apologize, mister: It's a sign 'a weakness."

In most war films, high value is set on the ability of a soldier to watch one's comrades die around him and yet appear not to weaken and suffer no apparent emotional trauma. In the 1958 Korean war film *The Hunters*, fighter group commander Richard Egan proudly dubs pilot Maj. Cleve Saville (Robert Mitchum) the "Iceman," because of Saville's ability to perform his lethal tasks in an emotionless manner, as if oblivious to the danger, suffering, and death around him.[2] One of your authors vividly remembers a time shortly after that film's release (well before the establishment of bike paths on roadways), when, threading his bicycle through fast city traffic, he adopted the persona of the "Iceman," imitating Saville's fearless cool to overcome his anxiety about the cars whizzing past him just a few feet away.

Decades later, demonstrating that wars and warriors may adjust to the times, but bedrock criteria for American maleness remain intact, in *Top Gun* (1986), Lt. Tom Kazanski (Val Kilmer), the most coolly efficient, emotionless pilot attending the navy's fighter weapons school, adopts the call sign "Iceman." Perhaps *Top Gun* screenwriters Jim Cash and Jack Epps Jr. also once fearlessly rode *their* bikes through heavy traffic.

TABOOS ABOUT GRIPING

Although it's acceptable for soldiers to gripe about the lack of warm food and decent lodging, an unspoken line is often drawn between

Korean War fighter pilot Robert Mitchum is the "Iceman" in *The Hunters. 20th Century Fox / Photofest © 20th Century Fox*

complaints that are acceptable and those that are taboo. In *Platoon* (1986), and only in his letters to his grandmother, Pvt. Chris Taylor (Charlie Sheen) admits that the physical and emotional stress of fighting the jungle war in Vietnam may be too much for him to endure. Around his comrades-in-arms, Chris quietly goes about his job without complaint.

> (voice-over) Somebody once wrote Hell is the impossibility of reason. That's what this place feels like. I hate it already, and it's only been a week. Some goddamn week, Grandma. The hardest thing I think I've ever done is to go on point, three times this week—I don't even know what I'm doing. A gook could be standing three feet in front of me and I wouldn't know it, I'm so tired. We get up at five a.m., hump all day, camp around four or five p.m., dig a foxhole, eat, then put out an all-night ambush or a three-man listening post in the jungle. It's scary 'cause nobody tells me how to do anything 'cause I'm new, and nobody cares about the new guys—they don't even want to know your name. The unwritten rule is a new guy's life isn't worth as much, 'cause he hasn't put his time in yet—and they say if you're gonna get killed in the 'Nam, it's better to get it in the first few weeks, the logic being [that] you don't suffer that much. I can believe that. . . . If you're lucky, you get to stay in the perimeter at night, and then you pull a three-hour

> guard shift, so maybe you sleep three/four hours a night, but you don't really sleep. . . . I don't think I can keep this up for a year, Grandma—I think I've made a big mistake coming here.

In *Platoon*, not even painful wounds are an acceptable reason for movie soldiers to resort to venting their emotions. After a firefight, a tough-as-nails sergeant confronts a soldier screaming in pain from a wound: "Shut up, shut up! Take the pain," he orders. Intimidated by the sergeant, the wounded soldier obeys. Leed (1989) characterizes this self-destructive self-delusion, saying, "Men become what they are, realizing a masculine character and a strength through what they lose rather than what they gain." In *The Longest Day* (1962), Lt. Col. Benjamin Vandervoort (John Wayne, of course) suffers a compound fracture of the lower leg in a parachute drop, but does he complain? No. Not the Duke! It doesn't even slow him down much. At first, he hobbles along, using a rifle as a cane. Later, Wayne orders the medic who is examining his injury to relace his combat boot tightly, so he can continue the march along with his men. In *They Were Expendable* (1945), Lt. J. G. Rusty Ryan (Wayne again) becomes indignant when he is ordered to stand down from a torpedo boat mission because of an injury to his hand. Despite being told that if he doesn't rest and submit to antibiotic therapy he may lose his entire arm to gangrene, Wayne impatiently orders the doctor to "slap a little iodine on it and let me get outta here."

THE IMMORTAL LEGION

Chaim Shatan (1989) writes that military trainers "fear that the death of a beloved buddy will render a soldier useless for combat. So military basic training often fosters 'antigrief' by maintaining that if killed, soldiers are absorbed into the ultimate men's club, the corporate entity of the 'immortal legion'" (121). Countless war films reinforce this myth, implying in subtle or not-too-subtle ways how unprofessional, unsoldierly, and detrimental to the mission it is to unduly mourn the death of a comrade. For example, in *Top Gun*, the death of Lt. J. G. Nick "Goose" Bradshaw, Lt. Pete "Maverick" Mitchell's (Tom Cruise) back seat electronic warfare officer and best friend, causes Maverick to lose his courage and self-confidence, rendering him unable to engage an enemy in aerial combat. The latter part of this film centers on Maverick's refusal to follow the soldier's manly code to "shake it off" and return to his former aggressive, confident self. Only when he is willing to "let Goose go" (read this as putting away his friend's death and not thinking about it anymore) can Maverick fight again.[3]

In war, succinctly described by gunboat captain Collins (Richard Crenna) in *The Sand Pebbles* (1966) as the "give and take of death," there must be some kind of carrot dangled in front of warriors to compensate for the possibility of having to give up their lives. Immortality is the great reward, allowing soldiers a form of denial of both the finality of death and the grief they suffer when a buddy dies. Also, every human being, regardless of gender, has the need to belong to the group. If the group is the biggest, toughest, most exclusive men's club in existence, such membership mitigates against the reality of death and grief. On graduation day in *Full Metal Jacket*, the D.I., Gunnery Sgt. Hartman (R. Lee Ermey) explains it in the following way:

> Today you people are no longer maggots. Today you are marines. You're part of a brotherhood. From now on until the day you die, wherever you are, every marine is your brother. Most of you will go to Vietnam; some of you will not come back. But always remember this: Marines die, that's what we're here for. But the Marine Corps lives forever, and that means *you* live forever.

To reinforce this concept, at the end of dozens of World War II combat films, a crescendo of patriotic music would rise, and appropriate narration—perhaps a quote from FDR, Winston Churchill, or Gen. George Marshall—would reinforce the gratitude of a nation for those who gave their lives. Then the happy, smiling faces of the heroes who died during the film would be superimposed, ghost-like, over the picture on the screen. Thus, as newly minted members of the immortal legion, the dead live on in glory, and there's not a dry eye in the audience.

MILITARIZED GRIEF AND VENGEANCE

But there still must be some manly outlet for emotion over lost buddies. Shatan (1989) describes the "authorized" manly alternative for grief and remorse at the death of a comrade as "militarized grief and ceremonial vengeance" (137–38). These behaviors can take the form of either dedicating the next enemy kill to the deceased comrade or generally raising the level of mayhem in subsequent skirmishes. Examples of both are found in *Destination Tokyo* (1943). An older, much-revered submarine crewmember named Mike is stabbed in the back by a downed Japanese pilot he attempted to rescue from icy waters. Witnessing this treachery, one of Mike's shipmates repeatedly and redundantly pounds the enemy pilot down into the water with slugs from a fifty-millimeter machine gun. Later, the crew paints the dedication, "For Mike, torpedoman first class, R.I.P.," on the next torpedo the sub fires at a Japanese ship. In the 1940's, skillful screenwriters routinely sanitized and thereby legitimized such vengeful enthusiasm; however, in recent years, Vietnam and Gulf War films have provided audiences with more starkly realistic portrayals of soldierly revenge. In such films as *Platoon* and the 1980 television miniseries *A Rumor of War*, soldiers and marines commit My Lai-like atrocities (killing innocent civilians) to extract vengeance for the loss of their buddies. Following the manly credo, Hollywood's contemporary soldiers prefer committing war crimes to sitting down and having a good cry over a lost friend.

But the practice of militarized, manly grief and vengeance is not new to war or war films from any era. Although the World War I film *Flyboys* was produced in 2006, the picture was based on a real group of U.S. airmen who flew for France in the Lafayette Esquadrille. In one scene, pilots are drinking and singing one evening following a mission in which three young members of the squadron lost their lives. Blaine Rawlings (James Franco), who had just returned from that mission, shouts in dismay at the veteran pilots, scolding them for not honoring his dead comrades. The veteran flying ace, Reed Cassidy (Martin Henderson), explains why the men appear to ignore the ultimate sacrifice their comrades made in the sky that day:

> This is how we honor them. It's how we've always honored them. None of us knows how much time we have left, and we can't waste it, sitting around, grieving over things we can't change. You can either join in, or you can go up to your room and cry like a little baby.

In one speech, Cassidy makes clear the only manly option for these brave flyers: Set aside the normal grief cycle, and, instead, drink and sing happy songs and pretend that their friends didn't die this day. And, of course, there's no crying in aerial warfare. At least Cassidy didn't say, "and cry like a woman."

Cassidy is a veteran who has lost all his friends in the war. Rather than cry, Cassidy, a three-time ace, flies extra, solo missions to exact revenge against the German flyers who shot down his buddies. Cassidy is especially interested in one particularly ruthless German pilot, the Black Falcon, who flies a black (they're usually red) tri-winged Fokker. The Falcon does not follow the usual code of chivalry practiced by pilots on both sides. We see this as he shoots down a French fighter plane, follows it down to the ground, and sees that the pilot has managed a crash landing and has safely gotten out of his aircraft. The Falcon dives and strafes the helpless pilot, killing him. At the end of the film, Cassidy dies in aerial combat against the Black Falcon, but Rawlings follows the Falcon to his aerodrome, challenges him to single combat, and eventually, with the help of his fellow flyboys, completes the ceremonial revenge for Cassidy by shooting down the malevolent German ace. For these men, revenge is not sweet, but somewhat satisfying. If manliness doesn't allow you to cry for your friends, you are permitted, at least, to coolly exact bloody revenge on their assassin.

In chapter 2, we will examine and explore an important U.S. cultural institution—organized team sports—and its relationship in war films to concepts of masculinity.

NOTES

1. Social learning theorists say that masculinity is learned directly through a system of positive reinforcement (rewards) and negative reinforcement (punishment). Indirectly masculinity is said to be learned through observation and modeling (imitation). Young males are reinforced for their maleness through gender-specific play, clothing, games, and even chores. In families where the father takes on the stereotype of the male, the son who does not emulate these behaviors often feels like he does not fit into the masculine role that his father has modeled. Pfc. Peter Conway appears to reflect these feelings of inadequacy and a lack of approval from his father.

2. The concept of the "Iceman" portrayed by Robert Mitchum in *The Hunters* and adopted by Lt. Tom Kazanski (Val Kilmer) in *Top Gun* reflects characteristics of a dissociative state in which the environment is blocked from their attention. The American Psychiatric Association's (APA) *Diagnostic and Statistical Manual of Mental Disorders* (1994) describes this blockage as the "protective activation" of an altered state of consciousness created to protect the individual from the overwhelming psychological trauma of the violence and trauma surrounding them. The audience views these characters as seemingly emotionless, when, in fact, they are merely internalizing their feelings. The continued barrage of pain and despair of war around them makes it too difficult for them to bear, so they have learned to create these altered states of consciousness as a protective barrier (519–33).

3. Maverick's need to "let Goose go" reflects the final of the eight stages of Elisabeth Kübler-Ross's grief cycle (1969). Of these eight stages, the five most often discussed in popular literature are denial, anger, bargaining, depression, and acceptance. The denial stage involves refusing to accept the inevitability and finality of death. The anger stage comes about as pent-up emotions erupt, and it is followed by the bargaining stage, which includes searching for a way to cheat death. The depression stage sets on as the inevitability and finality of death sinks in, and the acceptance stage entails finding the way to move forward. This final step in the grief process is the stage that military trainers teach soldiers to adopt. Soldiers are to skip the earlier stages of grief, accept the inevitable, and move on. In this stoic acknowledgment, soldiers can better focus on the belligerent job at hand. The key for military trainers is to teach soldiers how to move quickly to the acceptance stage. They stress how counterproductive the earlier stages can be to the task at hand—completing the mission, which, after all, is a soldier's "job." In effect, doing one's job refocuses men's minds away from grief, giving them at least a temporary sense of purpose. Training subtly emphasizes that a soldier must take on a hard shell, jump to the acceptance phase, and get on with the task at hand. The stages of denial, anger, and depression often haunt soldiers later—off the battlefield—when they are finally allowed to deal with their friends' deaths.

2

"Go, Team, Go!" Manliness and War/Sports Metaphors

Lucy Komisar (1976) writes:

> Little boys learn the connection between violence and manhood very early in life. Fathers indulge in mock prize fights and wrestling matches with eight year olds. Boys play cowboys and Indians with guns and bows and arrows proffered by their elders. They are gangsters or soldiers interchangeably—the lack of difference between the two is more evident to them than to their parents. They are encouraged to "fight back," and bloodied noses and black eyes become trophies of their pint-sized virility. (202)

This may help explain why war films are so popular among American boys: They're bred for it. After all, as Molly Merryman writes, the process of proving oneself a man is a "culturally prescribed construction in which men are willing to risk danger, dismemberment, and [even] death to prove their masculinity" (Creedon, 2004, 1). This also sounds a little like high school football, doesn't it? Samuel Stouffer (1976) writes, "In contemporary society, most men rarely have the opportunity to demonstrate their ability to be a 'real man.' Perhaps the only situation [that] allows them to express this aspect of their manhood is war" (179). But if, at the time, there is no war handy for American males to prove themselves, such sports as football, baseball, hockey, or boxing provide an alternative social venue, complete with the opportunity for selfless team effort, the thrill of conquest, and the chance for glory as well as physical injury—everything needed to transform a boy into a full-fledged warrior-man in our culture. Pam Creedon argues that in the absence of war, to provide an opportunity to achieve this manly status, American boys and men turn to sports like football for a substitute for armed conquest (2004, 1–14).

WAR METAPHORS IN SPORTS

Thomas Fiddick (1989) reminds us that the "use of helmets and such terms as 'the bomb' and 'the blitz' make football ideal as a central metaphor of war" (80). Paul Hoch's (1980) observations at a football game are similarly enlightening:

> The movements of the cheerleaders are plugged into what amounts to a set of stereotyped military drill routines. Watching the drum majorettes and girls' drill teams prancing about in their mini-skirted mock uniforms, in precision goose steps, it is hard to miss the symbolism of sexuality subordinated to militarism, sexuality used as an advertisement for militarism, and frustrated sexuality used as a spur to militarism and machismo generally. (10)

Sally Jenkins describes football in terms a general would understand, saying it involves "bullying the opposition into retreat with mob action" (Creedon, 8). There's even a sports pecking order for comparing football and baseball to war. George Carlin (1997) put it this way, in comparing and contrasting the two sports:

> Baseball and football are the two most popular spectator sports in this country. And as such, it seems they ought to be able to tell us something about ourselves and our values. . . . The objectives of the two games are completely different: In football, the object is for the quarterback, also known as the "field general," to be on target with an aerial assault, riddling the defense by hitting his receivers with deadly accuracy, in spite of the blitz, even if he has to use the shotgun. With short, bullet passes and long bombs, he marches his troops into enemy territory, balancing his aerial assault with a sustained ground attack that punches holes in the forward wall of the enemy's defensive line. In baseball, the object is to go home! And be safe! (52–53)

So an American boy can prove his readiness for manhood in two ways: If there's a war handy, he can become a soldier and fight bravely for his team. In the absence of a war, he can become an athlete and fight bravely for his team. For young men who have witnessed hegemonic masculinity and the subjugation and trivialization of women throughout childhood and adolescence, the continuation of their male-favored status in life is at risk unless they can find some way to "step up to the plate," "take their cuts," and "win one for the Gipper." The alternative, according to the mainstream voices of American male socialization, is too dreadful to consider: life as, at best, a sissified, unmanly male, or at worst, in the eyes of the male social establishment, a homosexual, on a par only with females, themselves considered by men as the inferior sex. The social construction by which boys become men, then, seems pretty simple, no more sophisticated than Native American rituals involving being hung by their pectorals to prove the endurance of a brave or counting coup in combat against an enemy of the tribe.

A "DIRTY DOZEN": KEY SPORTS/WAR VALUES

In modern America, the war film often blurs the distinction between war making and sports participation, effectively melding these two contemporary constructions of masculinity. One hand washes the other in the sports-war continuum: Sports metaphors inserted into the vocabulary used by soldiers in war serve to prime the combatants to remember the behavior expected of them during their boyhood socialization on the playing fields. They are cued to recall that above all, doing their duty for the team is required, and that they must complete all other requirements necessary to "get the job done." In Friedrich Nietzsche's *Thus Spake Zarathustra* (1999), the title character is asked about his happiness: "Do I then strive after happiness? I strive after my work" (194). Man *is* what he does: his *work*. So, as we heard in Carlin's recitation of football combat jargon, Hollywood's combat films stress most of the key values leading to success in sports, and, not surprisingly, vice-versa. The following are, excuse the pun, a "dirty dozen" of them:

1. Call the plays right.
2. Come in for the big win: Take your turn at bat.
3. Do a good job of work.
4. Appreciate your interference, don't hog all the glory, and sacrifice for the team.
5. "Americans love a winner and will not tolerate a loser."
6. Be bold, never too cautious.
7. To win, don't always face the enemy head-on: Be both strong and clever.
8. Females are losers.
9. Know the score.
10. The enemy team is inferior, so learn how to exploit their weaknesses.
11. Don't give up: Fight on to victory.
12. You gotta play hurt.

Analyzing the texts of a representative sample (see the filmography) of combat films produced in the United States, mostly from the 1940s to the present, half contain one or more sports metaphors that directly refer back to the conduct of war. Consider the following examples.

1. Call the Plays Right

In *Flying Leathernecks* (1951), in Col. Kirby's last advice to "Griff," the officer who will replace him as squadron commander, he predicts that Griff will do the same things all commanders do every night, "wondering . . . whether you called every shot right today." Later, Griff responds, "I'll try to call the plays right: I had a good coach." The theme of this movie is also important, because it portrays the conflict between the macho, "tough guy" approach to the job of warrior versus the humanistic man who tries to keep his sense of humanity amid the chaos of war. Along with many post–World War II films, and, as we'll discuss later in this book in more detail in the chapter on masculinity and the burden of command, *Flying Leathernecks* preaches that to be an effective commander in wartime, a man must at least outwardly appear quite heartless, covering up his emotions.

John Wayne, as Maj. Kirby, is tasked with toughening up his squadron's executive officer Griff, played by Robert Ryan, for the rigors of command (read toughening as improving Griff's manliness and thus his professionalism). Griff, among many similar characters often found in post–World War II films, doesn't come naturally to the tough guy persona that Kirby embodies: Griff finds it impossible to order men to their deaths while maintaining a cool isolation from the close friendships that develop between fellow pilots in his unit. Apparently, he should be taking behavioral notes from phlegmatic, calculating football coaches or baseball managers, who plan and execute their operations like spiders weaving their webs.

Likewise, as we learned in chapter 1, John Agar's Pfc. Conway, a member of Wayne's squad in *Sands of Iwo Jima* (1949), was also too much of a humanist—too sensitive and caring an individual—to be considered manly enough for war. At one point, Griff argues with Kirby, quoting John Donne, saying, "No man is an island." But the film demonstrates the opposite: that a squint-eyed, manly, frosty level of detachment (think Marlboro Man) is required to command a marine combat unit, or, for that matter, a football team. Like Griff, Conway eventually becomes a candidate for the Duke's Hollywood macho toughening-up course. And at the end, both Griff and Conway "get with the program"; adopt a tough, more detached John Wayne persona; "saddle up"; grit their teeth; and "lock and load" (choose your metaphor) to achieve victory.

The football metaphor of the quarterback calling the right plays is also found thirty-five years later in *Full Metal Jacket* (1987), when a newly minted squad leader, appropriately named "Cowboy," gets in an argument with an overly aggressive marine nicknamed "Animal Mother." Cowboy orders his squad to pull out, leaving two marines behind wounded and probably dead: "Back off, Mother," Cowboy shouts. "I'm calling the plays. I say we're pulling out."

Similarly, a submarine captain in *Up Periscope* (1959) is concerned about a difficult command decision he made on his last patrol. His judgment may have assured that the sub would not be detected and sunk by Japanese destroyers, but it may have cost a wounded sailor his life. Wrestling with the same humanism versus macho detachment issue as Griff in *Flying Leathernecks*, the captain asks his executive officer, "If you had been in my shoes and you were calling the signals, how would you have played it?" The honest exec says frankly that he would have done things differently. But, the exec adds, playing things according to the navy book (read playbook) is why they made him captain.

2. Come in for the Big Win: Take Your Turn at Bat

In *Full Metal Jacket*, a cartoonish, gung-ho marine colonel is outraged by Pvt. Joker's wearing of the peace symbol on his fatigue jacket while his helmet is decorated with the words "Born to kill." Joker tries to explain this contradiction as the "duality of man, sir, the Jungian thing." But the colonel, who sounds and acts more like a football coach than a battalion commander, is having none of this ambiguity, which he considers wishy-washy: "How about getting with the program?" barks the officer. "Why don't you jump on the team and come on in for the big win. . . . It's a hardball world, son. We've gotta try to keep our heads until the peace craze blows over."[1]

In *American Guerilla in the Philippines* (1950), Ensign Palmer spends two years organizing Filipino and U.S. guerilla actions against the Japanese. A U.S. submarine has just arrived full of supplies, guns, and ammunition. Palmer knows that Gen. MacArthur's return to retake the Philippines is imminent, and it's time to go in for the big win: He contacts his people to spread the word that the "football has arrived and the game is on as scheduled."

Switching to baseball, the notion of having to step up to the plate to bat has a twofold meaning in both baseball and war. Batting is one of the most individualistic acts one does in this team sport, yet one's actions can sometimes be strictly for oneself, or in others, a pure sacrifice for the team. This notion occurs in some of the other sports metaphors. As in sports, the motion of "momentum," piling on success after success, is significant. The first time up to bat can set the tone for the rest of the game. This concept is not lost on Gen. Omar Bradley (Karl Malden) in *Patton* (1970). Bradley and his aide survey the aftermath of the American defeat in the battle for the Kasserine Pass in North Africa. Amid dead Americans lying all about and destroyed U.S. tanks and other vehicles, Bradley says, "For the American Army to take a licking like that the first time at bat against the Germans . . ." (he finishes his sentence with body language and shakes his head in disgust). For Bradley, the U.S. Army has struck out, and the momentum of the "game" has shifted to the Germans.

In *The Enemy Below* (1957), an American destroyer captain is still recovering from injuries suffered during his last mission, but he must step up to the plate again (read "play hurt") to command his vessel in a desperate, deadly game of cat and mouse with an enemy submarine. The ship's doctor describes this dilemma to the ship's executive officer, saying, "He's weak as a kitten. A man that gets his ship torpedoed and spends twenty-five days on a raft in the North Atlantic oughtn't have to hit the ball again with only a few weeks in the hospital."

In the HBO Miniseries *Band of Brothers*, in an episode entitled "Carentan" (2002), one soldier's bazooka shot has just knocked out a German tank. Another soldier gleefully shouts, "You just hit a home run!" And in *The Big Red One* (1980), when the sergeant (Lee Marvin) orders one of his soldiers, Pvt. Kaiser (Perry Lang), to go on point (take over the duty of the forward man on his squad's combat patrol), the sarge barks, "Kaiser: It's your turn at bat."

In *Dr. Strangelove* (1964), a delusional Gen. Jack Ripper (Sterling Hayden) thinks there is a communist plot to disable his "precious bodily fluids." Ripper reasons that the only way to save the United States is to perpetrate a sneak attack on the Soviet Union. Since he commands a wing of B-52 bombers, he's capable of sidestepping the president's authority to order such an attack. Since only Ripper knows the code that will cause the bombers to cancel their attack and return to base, and since he plans to kill himself, he reasons that the president will be forced to order all U.S. units to attack the Soviet Union. This would save the United States from the expected Soviet nuclear assault in retaliation. Appropriately, the training exercise Ripper uses for this attack is called "Operation Dropkick." In American football, a dropkick is a surprise way to score a field goal when the opposing team is defending against another kind of play.

3. Do a Good Job of Work

An old adage—probably coined by a man—about the difference between the way men and women view themselves goes something like this: A woman is what she looks like, and a man is what he does. Fortunately for women, in modern times, new personal options have been added to the social construction of female identity that allow for additional, more substantial, ways to establish themselves. But for men, nothing much seems to have changed since the age of the Neanderthals:

Delusional General Ripper (Sterling Hayden), right, talks to Group Captain Mandrake (Peter Sellers) in *Dr. Strangelove. Photofest © Columbia Pictures*

Once boys become established as men, securing a job and succeeding at it, as Nietzsche might say, defines their potency. Both in sports and war, there is a job of work to be done. As discussed in chapter 1, Capt. Collins succinctly explains in *The Sand Pebbles* (1966) that a warrior's job of work is the "give and take of death." Men are uneasy unless they feel confident and competent in their jobs. Men out of work are more than financially challenged. Most go through periods of depression and great anxiety until they are once again employed. Men may not like it, but in war, Capt. Collins's definition becomes their job description, and most men are task oriented. Sports metaphors, those familiar terms from less chaotic times, help both to clarify the job at hand and remind soldiers of simpler days on the playing field.

Mixing baseball metaphors about their assigned jobs, the admiral (Charles Trowbridge) in *They Were Expendable* (1945), like a wise old baseball coach, explains to Cdr. Brickley (Robert Montgomery) why he can't permit the eager young skipper the opportunity to prove the effectiveness of his PT boats in action against a Japanese task force headed their way. The admiral explains, "Listen, son, you and I are professionals. If the manager says, 'sacrifice,' we lay down a bunt and let somebody else hit the home runs. . . . Our job is to lay down that sacrifice [fighting a delaying action against the Japanese in the Philippines]. That's what we're trained for, and that's what we'll do."

Conversely, many war movies demonstrate that the failure to conduct themselves in a professional manner can result in tragedy for the man or the mission. In *The Dirty Dozen* (1967), the dangerously unbalanced Pvt. Maggott precipitates a gun battle that results in the deaths of nearly everyone involved, when he kills a prostitute in the middle of a stealthy raid on a mansion in France used to entertain top German generals. In *Guadalcanal Diary* (1943), Pvt. Johnny "Chicken" Anderson (Richard Jaeckel) spots a dead Japanese officer and wants to snag the man's samurai sword as a souvenir. Chicken's sergeant orders him to leave souvenirs alone, because retrieving such items would expose him unnecessarily to enemy fire. Chicken later ignores his sergeant's advice and makes his way to the dead officer to retrieve the sword, but he is shot. In *Full Metal Jacket*, a sergeant who should have known better sees a bright-colored toy bunny in the wreckage of a burned-out building and decides to examine it. As he picks it up, the booby-trapped toy explodes, killing him. And in the Vietnam War drama *The Boys in Company C* (1978), a company of marines is ordered to lay flat on their stomachs, because there is a possibility of snipers just over the ridgeline. But one troop, a shutterbug, wants a picture for his scrapbook. Rising to his knees to get a good shot, he is picked off by a sniper.

Sometimes it's hard to differentiate between unprofessional behavior and Darwin Award stupidity. In *Jarhead* (2005), a story about the adventures of a squad of marines during Operation Desert Shield and Operation Desert Storm, there are many instances of unprofessional behaviors and their consequences. For example, one marine on sentry/lookout duty in Saudi Arabia on Christmas Eve is cooking sausages on a portable stove. He daydreams for a few moments, and while he is not paying attention, the stove sets a tent flap on fire, igniting three cases of aerial flares nearby. The resultant explosions turn the holiday night into a fireworks show, but result in major disciplinary action.

Earlier in the film, back in the United States, unprofessional behavior has a fatal result. In a live-fire exercise, trainees are crawling in the mud under a barbed wire enclosure while real machine gun rounds are fired over their heads. The purpose is to desensitize the men to acting in concert under fire, but one marine panics and starts to stand up. He is hit by the machine gun fire and dies instantly. Finally, toward the end of the film, an unstable young marine named Fowler comes across the body of an Iraqi soldier, who had burned to death. Fowler plays around stupidly with the corpse and makes jokes about it. Other rs, including their sergeant, object to this and take the body away from Fowler. Later, SSgt. Sykes (Jamie Foxx) tells Pvt. Swofford that the "army may pull this type of shit, but the marines don't. When we get back [to the rear], Fowler will be passin' out shit paper." This means that Fowler is too unprofessional (and probably mentally unbalanced) to trust in his current assignment as a marine rifleman and will be reassigned to supply duty behind the lines.

In *Full Metal Jacket*, we observe that the idea of doing a job of work even has shorthand: The sergeant assigns his men a risky plan of attack for the difficult objective facing them and then shouts, "Let's go. Let's get it done" (implying that "it" is their job of work). Most GIs excel in griping, and standard operating procedure for sergeants in World War II films is to let the men get it out of their systems en masse so they can get on with the business of killing. This is an analog to the football team that huddles together before the start of the game, arms extended into a pile of hands, followed by a huge shout of team unity. Such actions, on the football field and in the soldiers' huddle, serve dual purposes: a healthy release of emotion and a reminder to the men that their fears and worries—and enthusiasm for the task at hand—are shared.

So, Sgt. Kinnie (James Whitmore), the squad leader in William Wellman's *Battleground* (1949), and Sgt. Porter (Herbert Rudley) in *A Walk in the Sun* (1945) give their men the opportunity to complain about their difficult job as a group. After explaining to the men that they must once again risk their lives to achieve an ambiguous objective in a strange, unknown location, both sergeants bark, "It's a stinkin' situation, right?" And the men, in unison, shout, "Right!" Tension is relieved, and the men fatalistically proceed to complete their assigned job of work.

Some directors, especially ones like former World War I Lafayette Escadrille pilot Wellman, go out of their way to add incidents to their films that show the result of failure to do their job in a professional manner. Often in Wellman's films, the soldier who cuts and runs and won't listen to practical advice from their sergeant, or the humanistic soldier or flyer who fails to coldly kill and give no quarter often ends up paying for his lack of professionalism with his life.

4. Appreciate Your Interference, Don't Hog All the Glory, and Sacrifice for the Team

In war films, one of the most important connections made between combat and sports is the importance of teamwork, subordination of personal ambition, and sacrifice for the good of the team. The word *teamwork* is mentioned in some context in nearly every war film.

Among the American Volunteer Group (AVG) pilots in *Flying Tigers* (1942) is Woody (John Carroll), a lone wolf character who doesn't comprehend the importance of teamwork. After listening to Woody brag about his latest exploit in shooting down a Japanese plane, another pilot, Blackie (Edmund MacDonald), a normally quiet individual, finally blurts out, "How does it feel to be a one-man team? You aren't the first ball carrier that didn't appreciate his interference." But sacrifice for the sake of the team isn't in Woody's playbook. Since AVG pilots receive cash bonuses for each Japanese plane they shoot down, Woody is greedy. Blackie continues, saying, "Twice I've been on the trail of the Nakajima [Japanese aircraft] when you cut in for the kill—and the credit." Later, Woody finally learns—the hard way—the lesson repeated in so many war films: One must subordinate one's own needs and desires for the good of the team, or dire consequences occur.

Woody decides to go AWOL with a pretty nurse. Two other AVG pilots argue about who should fly a mission as Capt. Jim Gordon's (John Wayne) wingman in Woody's place. "Hap" (Paul Kelly) explains to "Alabama" (Gordon Jones) that he has considerable experience as Gordon's wingman and that he could serve as an offensive lineman to block opponents for Gordon, the running back. He states, "I know every one of his quirks, every one of his moves. We're a team, don't you understand? It's like he was the ball carrier and I was his interference." Hap flies the mission, but is shot down. Afterward, Woody, disgraced and repentant, finally takes one for the team: He redeems himself by replacing Gordon on a suicide mission.[2] If you asked Wellman, Woody was both a poor team player and unprofessional. Woody would have had the same problems if he had joined the Lafayette Escadrille.

Like Woody, in *They Were Expendable*, a feisty young PT boat commander named Rusty, this time played by John Wayne, decides he wants to transfer out. He wants to make a name for himself in the navy as an officer on a destroyer, so he's writing a letter to request a transfer. But Rusty's boss, Cdr. Brickley (Robert Montgomery), asks, "What are you aiming at, building a reputation or playing for the team?" That night, the men hear an announcement that Pearl Harbor has been bombed. Hearing this, Rusty crumples up the letter and, for the rest of the picture, unselfishly, if not a little petulantly, devotes himself to his "team," the PT squadron.

In *The War Lover* (1961), the colonel commanding a World War II bombing group in England has a problem pilot who intentionally disobeys orders meant for group safety during their daylight bombing raids over Germany. Despite the pilot's successes on these high-risk, lone wolf exploits, the colonel knows that in the long run, success requires a cooperative effort. So his briefing includes a few sports metaphors to remind the rest of the pilots to follow his game plan: "Remember," he says, gazing over toward his problem pilot, "no broken field running. This is a team effort."

And in *A Wing and a Prayer* (1944), a squadron commander chastises a pilot who becomes jealous of another pilot's recent celebrity and receiving the Navy Cross. "Remember," the commander says, "you're part of a team, and you'll play as the team plays."

Brick (Robert Montgomery), right, lectures Rusty (John Wayne) about teamwork in *They Were Expendable. MGM / Photofest © MGM*

In both sports and war, every team member knows he must subjugate his own wishes and desires to the final strategic goal. Typical of this ethic is a scene in *Task Force* (1949). Adm. Ames (Moroni Olson) and Cdr. Scott (Gary Cooper), his air operations officer, are sweating it out, waiting for word on how their aircrews are faring during the Battle of Midway. Scott is frustrated and hates having to stay behind and perform supervisory duties on the aircraft carrier. He wishes he was flying this crucial mission, leading his young pilots on an attack against Japanese aircraft carriers. The admiral reminds Scott, "You think things would be different if you were up there? Nobody's the whole team, Scotty. It takes the whole navy to make up a team. I'm bettin' on the boys that are carrying the ball."

In *Run Silent, Run Deep* (1958), after a submarine captain dies on a mission, his replacement, who lost his own sub a year earlier, takes command. But the new captain's executive officer—and indeed the entire crew—expected their popular exec to be in line for the command. The exec is told that because of his experience, he is to play "backstop" to the skipper for this one mission. Eventually, as in most of these kinds of films, the exec overcomes his personal disappointment and selfish attitude. When the captain is injured, the exec fulfills his backstop role and successfully completes the mission, guaranteeing himself a command of his own in the future.

In the famous flag-backdropped address to his troops in the beginning of *Patton* (1970), Gen. Patton (George C. Scott) touches on a number of subjects, including the importance of teamwork, saying the following:

> Now an army is a team. It lives, eats, sleeps, fights as a team. This individuality stuff is a bunch of crap. The bilious bastards who wrote that stuff about individuality for the *Saturday Evening Post* don't know anything more about real battle than they do about fornicating.

Object lessons in suppressing individuality for the good of the team abound in most of these films. In *Eagle Squadron* (1942), a new pilot named Coe dies because he acted independently (Wellman's unprofessional behavior again) and didn't follow squadron procedure. Pilot Brewer mourns his friend's loss but is told that Coe would not have died if he had followed procedure and not gone off as a lone wolf to strafe a target of opportunity. There, without the protection of his team of wingmen, he was set upon by three German Messerschmitts who shot him down. Brewer learns through his grief that teamwork is the key to success in the Battle of Britain.

In *The Purple Heart* (1944), captured Doolittle raiders vote to include a Chinese man who gave them assistance as an honorary member of their bomber crew. Achieving team membership, or "making the team," like the letterman jacket, is an indicator of athletic success and manliness. After all, one cannot excel in sports if they're cut from the squad. So just "making the team" is a signifier of acceptance into the male fraternity. The captain (Dana Andrews) announces, "I'd have him on my team any time."

In *Black Hawk Down* (2001), army ranger captain Steele (Jason Isaacs) tries in his own way to maintain order and a sense of military decorum amid an often-chaotic army barracks scene in the airport they've occupied in Mogadishu, Somalia. Steele and his men find themselves deployed as part of the U.S. intervention against Somali warlords and their followers. Steele recognizes that the young army rangers he commands, with an average age of twenty, are full of "piss and vinegar," spoiling for a straight-up fight to assert their manhood, and that currently, they're bored. Since boredom makes for trouble, Steele's answer is discipline. The trouble is that Capt. Steele's attitude, and appearance more than anything, resembles the stereotype of a high school principal or gym coach. Remembering the negative male authority figures of their not-too-distant high school days, the young men don't value most of what Steele has to say. Faced with the news that a soldier under his command has had an epileptic seizure, Steele tells a young sergeant, "He'll be fine . . . but not in this army. He's outta the game, he's epileptic, goin' home."

Later, upset with the all-too-casual behavior of a Delta Force sergeant, Steele dresses down the man, saying, "You Delta boys are a bunch of undisciplined cowboys. Let me tell you something, sergeant, when we get on the five-yard line, you're gonna *need* my rangers. So y'all better learn to be team players." Then, a young Ranger imitates Steele's airs and Southern accent to entertain his buddies with a mocking imitation of Steele's use of thoughtless sports metaphors, relaying, Hey! We're at the ten-yard line here, men, understand? Can you count? One, two, ten! [Laughter] Where are my running backs? [The men shout their grunted shorthand for "hoorah." It sounds like "hoo-ah"!] Where *are* my running backs? [hoo-ah]. The captain catches the ranger doing this impersonation and warns him that if he ever catches the young man doing it again, "you'll be cleaning latrines with your tongue."

Capt. Steele believes that the use of sports metaphors is the best way to assert key points about teamwork to his young men and chastise the Delta sergeant. More than anything else, Steele fears that a mission could fail because not everyone is willing to play the game by the army's rules. But there are times when men—for many reasons—refuse to play the game.

Lone Wolf

A "lone wolf" scenario such as this occurs in Howard Hawks's *Air Force* (1943). It's the job of the man in charge, Capt. Quincannon (John Ridgely), of the B-17 bomber, the *Mary Ann*, to lecture a crewman named Winocki (John Garfield) who won't play ball. Because Winocki washed out of flight school and was reassigned the less glamorous job of machine gunner, he plans to quit the U.S. Army Air Corps in a few weeks when his enlistment runs out. In the meantime, he is displaying a considerable amount of antiteam attitude. Quincannon makes it clear to Winocki that sportslike teamwork is expected on the *Mary Ann*, regardless of the crewman's feelings, when he says, "You've played football, Winocki. You know how one man can gum up the whole works? You've got to play ball with us and play the game or I'll have to get rid of you." This is not exactly a Knute Rockne oration, but the point has been made: Play ball with us or you're cut from the team.

However, after witnessing the attack on Pearl Harbor, Winocki is a changed man. He rededicates himself to his job, but still exhibits occasional moments of nonteam-sanctioned individualism. On one occasion, the *Mary Ann* must set down on a remote landing strip. Japanese fifth columnists begin firing on the aircraft, and the captain orders everyone back inside the plane and plans to take off. But Winocki ignores the order and runs a few yards into the jungle, shooting angrily—and wildly—at the hidden Japanese. The crew chief (Harry Carey) forcibly restrains Winocki, knocking him unconscious and carrying him to the ship. Once airborne and Winocki awakens, the crew chief, who always wears a Cincinnati Reds baseball cap, explains his actions in strictly baseball terms, declaring, "They'd have cut you down before you got to first base."

5. "Americans Love a Winner and Will Not Tolerate a Loser"

This key sports value is a quote from that famous opening speech in *Patton*. It speaks directly to the socialization of American boys in sports, the importance of successful competition, and the winning imperative:

> PATTON: When you were kids, you all admired the champion marble shooter, the fastest runner, the big league ballplayers, the toughest boxer. Americans love a winner and *will not tolerate* a loser. Americans play to win all the time. I wouldn't give a hoot in hell for a man who lost and laughed. That's why Americans have never lost and *will never lose a war*, because the very thought of losing is *hateful* to Americans.

If one agrees that films are cultural artifacts and that popular feature films can be said to mirror contemporary societal mores and culture, consider the preceding speech in *Patton*, released in 1970, written by screenwriter Francis Ford Coppola at the height of the killing and American youth protests over the unwinnable war in Vietnam and the Johnson and Nixon administrations' unwillingness to leave Vietnam without some semblance of victory.

As previously mentioned, in *Sands of Iwo Jima*, Sgt. Stryker's job was to turn his squad into winners, but in these films, there seems to always be one soldier in a squad who poses a particularly thorny problem. One of Stryker's men is particularly clumsy and uncoordinated on the bayonet course. The platoon leader sarcastically asks the private what he thinks he's doing. "Running the bayonet course, sir," he replies. "Not in this league you're not," the lieutenant quips. In this officer's eyes, the marines are the big leagues, and the soldier's work on the bayonet course is definitely minor league material. Later, after other unsuccessful attempts to turn the marine into a winner, Stryker finds a way, using music, to teach the man some rhythm and improve his performance with the bayonet.

Boxing is a sport of both punches and counterpunches, and in the sports metaphor-rich *Air Force*, screenwriter Dudley Nichols manages to get in a few jabs: The crewmen of the *Mary Ann* talk with the commander of Hickam Field in Hawaii just after the Japanese attack. Commenting on the initial Japanese success, the commander makes it clear that the next time the result will be different, uttering resolutely, "They took the first round, but there'll be others." In *Thirty Seconds over Tokyo* (1944), the famous Doolittle raid is described as "Uncle Sam's first counterpunch in this war." Countless motion pictures describe their particular war mission as the one that will provide the "knockout punch" against the enemy.

6. Be Bold, Never Too Cautious

Again in *Patton*, the importance—at least to the great general—in moving boldly and decisively is brought home to viewers in the contrast between the studied caution of Gen. Lucien Truscott (John Doucette) and Gen. Omar Bradley (Karl Malden) versus Patton's own impulsiveness. Truscott warns his commander (George C. Scott) that he needs an extra day to prepare for the amphibious "end run" Patton requires in his quest to capture the city of Messina before British field marshall Montgomery. "You're too old an athlete to think that you can postpone a match that's already been scheduled," Patton says to Truscott. Responding in metaphor, Truscott verbalizes, "You're an old athlete yourself, sir. You know matches sometimes *are* postponed." Gen. Bradley chimes in, saying "George, if Lucien's right and we can't back him up by land, our end run could be a disaster." Later in the argument, Patton, irritated, gets formal with Truscott. "General," Patton says, "if your conscience will not permit you to conduct this operation, I'll relieve you and find somebody who can." Truscott replies, equally formal, "General, it's your privilege to relieve me any time you want to." Backing away from that kind of confrontation, Patton concludes this argument by reiterating, "Well, this match will not be postponed."

In the comedy-drama *Kelly's Heroes* (1970), ironically released the same year as *Patton*, there is an equally impulsive, Pattonlike general. Referring to the German general he faces on the battlefield as his "opposite number," he is listening in at his headquarters to radio traffic in what he assumes is a bold incursion across German lines by some units under his command. Although there is an incursion in progress, the attack is Kelly's (Clint Eastwood) caper, undertaken to steal millions in German gold bullion stashed in a bank behind German lines. The general (Carroll O'Connor) leans over the radio set as his orderly arrives with coffee on a tray. Enthusiastic as a football fan, the general dismisses the orderly, exclaiming, "Get the hell outta here, Barnes! We've got the game on!" Later, the general hears Sgt. Bellamy, an NCO in the engineers, radioing Kelly with the news that they can't speedily bridge a river because its bed is too soft. "So what do we do?" Bellamy asks. The general, by this time frothing at the mouth like a true football fanatic and hoping his team won't meekly fall back, shouts, "Go, team, go!"

George C. Scott as Patton speaks to troops at the beginning of the film. *20th Century Fox / Photofest © 20th Century Fox*

7. To Win, Don't Always Face the Enemy Head-On: Be Both Strong and Clever

Success in sports isn't always about brute strength: Manliness and winning not only require an encyclopedic knowledge of sports rules, but also of sports strategies and tactics. Winning in a sport such as football does not always mean a frontal attack, regardless of what the general in *Kelly's Heroes* thinks. The sports metaphors found in combat films provide instances that make this point. As he often does in *Patton*, the general explains to his chief of staff that understanding the history of warfare (reading the playbook) is essential to success in the present. To solve the post–D-Day problems the Allies are experiencing in French hedgerow country, the U.S. command should simply look to the past, but in sports terms. He explains, "What they should do now is pivot the way von Schlieffen planned it in the First World War. Then we might get a chance to do some real broken field running." Shortly after this scene, Gen. Bradley explains "Operation Cobra" to Patton, a plan similar to von Schlieffen's, which Bradley calls a "sweeping end run," which he has assigned to Patton's Third Army.

As introduced earlier, in *Thirty Seconds over Tokyo*, reciprocity in boxing is compared to the United States' bold strike on the Japanese mainland. With their fleet devastated from the attack on Pearl Harbor, rather than attempt an open attack, the Americans used another more clever approach. In the film, Lt. Col. Doolittle calls this daring raid "Uncle Sam's first counterpunch of the war." And like a short jab of a counterpunch, the Doolittle raid was meant to prevent the Japanese from rushing headlong across the Pacific and overrunning Hawaii. Instead, the unexpected counterpunch into the Japanese mainland made the enemy unsure about their own rear echelon. It took many months for the Japanese military, off balance from the Doolittle counterpunch, to discover that the Americans did not attack Japan from a secret base in "Shangri-La," somewhere in the Japanese rear. Rather, these light U.S. bombers flew off the deck of the aircraft carrier the U.S.S. *Hornet*.

Part of any sports strategy is to intimidate the opponent. Counterpunches may be one way, but another, with shouts and grimaced faces, as useful in football as in Indian attacks or a Confederate charge, is pure vocal intimidation. This kind of threatening is as old as Homo sapiens. Consider the first terrible oration Gunnery Sgt. Hartman (R. Lee Ermey) hollers at his men in *Full Metal Jacket*. He has just explained to his marines that he will be their drill instructor (DI) and that they will hate him. One recruit (Matthew Modine), whom Hartman soon nicknames Pvt. Joker, makes a poor attempt at humor. When Joker picks himself up off the floor following the DI's punch in the stomach, Hartman yells the following (the entire conversation is yelled at the tops of their voices):

> HARTMAN: Pvt. Joker, why did you join my beloved corps?
>
> JOKER: Sir, to kill, sir.
>
> HARTMAN: So you're a killer?
>
> JOKER: Sir, yes sir.
>
> HARTMAN: Lemme see your war face!
>
> JOKER: (confused) Sir?
>
> HARTMAN: You gotta war face? (He gives Joker an ugly face and screams) Aaaah! That's a war face. Now lemme see your war face.
>
> JOKER: (Grimaces as best he can and screams) Aaaah!
>
> HARTMAN: Bullshit. You didn't convince me. Lemme see your real war face.
>
> JOKER: (Screaming even louder and with more grimacing) Aaaah!
>
> HARTMAN: You don't scare me. Work on it.

With that, the DI walks away to terrorize someone else.[3]

8. Females Are Losers

To men, winning is everything, and in the socialization of American boys, winning at any cost might be acceptable under certain conditions. The way women and girls might approach winning might be less testosterone laden, more likely to be philosophical, perhaps adopting the notion that "it's not whether you win or lose, but how you play the game." But male norms classify losing as lacking sufficient male hormones or large, metal-hard genitalia, and it is classed as equal only to the female. When a boy plays golf with his dad, he's likely to hear someone in the group whose putt stops woefully short of the hole or his miss-hit drive that doesn't travel down the fairway as far as the ladies' tees referred to as an "Alice," a classic reference to the weakling younger sister in James Fenimore Cooper's *Last of the Mohicans*. In the case of a dribbled drive that does not travel past the ladies' tees, some macho golfers insist that the testosterone and anatomically challenged member of their group march up to the ladies' tee box and lower his trousers in penance.

Consider a recent Top-Flite golf ball campaign in which a mythical professional golfer is criticized by commentators for hitting a lay-up shot short of a greenside water hazard on a par-five hole rather than attempting to go for the green. The on-course commentator approaches the golfer, calls him a "Sally," and tells him to "man up" and go for the green with Top-Flite D2 golf balls, which presumably will assist the golfer in hitting the ball farther. Visiting Top-Flite's "Man Up" website, we found statements such as the following:

> Never lay up, never wuss out.
> We're for 'no guts, no glory' golf.
> Teaching the pin a lesson.
> Letting the big dog eat.
> And for those "wusses" [Top-Flite's euphemism for less manly, sissified golfers who don't go for it], we believe in calling them out—mercilessly. We can, because when it counts, we have the balls to go for it. (www.theballstogoforit.com/base.html)

In this interactive website, if the reader clicks on the link to "play it safe," a pink graphic opens, featuring a cute kitten and the words, "Aww, your 'play it safe' golf is a cute as a kitten. Once you're ready to man up and go for it with your golf game, click here." If the reader does "click here," the next screen says, "Now that we've ditched those mama's boys, here: Don't let the dimples fool ya: This'll put hair on your game's chest."

Encouraging golfers to adopt their macho ethic and avoid acting in any way like a female, Top-Flite's website has an "insults" link, which includes an announcer describing a "penalty" for a golfer who can't consistently hit his drives past the ladies' tees. He is forced to tee it up from the ladies' tees. Top-Flite admonishes the golfer to, "Man up and play golf, dude!" The announcer also says that a golfer who constantly lays up with a four-iron, rather than attack a green guarded by hazards with his driver, no longer can be a member of the (implied) men's club and must heretofore use pink tees and go by the name of "Irene." One link even shows a wussy golfer dressed in pink pedal pushers, standing in front of his pink golf cart and holding a club covered with a fuzzy animal head cover. You arrive at this link by clicking an icon shaped like a pink purse. Another link makes a not-too-veiled allusion to male impotence by describing any player who consistently can't get his ball up in the air as "projectile dysfunctional" (www.theballstogoforit.com).

It's not just in advertising campaigns where we find male–female comparisons in golf (What is it about golf, anyway? Is it because golf, compared to, say, full-contact football, is considered a sissy sport?) In the November 2010 issue of *Golf Digest*, there's a seemingly innocent article about the new driver golf clubs that guarantee that golfers will hit their drives farther, thus not being humiliated by their lack of manly ball-striking power in front of their peers. The article begins with a full-page cover picture, featuring a scrabbly bearded, manly looking golfer wearing a pink golf shirt, a pink golf glove, and a string of pearls. To top it off, he is in the process of applying lipstick. The headline on the page says, "Tired of Being the Short Hitter?" (Adler, 2010, 67). The article and picture clearly imply that if you purchase one of these new long drivers, you won't be the one who hits your tee shot embarrassingly short, as if struck by a woman.

Lucy Komisar (1976) writes the following:

> Boys are encouraged to roughhouse; girls are taught to be gentle ("ladylike"). Boys are expected to get into fights, but admonished not to hit girls. . . . Men are aggressive as they "take" or "make" women, showing their potency ("power") in their conquest. Women, on the other hand, "submit" and "surrender," allowing themselves to be "violated" or "possessed." (203)

Until recently, in sports, women were considered inferior weaklings, due to the strength differential between genders. It's a little-remembered fact that in the 1950s, there was a rule in schoolgirl basketball that prevented females from dribbling the ball all the way down the court, since it was assumed that girls were too weak to run that distance. Girls were limited to dribbling three steps before being required to stop (presumably to take a ladylike breath or two) and then pass off the ball.

In the testosterone-laden *Top Gun* (1986), the entire training setup at the Top Gun school for advanced aerial combat training is analogous to a men's athletic competition. Points are earned for victories over opponents in mock aerial dogfights. Scoring is announced with the regularity of a sports stadium PA system. Early in the competition, while examining the prize, the Top Gun trophy, one of the flyers, "Slider" (Rick Rossovich), whose call sign (nickname) is itself sexually suggestive, quips, "The second place trophy is down the hall, in the ladies' room."

As introduced in chapter 1, in *A Guy Named Joe* (1943), Pete (Spencer Tracy), the ghost of a World War II bomber pilot killed in action, becomes a guardian angel to another pilot, Ted (Van Johnson), helping him learn to fly and coaching him. Pete can't be heard or seen, but Ted senses Pete's instructions and reacts, as if by instinct. Eventually, Ted is successful and becomes an ace. Pete's former girlfriend, Dorinda, also a pilot, is not allowed into combat, despite her expert flying ability. She is permitted only to shuttle planes back and forth for the men.

As the screenplay would have it, Dorinda falls in love with Ted. She overhears plans for Ted to fly what may be a suicide mission to bomb a Japanese emplacement. Out of love for Ted, Dorinda (Irene Dunne) steals Ted's plane and flies the mission herself. Of course, this is 1943, so the ghostly Pete flies along as Dorinda's coach, coaching her like a modern day offensive coordinator radios plays into the quarterback's helmet. To bolster his ego, a male must feel superior to someone. The female provides this "inferior" comparison, and men would like to keep women in this role. That's one of the reasons at the beginning of the twentieth century that so many American men fought so hard against permitting women to vote. Let suffragette Alice Duer Miller's 1915 rejoinder to male arguments against the vote for women—complete with views on men and sports and war—to complete this section:

Why We Oppose Votes for Men

1. Because man's place is in the army.
2. Because no really manly man wants to settle any question otherwise than fighting about it.
3. Because if men should adopt peaceable methods, women will no longer look up to them.
4. Because men will lose their charm if they step out of their natural sphere and interest themselves in other matters than feats of arms, uniforms, and drums.
5. Because men are too emotional to vote. Their conduct at baseball games and political conventions shows this, while their innate tendency to appeal to force renders them particularly unfit for the task of government. (215)

9. Know the Score

This precept is voiced in many ways in these films, but it usually adds up to the importance of understanding what is going on, the big picture of what is at stake at any given time in a battle or war. Again, to be successful in sports or war, real men "know the score" and understand what's happening and what must be done at all times. For example, in *The Longest Day* (1962), Brig. Gen. Norman Cota's (Robert Mitchum) pep talk to his men, who are pinned down by murderous fire on Omaha Beach, urges them to attack, rather than just sit there, when he says, "I don't have to tell you men the score. You all know it. Only two kinds of men are going to stay on this beach, those who're already dead and those who're gonna die. Now get off your butts!"

In *Bombardier!* (1943), knowing the score for a tough bombing raid for which they have been training for months is a simple statement of fact: Training is over, and it's time to commence the football game. So right before the big raid, the group commander and his flyers gather in a football-like huddle, reach in, place their right hands on top of the commander's in the middle of the huddle, and listen to the commander's (read quarterback's) words: "Of course, you've all played football: This is the kickoff." Of course, the commander/quarterback was Pat O'Brien, who played the title character, a famous football coach in *Knute Rockne, All American* (1940). And it's interesting that he just automatically assumes that all his men have played football. No sissies, water boys, or chess club members on his team.

In these combat films, clever players sometimes use American sports terms to confuse the enemy. As previously introduced, in *American Guerilla in the Philippines*, the Japanese have been listening to U.S. radio transmissions. So Ensign Palmer uses mixed football and baseball terms in a coded report on enemy shipping: "Two large wolves on the twenty-yard line, going down center field." Likewise, in the Vietnam War film *Bat-21* (1988), air force officers use golf terms for map references to locate a downed flyer, because they were sure that the Viet Cong, who were listening, could not comprehend the game.

Sports terms in combat films are not limited to those tactical phrases used during a game, but they are also utilized to describe war as a kind of grand spectator sport. Manliness, it seems, extends beyond a player's active role in the game to the role of fan (short for fanatic, which best describes some men's allegiance to the games of their youth). As mentioned, the general in *Kelly's Heroes* listens to the "game" on his radio and acts every bit as fanatic as any twenty-first-century tailgate party participant. In *A Walk in the Sun* (1945), one soldier gripes about only being able to hear the fighting from the gully in which he and a sergeant are hiding, saying, "You get a grandstand seat, but we can't see nothing." In *One Minute to Zero* (1952), from high ground, U.S. soldiers watch as their own planes bomb a column of enemy tanks. "This time we got box seats," one officer says.

Sometimes, "knowing the score" simply means, in 1940s slang, "getting wise" to the situation. In *They Were Expendable*, a dying crewman's question to one of his shipmates is couched in a sports metaphor when he asks, "What's the score?" It's somewhat unclear for a moment whether he's asking his shipmates how well the squadron did on their mission (incredibly, two PT boats' torpedo attacks sank *both* a destroyer and a large cruiser), or whether he was asking if his wounds were mortal. But his honest shipmate's answer is, "Ninth inning, kid." The crewman turns his head and dies.

Likewise, in *Destination Tokyo* (1943), one crewman on board the submarine *Copperfin* hands an injured sailor a grease pencil so he can "keep score" on the bulkhead near where he's lying in his bunk. He's counting the number of times Japanese depth charges miss the sub.

10. The Enemy Team Is Inferior, So Learn How to Exploit Their Weaknesses

This characteristic, in which the enemy, the Indians (versus the cavalry), the villains (versus James Bond), and so forth, are incapable of the manly skills of shooting straight or waging an intelligent battle, is found in many kinds of action/adventure films. Virtually all combat films made during World War II made it clear to U.S. audiences that the enemy was inferior to Americans in all aspects of war making, and, by inference, were not as deft at the manly arts as the Yanks.

In *A Walk in the Sun*, a soldier makes a sportscaster's appraisal of the enemy's accuracy after an artillery shell misses the platoon's landing craft, stating, "Ball one, too high. . . . At [the battle at] Messina they pitched a few strikes. But here, no control, no control." In *God Is My Co-Pilot* (1945), Gen. Chennault (Raymond Massey) describes the imminent Japanese air strike in boxing terms, declaring, "The old one-two. Lead with six [planes] from the east and cross with twelve from the west." Because the enemy never changed their "playbook," the Flying Tigers were able to anticipate the opponent's moves and easily shoot down most of the Japanese planes.

11. Don't Give Up: Fight on to Victory

Sports jargon is regularly used to remind soldiers to stay the course, that the manly path is not to be abandoned because of momentary setbacks or other discouraging events. In *Bombardier!*, when the bomb school commandant asks a cadet how his studies are going, the cadet says that it's tough, but he'll be all right. The commandant (Pat O'Brien) replies, "That's right, keep punching."

Similarly, in *Wake Island* (1942), another commander, a marine, congratulates a subordinate for a job well done by simply saying, "Keep pitching." And in *Battleground* (1949), Pvt. Jarvess (John Hodiak) explains to his squadmates why he enlisted, declaring the following:

> The real meaning of the war against fascism, why every American had to get in there and pitch, the logic was magnificent. I couldn't resist it. The next thing I knew I was on a troop train waving bye-bye to my wife.

As previously mentioned in *Air Force*, aircraft gunner Winocki has a bad attitude, which he discusses with a young, inexperienced crewman. Winocki advises the youngster against making the U.S. Army Air Corps his career. The crew chief (Harry Carey) hears this and tells the youngster not to listen and to "Stay in the box, son, and keep on pitching." Later in the film, the commander of the bomber is told that unless their disabled B-17 can get off the ground in a few hours, it must be destroyed to avoid it falling into the hands of the enemy. "Can you get that engine [that you are working on] running right?" the captain asks. The enthusiastic crew chief boasts, "We'll have her hitting home runs in ninety minutes flat!" Likewise, in this film, the marine air commander at Midway Island tells the crew of the *Mary Ann* that if they see his old boss, Gen. MacArthur, to tell him this non sequitur: "that we'll be in there pitching until they strike us out." This oxymoronic metaphor is because the marines on Midway assumed that it was only a matter of time before they would be overrun by the Japanese.

In *Gung Ho!* (1943), on two occasions, things looked bad for Carlson's Raiders. Pinned down by the Japanese, "Frankie" (Harold Landon), a young marine, decides to use his track skills to surprise the enemy and destroy their gun emplacement. He strips to the waist, announces that he "used to run the hundred yard dash in ten seconds flat," and sprints to the objective, evading enemy fire, and he destroys it with hand grenades. He's wounded but survives. Later, another marine, Kozzaroski (Peter Coe), has an idea. Again, the raiders are pinned down until he commandeers a bulldozer and uses it as if it was a tank, providing cover for the marines to advance. As he explains to his sergeant, "Good old Dubuque [the bulldozer] here is carrying us over for a touchdown." The marines score their touchdown, but Kozzaroski is killed.

12. You Gotta Play Hurt

It should first be understood that in sports talk, playing hurt isn't exclusively about toughing out a physical injury. As Dan Jenkins writes in his book of the same name, *You Gotta Play Hurt* (1991) takes its title from an old saying among athletes. Sportswriters use it to sum up problems in their daily lives. Mostly, they use it as they stare at their writing machines, on deadline, hungover.

But in most references in war films, the saying refers to the manly art of ignoring pain and injury—both physical and mental—to carry on for the team. Most readers are aware of John Wayne's war film characters' superhuman abilities to withstand pain and punishment. As you recall in chapter 1, in *The Longest Day*, Wayne's character, Lt. Col. Benjamin Vandervoort, suffers a compound leg fracture in a parachute jump, but this undaunted alpha male marches along with his men, using a rifle as a crutch. This is not pure military sacrifice. It is the ethic of the athlete, who, although injured, will continue on for the sake of his team's victory.

In *The Purple Heart*, this "play hurt" ethic is lionized. POW Sgt. Skvoznik (Kevin O'Shea) is led away from his cell by the Japanese, almost certainly to be tortured, but the rest of the crew isn't worried that Skvoznik will talk, because, as one flyer points out, the sergeant is a former college football star and once "played the best game of his career with three broken ribs."

Of course, there are countless war films in which the hero, although wounded, still musters up the strength and wards off the shock to get the job done. Among the more bizarre moments that come to mind are the last few minutes in the life of Lt. Joe Costa (Jack Palance) of Fox Company in the film *Attack!* (1956). Although his left side was crushed and bleeding profusely when he was literally run over by the treads of a German tank, Costa musters up the strength to hobble through the streets to seek out and shoot Capt. Cooney (Eddie Albert), whose cowardice and mendacity needlessly sent Costa and his men into harm's way.

As previously mentioned, in *Top Gun*, before he is able to engage in combat with the enemy, Lt. Pete "Maverick" Mitchell (Tom Cruise) must overcome the psychological trauma of feeling responsible for a friend's death. At the climax of the film, struggling with his feelings as well as what his Top Gun commander calls a "confidence problem," Maverick "plays hurt" and overcomes his handicap, saving other flyers and shooting down enemy planes.

There are numerous stories in which a critically wounded soldier, sailor, or pilot, playing hurt and realizing that he is likely to die of his wounds, chooses to gut it out and perform a kamikazelike act of heroism in support of his buddies or for the cause. For example, in *Bataan* (1943), a pilot, Lt. Bentley (George Murphy), wounded and sure to die, dives his dynamite-packed plane into a bridge, destroying it, and preventing the Japanese from using it to resupply and reinforce their fight against the Americans.

BEYOND THE WAR GENRE

There are other examples beyond the war film genre in which modeling behavior and speech clarify and reinforce the prerequisites of manhood. Adventure films and westerns, to name two, are rich with them, and, often, narrative sports films reverse this process, using the nomenclature and vocabulary of warfare to describe, as George Carlin has demonstrated, their interchangeability. Beginning in World War II, even documentary and training films reinforced the messages found in narrative films. Referring to such Hollywood-produced "Victory Films" as *Target Tokyo* (1945), starring Ronald Reagan, and *Winning Your Wings* (1942), starring U.S. Army Air Corps lieutenant Jimmy Stewart, Thomas Doherty (1993) writes the following:

> Sports were a wellspring of reference. Baseball and football metaphors ("Hand off the ball," "Lay down a sacrifice bunt," "Set up the defense," "Wait your turn at bat") sweep through the instructional dialog [in the same manner as they prevail in many narrative films]. (110)

Limited by time constraints, film and television production requires writers and directors to present exposition in very little time, compared to the more leisurely pace in books. A filmic shorthand, stereotyping, is often used to achieve this succinctness. In the next chapter, we investigate how such stereotyping contributes to the social construction of manliness in war films.

NOTES

1. The contradiction of Joker's wearing a peace symbol on his fatigue jacket and scribbling the phrase "Born to Kill" on his helmet is best explained by Carl Jung (1968), as Joker mentioned. Jung's archetypes of the *anima* and *animus* act as a guide to our unconscious unified self. Jung theorized that humans, regardless of gender, are made up of unconscious feminine and masculine components that theoretically give us a balance in decision making. The *anima* (feminine component) is strongly connected with feelings. The *animus* (masculine component) is strongly connected with the functions of thinking, courage, and objectivity. Therefore, the peace symbol on Joker's jacket reflects his *anima* (feminine) side, and the message on the helmet reflects his *animus* (masculine) side.

2. Woody attempts to redeem himself by flying—and dying—on a suicide mission. A soldier's suicide is often related to survivor guilt, and Woody was certainly guilty over Hap's death. But even in more normal circumstances, this kind of guilt is often felt by a surviving soldier when one of his buddies is killed. The surviving soldier feels an overwhelming remorse because his buddy is dead and he is still alive. Both suicide and guilt are manifestations of post-traumatic stress disorder (PTSD). Woody felt out of control emotionally because of fear and rage. This lack of control and helplessness led to his self-destruction. In a study by Hendin and Haas (1991), PTSD among Vietnam combat veterans emerged as a psychiatric disorder with characteristics of considerable risk for suicide and intensive combat-related guilt. The character of Woody and his guilt and subsequent suicide mission is a personification of the results of this study.

3. In *Full Metal Jacket*, Hartman urges his men to adopt savage expressions and develop "war cries." Beth Azar, in her article "A Case for Angry Men and Happy Women" (2007), describes a series of experiments conducted by D. Vaughn Becker, a cognitive psychologist from Arizona State University. In Becker's study, a face was described to be masculine if it was making an angry expression. His research suggests that there is a perceptual bias in evidence related to cognitive processes that identifies the male with anger and the female with happiness. Becker wrote that this perception may have begun in our evolutionary past, when an angry man was considered dangerous. In fact, today, men commit 80 to 90 percent of all violent crimes. Hartman's objective, to turn his marines into true "warriors," appears to agree with Becker's gender description and brings to one's mind the perception of an angular, angry face with a heavy brow. These features caused the participants of Becker's study to perceive the faces shown to them as "masculine." Becker related his findings to the brain possessing what he called an "angry male detection module that allows 'fast and accurate' detection of what would have been one of the most dangerous entities in our evolutionary past" in which the signals for detecting masculine facial expression have emerged over time (18).

3

Stereotypes of Manliness

One of the great limitations of both film and television is time. Television series episodes usually run half an hour to an hour. Motion picture producers know that it's rare when a film that runs much more than two hours can hold its audience's attention. Many times, prior to release, a film's producer chops the first (director's) cut from more than two hours to less than two. Books rarely have similar restrictions and thus can develop characters, along with "French" scenes (of incidental action) in a more detailed, leisurely fashion. So economical film and television production requires writers and directors to find ways to lay out the setting, plot, and character sketches in as short an amount of time as possible.

In this often-retold example from his classic text, *Film Technique and Film Acting* (1954), Vsevolod Illarionovich Pudovkin describes the brutish character of a villainous thug in Henry King's 1921 silent film *Tol'able David*. The villain's nature is clearly and quickly established when the man is about to enter a cottage. On the stoop he, "spies a tiny, fluffy kitten, asleep in the sun. He raises a heavy stone with the transparent intention of using it to obliterate the sleeping little beast, and only the casual push of a fellow, just then carrying objects into the house, hinders him from carrying out his cruel intention" (27–28). There is no need for a title to announce that this man is full of mindless violence and hate. That brief moment is all audiences require to understand what kind of man he is. Similarly, thanks to clever montage, in Sergei Eisenstein's *October* (1928), shots of Prime Minister Aleksandr Kerensky in the Winter Palace are crosscut with shots of a gilded mechanical peacock, suggesting Kerensky's vanity.

Such filmic shorthand as this has become as much a part of the language of the motion picture as punctuation marks are in English grammar. But in the social constructions of masculinity found in war films, stereotypes take on meaning beyond manipulations of cinematic grammar: They describe the archetypes of appropriate masculine behavior for their viewers. This chapter is devoted to a detailed typology of masculine stereotypes in war films and a discussion of their impact in the socialization of American males.

For the purposes of this discussion, the key stereotypes of manliness in war films discussed are the mama's boy, the wolf, the lothario, the father figure, the rebellious son, the gay soldier, the mate, battling brothers, the virgin, the rapist, the woman hater, the psychopath, the FNG, the courageous boy, the coward, the sissy, variations of a kind of character known as the "REMF," and the hero.

THE MAMA'S BOY

In American and many other cultures, cutting mother's apron strings means stepping away from the world of childhood and making one's first steps toward manhood. As we have already discussed, the external appearances, emotions, and culture of women are often portrayed to males as an undesirable "other." In the world of men, things female are used as negative comparisons, are characterized as inferior, and thus should be avoided.

Adult males who have not established their own domiciles and still live with their mothers are often suspected of being either "mama's boys" or perhaps homosexuals, or both. For example, in *This Land Is Mine* (1943), Albert (Clarles Laughton) is a prototype of the mamby-pamby mama's boy. A schoolteacher, he lives with his mother in a village in occupied France. Afraid of his own shadow, Albert doesn't even earn the respect of the young boys he teaches. Albert admires and loves fellow teacher Louise Martin (Maureen O'Hara) from afar, but he is too timid to approach her. He knows that the French Resistance is active in his village, and Albert is sympathetic, but he is too afraid to do anything to aid the cause. But when his father-figure and mentor, the school's venerable headmaster, is murdered by the Nazis for spreading anti-Nazi propaganda, Albert, angered to action for perhaps the first time in his life, suddenly grows a backbone. He openly stands up and opposes the Nazis, and in the film's denouement, he is led away by the Nazis to be shot, becoming a hero to both Louise and his pupils.[1]

Thanks to a culture that both denigrates women and demeans men who refuse to make the break with their mothers, men know full well what is expected of them. They also understand that too close an association—

regardless of how insignificant—with their mothers is a cultural taboo. In *Biloxi Blues* (1988), Pvt. Eugene Jerome is about to engage in his first sexual encounter. He and his friends have contracted the services of a world-weary but caring prostitute named Rowena. After some verbal sparring, the extremely nervous Jerome is finally ready to consummate his first love making. Rowena has divested herself of most of her clothing and lies on the bed. She beckons to Eugene, still nervously standing nearby, weight shifting from foot to foot, "All right, now . . . come to mama." Jerome replies, suddenly petrified with that maternal image, "Please, don't say come to mama."

At the outset of Howard Hawks's *Air Force* (1943), Pvt. Chester, the youngest member of the bomber crew, bids farewell to his mother. She, rather than a girlfriend, is at hand to see him off on his first mission. The mother asks to speak to the captain of the bomber, and asks him, in essence, to protect her boy and return him safely to her. In this short scene, it's made clear that unlike the other crewmen on board the B-17 bomber *Mary Ann*, the fresh-faced Chester is the only one who has not yet completely cut the apron strings and thus has not yet achieved full manhood.

Later, Chester's character is used by screenwriters Leah Baird, Dudley Nichols, and William Faulkner as their "how to explain things to a newcomer" exposition device. This permits aircrew conversations with neophyte Chester to smoothly set up important character and plot exposition. But Chester remains the novice, the beginner of lesser status (see a more thorough discussion of newcomers under the heading "The FNG" later in this chapter), until later in the picture, when he's tested in battle. But even then, these wartime screenwriters use this sympathetic newcomer to create propaganda through pathos. Chester finds himself temporarily assigned as a tail machine gunner aboard a pursuit plane, engaging Japanese zeroes in air combat. The plane is hit, the pilot is killed, and Chester bails out and successfully opens his parachutes. A sadistic Japanese pilot swoops down and machine guns Chester as he floats helplessly down in his 'chute, holding out his hands in front of him as if to beg for mercy. As often seen in war movies, young, inexperienced characters are expendable and add pathos to the other audience emotions. In this scene, the enemy is shown to be heartless and savage. The contrast is heightened by the fact that the victim is a youngster, not yet individuated from his mother, effectively a boy, not yet a man.

In *The Caine Mutiny* (1954), a somewhat similar character, Ensign Willis Keith, fresh from college and naval officers' candidate school, is chauffeured to the dock by his wealthy mother to report on board his first ship. Unlike Chester, whose mother is not subsequently seen in *Air Force*, Keith's mother appears again as the subject of conflict between Keith and his fiancé, May. This conflict is an old one, as Keith is clearly still enough

In *Air Force*, mortally wounded Pvt. Chester (Ray Montgomery) is tended to by Crew Chief White (Harry Carey Jr.) and Lt. Hauser (Charles Drake), while Winocki (John Garfield) deftly shoots down the Japanese plane that strafed Chester. *Warner Bros. / Photofest © Warner Bros.*

of a mama's boy that he can't break the primary link between himself and his possessive mother, who resents the competition May introduces into the close mother–son relationship. Finally, after Keith matures through experiences in combat, a mutiny, and the court-martial of some of his fellow officers, he is able to cut the apron strings, give himself completely to May, and establish a new, more mature relationship with his mother.

Close relationships with their mothers are not always used to identify the unmanly. As with Chester, other mother–son relationships are used by screenwriters to create moments of pathos, as when navy gunboat crewman "Clean" Miller is killed in *Apocalypse Now* (1979). In a moment reminiscent of a similar scene thirty-six years earlier (the aftermath of sailor Mike's death in *Destination Tokyo* [1943], discussed in chapter 1), Clean's shipmates hear an ironic cassette recording of his mother's voice professing her love for her son, along with a hope that Clean will soon return safely to home and hearth.

Screenwriters sometimes add pathos to a scene with a mama's boy reference, the pathetic cry of the dying young soldier, writhing in pain, who cries out, "Mama!" Two examples occur in Steven Spielberg's *Saving*

Private Ryan (1998), the first in the horrific D-Day sequence. Amidst the chaos of blood, death, and mayhem, the director cuts to a shot of a dying young soldier lying on the beach, his bloody entrails strewn about, crying in pain and screaming for his mother. Later, the squad's medic is mortally wounded, and, in his last moments, he also calls out for his mother, pleading, "I want to go home."

Another youngster thrust into combat, Johnny "Chicken" Anderson, is the youngest marine in *Guadalcanal Diary* (1943). The nickname "Chicken" does not refer to cowardice, but to the fact that Johnny is so young he's considered—in 1940s slang—a "spring chicken" by the older members of his platoon. On the troop ship taking them to Guadalcanal, another marine notices that Chicken is writing a letter. The older man assumes the note is to Chicken's girlfriend, and he asks about her. Embarrassed by the fact that the letter is actually addressed to his mother, Chicken lies to his friends and describes his nonexistent girlfriend as someone "who gives me no back-talk." Even in 1943, Chicken understands that to be considered an equal by his fellow marines, he must have previously established sexual and interpersonal dominance over a female. That his closest relationship is with his mother, instead of a girlfriend, is an indication that he has not yet transitioned into a man. Later in the picture, to enhance his bid for more manly status, Chicken locates a newly grown whisker on his chin and proudly asks a fellow marine to borrow a razor. Of course, Chicken's older comrades find this amusing.

THE WOLF

As was discussed briefly in the previous section, establishing sexual and interpersonal dominance over a female is part of the social construction of manliness. Thus, to soldiers, an indicator of manliness is one's ability to attract and successfully seduce and/or win over women. Many war films, such as *Pearl Harbor* (2001), feature a subplot of a love triangle and fierce competition between two male protagonists for a female. In *Pearl Harbor*, Capt. Rafe McCawley (Ben Affleck) and Capt. Danny Walker (Josh Hartnett) are close, boyhood friends, until they both fall in love with the same woman, at which point this best of friendships becomes strained. But the wolf stereotype in war films goes beyond this rather normal male condition. Not content to pursue and love a woman in a monogamous manner, the stereotypical wolf stalks females simply for the sport of the conquest and then moves on, like a fisherman who releases his catch. Like Steve McQueen's Capt. Buzz Rickson in *The War Lover* (1961) or Kirk Douglas's Capt. Paul Eddington in *In Harm's Way* (1965), the wolf may also be some kind of woman hater.

Bomber pilot Rickson's disdain for women may come from his lack of a family life, a backstory referenced in his comments to another flyer. He has been on his own since the age of thirteen, and his first lovemaking experience was a chance encounter (twenty-four hours of continual lovemaking) with a woman old enough to be his mother. Rickson objectifies women in the same manner as he did the woman who introduced him to sex. He comes from the wrong side of the tracks and knows it and carries a huge chip on his shoulder to hide his low self-image. Rickson has no claim to fame, no anchor for his ego, until he discovers—and is decorated for—his special talent for flying.

In this arena of socially approved manliness, Rickson has no equal, and he is proud of his status as the expert hunter and "top gun" among his bomber group's pilots. His navigator, who disapproves of Rickson's extremely aggressive approach to flying missions, sarcastically refers to him as "Superman." Rickson's commander dislikes him because he is insubordinate, but he reluctantly admits to his flying skill and ability to reach the bombing target when other pilots give up. Known for sometimes taking unnecessary risks, Rickson prides himself on his steely cool under fire and skill at bringing his often-damaged bomber back from each mission. For Rickson, these achievements let him dominate both the enemy and the airplane, which he has objectified as female by nicknaming it the "Body."

Maintaining dominance and an obsession with winning is vital in all of Rickson's activities: He must always be the best. Successful in war against the enemy and growing more smug with each victory, Rickson extends his macho pursuits to women, whom he seems to have very little use for beyond winning the battle of the sexes. His comments display his disdain for the female in that he describes women as merely objects, "bombing targets" to attack and overcome, rather than people. Even Rickson's smiles are peppered with his disdain for the opposite sex. Seeing his aircrew standing idly around the plane, gabbing, Rickson equates them to the inferior "other" by comparing them to a women's sewing circle.

On one occasion, while on a pass from their Southern English air base, Rickson and his crew are drinking in a pub. Just for sadistic pleasure, he cruelly tries to make a romantic match between a young bomber crewman called "Junior," whom he assumes is still a virgin, with a plump, shy English barmaid. When Rickson practically pushes the two together, Junior is embarrassed, and the reluctant barmaid is in tears, humiliated. Fortunately for all, a German bombing raid interrupts the incident.

Rickson accumulates a growing list of female conquests but is incapable of any lasting relationship. He attacks, conquers, and moves on to his next endeavor. To advertise his sexual prowess, he maintains a gallery of photos of women, presumably his sexual victories, on the bulletin board

Lt. Bolland (Robert Wagner), left, is the copilot in *The War Lover*, and Steve McQueen is Captain Rickson, who commands the crew of the B-17 bomber named *The Body*. *Columbia Pictures / Photofest © Columbia Pictures*

of his barracks room. When he decides to go out on the town, he closes his eyes and randomly points at the board to decide which female will be the lucky recipient of his attention that evening. As mentioned earlier, Rickson nicknamed his bomber the "Body." A cartoon of a near-naked woman is painted on the nose of the plane. Apparently only with the "Body" is Rickson capable of any kind of true affection. During the climactic final bombing mission, he talks affectionately to the "Body" while he flies, urging this female, over which he has achieved total dominance, to once again keep him in the air and get him safely home.

In contrast, Rickson's copilot, Lt. Ed Bolland (Robert Wagner), who is no wolf, falls in love with an English woman named Daphne. To prove both to Bolland and himself that he is the alpha male aboard the "Body" and throughout the bomber group, Rickson attempts to steal Daphne's affections, but she rejects him. Rickson resorts to a halfhearted attempt at rape but is not successful. Daphne insults him by asserting that Rickson "can't make love, you can only make hate!" Crushed by his striking failure to conquer a female objective, Rickson overcompensates by attempting a spectacular feat of piloting the "Body" on his next combat mission. His bomber is badly damaged, and good sense suggests that the aircrew bail out before the plane crashes into the English Channel. But Rickson insists on trying to bring his bomber home, despite major damage to the plane and its engines. All the crewmembers safely bail out, except Rickson, who stays at the controls of the "Body" as it crashes into the Cliffs of Dover.

Alpha males in *Dr. Strangelove* (1964), such as Gen. Jack D. Ripper (Sterling Hayden) and Gen. Buck Turgidson (George C. Scott), should also be classed as wolves. Ripper brags of his prowess with women (when he says, "Women feel my power"), although in his madness he denies them his "essence." Turgidson keeps his young, beautiful secretary as his mistress and insists that she "never call me when I'm in the War Room." Both generals are convinced that it is their manly prowess as military leaders that makes them naturally dominant over women.

Director Stanley Kubrick implants a number of sexual innuendos throughout the film to reinforce this male military Übermensch myth. For example, the film's opening visuals feature the phallic boom arm on the mighty KC-135 tanker penetrating the vaginalike receptacle on board the B-54 bomber during air-to-air refueling (complete with a noticeable limpness on the boom arm postcoitus). Later, as Turgidson stands by, grinning with approval, Dr. Strangelove explains to the president that in the years that follow the nuclear Armageddon they've just created, such alpha males as current government leaders, and, of course, generals like Turgidson, will survive in deep mine shafts to avoid nuclear fallout, tasked with having sex with as many as ten women each to repopulate the species.

In *In Harm's Way*, Kirk Douglas's Capt. Paul Eddington is executive officer of a navy cruiser but is close to losing his job. Eddington spends his time drinking away his troubles, caused mostly by an unfaithful wife. At the outset of the film, his wife is cheating on Eddington with a marine officer. She is among the many civilians killed during the Japanese attack on Pearl Harbor. Retrieving her belongings from the morgue, Eddington becomes unstable. He enters a bar, and when a friendly marine officer offers him a drink, he becomes enraged and attacks him. Later in the film, Eddington becomes attracted to a young woman, Annalee (Jill Haworth), but in his mind she also is unfaithful to him. A navy nurse, she is engaged to another man, but, as a girlfriend cautions her, she is attracted to the danger she senses in Eddington. Inexperienced, Annalee flirts with and teases Eddington, and the old anger within him wells up. Something inside him snaps, and he forcibly rapes her. Later, in despair and pregnant, Annalee kills herself. To redeem himself, Eddington flies a suicide mission. Like Rickson, Eddington tries to drown his failures with women in heroic, manly acts.

THE LOTHARIO

The character named Lothario first appears in literature in Nicholas Rowe's 1703 play *The Fair Penitent*. In this play, Lothario seduces and betrays the female protagonist. Since then, in literature or real life, a man whose life seems to be totally absorbed with the pursuit of women has been referred to as a lothario. Whether it is to seek comfort from women in the midst of the chaos of war or, like Rickson or Eddington, for some darker personal purpose, war films abound with lotharios. In the civil war melodrama *Gettysburg* (1993), Gen. Lewis Armistead (Richard Jordan) is never shown with a woman, but in this film's talky exposition, his fellow generals constantly refer to him as "Lo" Armistead, and they tell a British exchange officer that "Lo" (for "Lothario") has earned his nickname due to his prowess with the ladies. (In actuality, Gen. Armistead has been described as a shy man, especially around women.)

In *The Naked and the Dead* (1958), Lt. Robert Hearn (Cliff Robertson) is a hedonist and relentless lothario. While the rich, spoiled Hearn serves as a general's aide in a combat zone, he has a lot of time on his hands, which he spends daydreaming about his female conquests. In a sexy montage—at least by 1950s film standards—he is shown romancing a bevy of beautiful women, all dressed in revealing outfits. In one scene, he tries to dance a twosome of beautiful women on a conga line toward his bedroom.

Actual pursuit of women as subplots in war films is more evident in the romantic activities of Lt. J. G. Ward Stewart (Tyrone Power) in *Crash Dive* (1943) and Capt. Buck Oliver (Randolph Scott) in *Bombardier!* (1943). In the case of Stewart, he pursues his prey, Jean Hewlett (Anne Baxter), across three states, despite her protests. Although Stewart does not know it, Jean is close to becoming engaged to Stewart's commander and friend, Lt. Cmdr. Dewey Connors (Dana Andrews). More honorable than Rickson in *The War Lover*, Stewart would have reluctantly withdrawn from competition for Jean had he known about her relationship with Connors, but since he is unaware, he spends half the film pursuing her and finally succeeds.

Typical of strong males, Stewart and Connors have great difficulty expressing their feelings on the matter to each other, and they quietly feud for the next two reels. But later in the film, in the heat of battle against the Nazis, Stewart's brave deeds break the macho impasse. To Connors, Stewart's heroic actions demonstrate his superior manliness, which to Connors signals an acceptance of Stewart as the alpha male in this love triangle. And, as if they were two stags locking horns in competition for the same doe, Connors abandons the field—and the sexual prize—to Stewart.

Capt. Oliver (Randolph Scott) in *Bombardier!* is a little less honorable. He pursues a young woman nicknamed "Burt" (Anne Shirley), although he knows that his best friend, Maj. Chick Davis (Pat O'Brien), is also attracted to her. But later, Burt's brother is killed during a training mission in a plane piloted by Oliver, and there is some temporary doubt whether the young man's death was Oliver's fault. Burt and Oliver do not see each other for some months, but at the end of the picture, the flyer reads a letter from Burt, who says she does not blame him for her brother's death. But Oliver, flying a dangerous mission akin to Eddington's in *In Harm's Way*, is killed in the climax, and like McCawley and Walker in *Pearl Harbor*, only one flyer—Chick—will return home to claim the heroine.

Sometimes this wolf stereotype is a legend only in his own mind. In *Destination Tokyo*, such a character is a crewman whose nickname is "Wolf" (John Garfield). Wolf spends much of his screen time telling outlandish stories of his sexual exploits to sex-starved submarine crewmembers. But while Wolf narrates a story to the crew about an amazing sexual adventure, on the screen the audience sees flashbacks of the *actual* happenings he describes, in which Wolf strikes out much more often than he "scores."

Some soldiers who are would-be lotharios provide comedy relief, either as their principal role in the screenplay, like Wolf, or as an additional character attribute for a protagonist. Typical are two would-be seducer

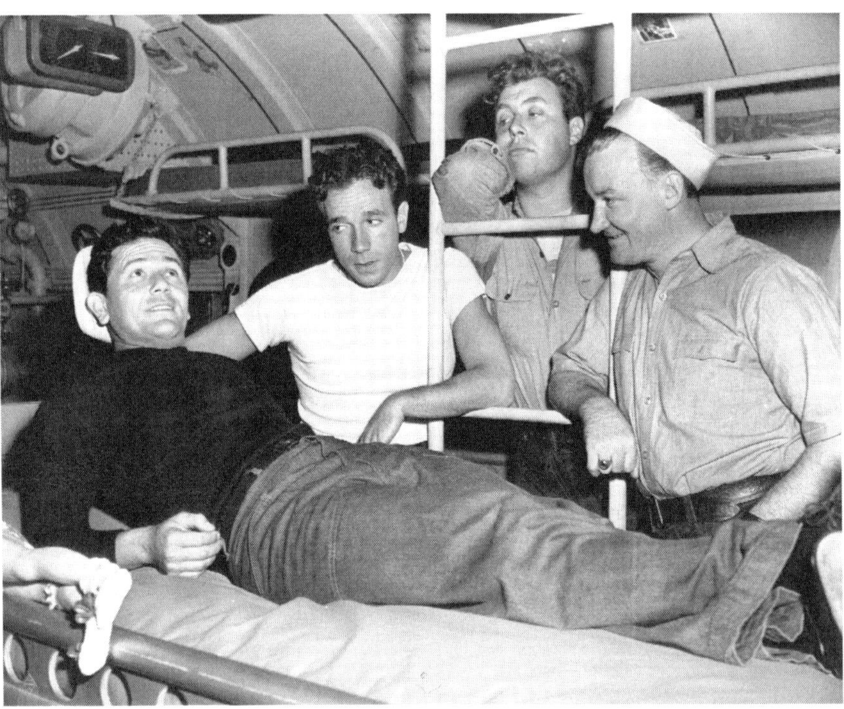

In *Destination Tokyo* "Wolf" (John Garfield) brags about his romantic exploits to shipmates. *Warner Bros. / Photofest © Warner Bros.*

characters, both played by Van Johnson, in the films *Battleground* (1949) and *Go for Broke!* (1951). In both motion pictures, as an infantryman whose unit was occupying towns in Belgium and Italy, Johnson attempts to bribe his way into the boudoirs of women with Hershey bars or silk stockings. In both instances, the army's needs intervene, his unit is moving out, and he has no time to consummate any romance.

Another would-be lothario is "Rascal" (Sean Astin), a bomber crew-member in *Memphis Belle* (1990), who concocts a pathetic scenario in his attempt to seduce a young woman at a dance. He appeals to her motherly side by reminding her that his "young life" could end the next day while on his assigned bombing mission over Germany. Unfortunately for Rascal, this jaded English girl has heard this story before and seems rather bored by it, and before long, she ditches him for another airman.

In Steven Spielberg's World War II comedy *1941* (1979), Capt. Loomis Burkhead (Tim Matheson) is obsessed with seducing a general's aide, Donna Stratton (Nancy Allen), with whom he cannot "get to first base" with (sports metaphors are used in both love and war). Burkhead learns that Stratton, an otherwise frosty customer, has a reputation of being enamored with flying to the point of sexual excitement. But Burkhead is no longer a U.S. Army Air Corps pilot, having washed out due to some unrevealed high jinks during flight training.

Burkhead manages to lure Stratton into the cockpit of a B-17 Flying Fortress parked on the ground and nearly succeeds in seducing her by simulating flight with imaginative stories and sound effects. They begin some spirited foreplay but only manage to accidentally release a bomb, which rolls away from the plane, nearly killing a general giving a speech nearby to a group of people. Later, Burkhead realizes that the only way to consummate his lust for the lady is to get her up into an airplane and have sex with her mid-flight. Although only a neophyte pilot, Burkhead is completely ruled by lust, so he commandeers an airplane. With great difficulty, the two manage to copulate during a flight, but when the unauthorized sex flight strays into Los Angeles air space, it triggers a citywide civil defense alert and a hilarious movie "climax" involving a tank, a ferris wheel, a Japanese submarine, and the La Brea Tar Pits.

THE FATHER FIGURE

Another prevalent male stereotype in war films is the father figure. Usually an older or at least more experienced soldier, aviator, or sailor who has been bloodied in battle and is often wise beyond his years, this character provides role models of manliness for the younger troops. In *Destination Tokyo*, Mike Conners (Tom Tully) is the father figure whose death at the hands of a Japanese flyer was described in chapter 1. Until that point in the film, Mike provides guidance and mentorship most specifically to Tommy Adams (Robert Hutton), "the kid," on his first submarine voyage, but also to other, less experienced sailors. Mike is the voice of moderation and maturity and provides the young men with a mature, manly role model. When he is stabbed by the enemy flyer he was trying to rescue, the entire crew mourns.

Both Sgt. Clell Hazard (James Caan) and Sgt. Maj. "Goody" Nelson (James Earl Jones) are senior sergeants and mentors to young infantryman Jackie Willow (D. B. Sweeney) in *Gardens of Stone* (1987). Both sergeants are decorated combat veterans and act as surrogate fathers and army mentors for Jackie, whose late father, also an army sergeant, had served with both Hazard and Nelson. At some points in the film, Nelson, who also refers to himself as the "bear" (as in "sometimes you eat the bear, sometimes the bear eats you"), becomes a towering authority figure who delights in making young troops tremble in their boots. His white glove inspections of the barracks are legendary.

Likewise, Hazard considers it his personal responsibility to ensure that each soldier under his command is trained well enough to survive in the jungles of Vietnam. To him, the manly, John Wayne-style hero is a remnant of another war: The two-tour veteran in Southeast Asia believes that the Vietnam War is unwinnable. This calls for a new definition of the manly duties of the soldier for this theater of operation: Since the mission can't be accomplished, the best thing you can do is know and understand the enemy and the jungle so you and your men can survive.

But at times these two senior sergeants act like black sheep uncles or older brothers to Jackie. For example, they join the young man in a bar fight with some soldiers from another unit just for the fun of it. And after Jackie has borrowed money and a car from Hazard for an important date, the phone rings with Jackie saying over the phone, "Hey, Sarge! I need another favor." Hazard replies, "Oh, great. Let's see . . . you got my money, you got my car. I guess now you need my dick to seal the deal!"

Not all father figures are as prominent in their films as Conners, Hazard, and Nelson. Pvt. Ernest J. "Pop" Stazak (George Murphy) plays a supporting but noteworthy role in the rifle squad whose experiences during the Battle of the Bulge in World War II are chronicled in *Battleground*. "Pop" gets his nickname because he's the oldest soldier in the squad, perhaps a little too old for combat. By the time Pop's hardship discharge orders arrive, those who were defending Bastogne are surrounded by the Germans, so he must remain with the squad and try to survive the battle and the harsh winter conditions. He befriends and fathers young Pvt. Johnny Roderigues (Ricardo Montalban) and looks after the young soldier. When Roderigues is killed, he quietly mourns the young man as if he had lost a son.

Another supporting actor who serves as a manly father figure and role model is "Boats" Mulcahey, (Ward Bond) a fiftyish torpedo boat squadron chief petty officer in John Ford's World War II classic *They Were Expendable* (1945). Boats is the senior chief of the squadron, a leader whom the young sailors look to for guidance. Boats is the same kind of senior NCO/father figure that Bond would play again opposite John Wayne in Ford's U.S. cavalry saga *Fort Apache* (1948). In *They Were Expendable*, in the final days before the fall of the Philippines to the Japanese, the torpedo boat squadron must be disbanded. The remaining officers are being evacuated and ordered to return stateside to teach others what they learned about PT boat tactics during their many victories against the Japanese Navy. But there is no room on the plane for the squadron's enlisted men, so Boats is put in charge of these young sailors and instructed to guide and protect them as they join army troops to fight a guerilla war against the Japanese until Gen. MacArthur and the Allied forces return to the Philippines. The last image in the film is of Boats leading his men, marching along the seashore, and looking up to watch the last transport plane, with their officers on board, fly off into the sunset.

In contrast to Daskal, his evil, "bad father" sergeant role in *The Beast* (1988), George Dzundza plays a wise but firm "good father" figure, the "Chief of the Boat," or "COB," in *Crimson Tide* (1995). As senior NCO on a nuclear submarine, the chief demands the greatest of respect from officers and enlisted men alike. But on this cruise, this nuclear missile-launching sub is in the middle of an international crisis. Dzundza's chief, who is truly a latter-day Ward Bond, finds himself in the middle of a war of words and wits between the captain (Gene Hackman) and the sub's young executive officer (Denzel Washington) over whether to immediately fire their nuclear weapons without first ascertaining if an ambiguous launch order is still valid. The chief is terribly conflicted, but regulations force him to side with the exec, even though the exec's actions might be later construed as a mutiny. Highly displeased with his situation, the chief tries unsuccessfully to serve as sage and conscience for both the exec and the captain. At one point, the exec, whose screen name is Hunter, thinking he has found an ally in the chief, expresses his thanks for the chief's support. But like a father irritated with his young son's rash actions, the chief surprises the exec, cursing at the young officer for putting him, the captain, and the boat in such a compromising situation:

HUNTER: Chief of the Boat.

CHIEF: Sir?

HUNTER: Thank you, COB.

CHIEF: (amazed) Thank you? Fuck you! Get it straight, Mr. Hunter, I'm not on your side. Now you could be wrong! But wrong or right, the captain can't just replace you at will. That was completely improper! And that's why I did what I did. By the book.

HUNTER: I thank you anyway.

First Sgt. "Buster" Kilrain (Kevin Conway) acts as much like a mother as a father to his colonel, Joshua Lawrence Chamberlain (Jeff Daniels) commanding an infantry battalion in the miniseries *Gettysburg* (1999). An Irishman, he refers to Chamberlain as "Colonel Darlin'," and he routinely tries to make the exhausted officer ride his horse rather than march alongside his men. Chamberlain refuses, because he feels he must experience what his men undergo so he knows what he can expect of them. Kilrain does everything but tuck Chamberlain in at night, making sure his commander has his coffee, eats, and gets enough sleep.

The screenwriters also use Kilrain's monologues to hold forth at some length on some of the themes of the film, adapted from Michael Shaara's novel *The Killer Angels*. These include the Jungian duality of man and that in America (as opposed to in Europe), a man is judged by his achievements, not by his class. But Kilrain's principal role is as Chamberlain's protector and doting parent.

In *A Rumor of War* (1980), Sgt. Ned Coleman (Brian Dennehy) portrays another classic top sergeant/father figure, this time for a young platoon leader, Lt. Phil Caputo (Brad Davis) of the marines. The young officer is immature, unsure of himself, and still rebelling against his own father, so Caputo's relationship with Coleman begins problematically. But Caputo soon realizes that the best thing that happened to him in Vietnam was to be mentored—and fathered—by the wise and crafty Sgt. Coleman.

A similar mentoring/father relationship develops in *Platoon Leader* (1988). Mac (Robert F. Lyons), the platoon sergeant, is tasked with keeping young Lt. Knight (Michael Dudikoff) alive long enough to learn how to survive and lead a platoon in Vietnam. Although inexperienced when he arrives, Knight first resists Mac's advice and mentoring but quickly learns how beneficial Mac's knowledge and maturity can be when you're in the "bush." Like Sgt. Kilrain, Mac is also used by the screenwriters to dispense philosophy, in this case about faulty U.S. policy and objectives in Vietnam.[2]

In *Saving Private Ryan*, both Capt. Miller (Tom Hanks) and Sgt. Horvath (Tom Sizemore) serve as parental figures to the men of their squad, the battle-weary remains of the company Capt. Miller brought ashore on D-Day in France. In a way, Miller is the somewhat distant father figure, while Horvath plays the mother/disciplinarian. Both patiently (more Miller than Horvath) provide wisdom, guidance, and structure to their men, who have seen and experienced too much for their young age. To the men, their mission (to keep an Iowa mother's fourth and last surviving son from being killed in the war) makes no sense, not after the carnage and devastation they have lived through in North Africa, Sicily, and D-Day. It's up to Capt. Miller to explain the reasons, and Sgt. Horvath, the disciplinarian, to insist that all the men obey their orders. At one point, Horvath draws a gun and threatens to shoot a soldier who temporarily refuses to continue the mission.

Another older, grizzled sergeant type may serve as a father figure but doesn't act all that fatherly toward his young troops. In *The Big Red One* (1980), Lee Marvin's character, never referred to by his surname and just called the "Sergeant" or "Sarge," is a World War I veteran serving in his second war in Europe. Haunted by his own demons from the first war, Sarge is the kind of mentor who suggests that the best use of condoms is to keep an infantryman's rifle barrel dry. Less warm and fuzzy than other father figure sergeants, in more than one scene the Sarge seems cold-blooded and insensitive. For example, a young soldier trips a land mine and loses a testicle in the explosion. The Sergeant locates and casually throws away the testicle, flippantly remarking, "It's just one of your balls, Smitty. You can live without it. That's why they gave you two." Later, the squad is ordered to assault an insane asylum in Belgium, because the Germans are using it as an observation post. One of the Sergeant's troops complains, "Why not just bomb it?" The sarcastic Sergeant replies, "It's not good public relations to kill insane people." Another troop says, "Killing sane people is okay?" "That's right," the Sarge replies. But later in the film, the Sergeant sheds a tear for a little boy he rescues from a Nazi concentration camp. He carries the boy on his shoulders for some time, reminding viewers of statues of St. Joseph carrying Jesus. A short time later, the boy dies, and the Sarge shows his humanity as he quietly mourns.

THE REBELLIOUS SON

Another male stereotype is the young, immature soldier who rebels against his father or father figure, but then realizes his error and amends his ways. This real-life father–son melodrama usually ends by reinforcing the manly values of the older generation, no matter how eloquently the younger makes his case to the contrary. As discussed in the beginning of chapter 1, Pfc. Peter Conway (John Agar), in *Sands of Iwo Jima* (1949), was such a character. Despite his father's (Col. Sam Conway) death at the Battle of Guadalcanal, the younger Conway's issues with his father still fester, made worse by serving in the same squad as his father's favorite marine, Sgt. Stryker (John Wayne), who seems to Conway to be channeling all his father's words and values. To Stryker, Conway exhibits elder sibling rivalry, as if the sergeant was the kind of son his father always wanted.

As discussed in chapter 2, Conway articulates a more masculine–feminine balanced, cultured, humanistic philosophy than is shown to be practical in the marines. But, as always in these kinds of character conflicts in war films, the dominant male ethic must overcome humanistic sentiment if the bloody job of war is to be performed successfully. So Conway gradually and begrudgingly adopts his father's values and learns respect for his surrogate father/brother, Stryker. In the final scene, with the seemingly invincible Stryker lying dead in the middle of a circle of stunned marines, Conway suddenly channels both his father and Stryker as he grits his teeth and growls orders to his squad, saying, "All right. Saddle up! Let's get back in the war!"[3]

Channeling Conway's character sixteen years later, Brandon De Wilde plays Ens. Jere Torrey in *In Harm's Way*. At first, Jere seems only to be a spoiled rich kid, estranged from his father, Rear Adm. Rockwell Torrey (John Wayne), by divorce when he was a boy, with little contact since. When the two are reunited, serving together in the South Pacific, "Rock," as the elder Torrey is appropriately called, realizes that Jere has been raised with and now voices the effete values of his spoiled, rich mother.

As befits his rigid nickname, Rock first finds Jere's values and haughty attitude revolting. This alienation becomes even more apparent as Jere allies himself with a congressman turned press agent for Adm. Broderick, Cmdr. Neil Owynn. Both Owynn (Patrick O'Neill) and Broderick (Dana Andrews), whom Rock has relieved as operational commander, as evidenced by their mamby-pamby game of croquet on the lawn of Broderick's headquarters, are what the present governor of California would later refer to as "girly men," the polar opposite of the manly Rock. To Jere's credit, and following in the thematic footsteps of Conway and Stryker, the young man eventually realizes the superiority of his father's character and values and requests a transfer from his safe, rear echelon staff job with the admiral back into harm's way as the second-in-command of a PT boat. There, in the climactic sea battle of the movie, Jere exhibits Rock's virtues and fights bravely, but is killed.

THE GAY SOLDIER

"Don't ask, don't tell, don't pursue" may be the currently disputed rule regarding the treatment of gays in the U.S. armed forces, but war films usually give no quarter to homosexuals. Generally considered security risks as well as being unmanly, in war films, gay soldiers are relegated to the second-class status of women. Burdened with ignorant, homophobic fears of gay men propositioning or raping straight men, soldiers in war films either shun or assail gays and purge them from their midst at every opportunity. After all, since the conduct of war is one of the ultimate male gendering activities, homosexual behavior is deemed antithetical and counterproductive.

Consider Mark Fleetwood's review of Rod Steiger's character in *The Sergeant* (1968) as found in the Internet Movie Database:

> The dark inner struggle of Master Sgt. Albert Callan to overcome the overwhelming attraction he feels for one of his charges, in the staid and stifling environment of a post–World War II army post in France, Callan's deeply repressed attraction to other men surfaces when he encounters handsome Private Swanson. Maintaining the rugged "man's man" image of a war hero, Callan barks orders to his underlings. Later, lonely in his solitude, he recalls the frightening experiences of war and the events that led to this crossroads. Filled with self-loathing and unable to act on the natural attraction he feels for Swanson, Callan's affection festers into antagonism. He pushes Swanson constantly with verbal assaults and undeserved punishments. Oblivious to Callan's attraction to him, Swanson finally comes to feel enmity for his master sergeant.

As regulations of the Roman Catholic Church root out homosexuality within potential members of the clergy while men are still candidates for ordination, military trainers remain on guard against letting a gay trainee slip through their grasp. In spite of current policies that vaunt "Don't ask, don't tell, don't pursue," some version of the 1940s scenario discussed earlier in *Biloxi Blues* remains more likely. When a recruit is discovered to be homosexual, he is immediately arrested, handcuffed, and whisked away from the platoon as if he were a dangerous criminal or Nazi spy who also suffers from leprosy.

As discussed in chapter 1, the opening sequences of *Full Metal Jacket* (1987) are replete with scenes in which a marine drill instructor (DI) hurls sexually abusive epithets at his recruits. An easy way to embarrass any impressionable young man in front of his equally immature peers is by attacking his manliness. To toughen them up, this film's DI routinely accuses his young trainees of real or latent homosexuality. Typical is the exchange quoted in chapter 1, when Pvt. "Cowboy" receives such harassment. Of course, Cowboy vehemently denies it, knowing that a fate worse than death awaits a gay marine. A virtually identical scene occurs eighteen years later in a basic training scene in *Jarhead* (2005).

Rod Steiger's character in *The Sergeant* notwithstanding, in war films, there are nearly no examples of gays peacefully coexisting with straights in war films; however, there are many instances in which men appear to cross that "macho line" between heterosexuality and the display of suspect levels of affection for another male. As Anthony Easthope (1990) reminds us,

> In the dominant versions of men at war, men are permitted to behave toward each other in ways that would not be allowed elsewhere, caressing and holding each other, comforting and weeping together, admitting their love. The pain of war is the price paid for the way it expresses the male bond. War's suffering is a kind of punishment for the release of homosexual desire and male femininity that only war allows. (66)

For example, in *Wings* (1927), flyers Jack (Buddy Rogers) and David (Richard Arlen) are close friends. In the denouement, Jack mistakes David for a German, because David has stolen a plane from the enemy. Jack shoots him down. As Joan Mellen (1977) writes, Jack

> shoots down the person he loves best in the world. . . . Before David expires, the two buddies are reunited in one of the most resonant love scenes between two men to appear in the American cinema. . . . Jack cradles David's head and their hands touch. Both men cry, able at last to express their concealed emotions now released by the imminence of death. Their arms are entwined as they caress each other gently. Each hungers for the other's consolation and each receives it. "You didn't kill me," says David. "You destroyed a Heinie ship." Jack presses his lips against David's face and allows words to surface that express what all these gestures have meant, what male impassivity struggles to conceal: "There is nothing in the world that means more to me than your friendship." On this note, David dies. Jack bends his head close over David's body and cries, his hand resting on the top of David's head. He lifts David's body in his arms and carries him off, David's arm around his neck. (86)

As previously mentioned, in *Pearl Harbor*, throughout the second half of the film, boyhood friends Rafe (Ben Affleck) and Danny (Josh Hartnett) have become estranged because they're competing for Evelyn's (Kate Beckinsale) hand in marriage. Finally, before the two flyers leave Hawaii to participate in the Doolittle raid on Tokyo, Evelyn tells Rafe that although she loves him, she has chosen Danny, because she's pregnant with his child. She begs Rafe not to tell Danny so he won't worry, but after the raid, Rafe and Danny crash in Japanese-held territory in China, and Danny has been mortally wounded. Rafe holds Danny lovingly in his arms, and the following dialogue ensues:

> DANNY: Rafe, I'm not gonna make it.
>
> RAFE: (insistently) Yes, you are.
>
> But Rafe inspects Danny's wound and knows he won't.

RAFE: (continuing) Danny, you can't die. You know why? Because you're going to be a father. . . . You're gonna be a daddy. I wasn't supposed to tell you. (he begins to cry)

DANNY: No, you are [going to be a daddy]. (he dies)

RAFE: (sobbing) Danny, Danny, please!

But Danny has expired. Rafe looks up in agony and utters little cries of despair. Only in the throes of death is a manly man allowed to hold his friend and sob out loud.

Upon Rafe's return to Hawaii and Evelyn, there is no more ambiguity. Rafe willingly does his expected manly duty, marrying Evelyn and becoming father to Danny's son. As the film ends, Rafe is teaching the boy to fly, perhaps priming another pilot to do his duty in the next war.

In *Apocalypse Now* (1979), it's unclear whether the "funeral" in the river that crewman Lance (Sam Bottoms) gives Chief (Albert Hall) is a result of heartfelt male affection for his shipmate or the lingering effects of the LSD he's taken, but the way Lance gently cradles his shipmate in death and kisses Chief's forehead is reminiscent of Jack's affection for the dying David in *Wings*. A somewhat similar scene occurs in *Platoon Leader*: Mac, the platoon sergeant, is badly wounded and in the hospital in Saigon. Lt. Knight is also wounded, but he is able to stand at Mac's bedside. Only with Mac lying in bed amidst bloody bandages, stitches, and tubes can Knight feel free to cry a little, hold Mac's hand, hug (gently because the sergeant is in pain), and touch foreheads in lieu of a kiss.

At the conclusion of the movie, both have recovered from their wounds. Knight is back at the firebase, and Mac also returns. Between these two brothers-in-arms, circumstances now are now back to army normal—no tears, no hand-holding, and certainly no touching of foreheads. Knight sees Mac coming and, in a manly way, tosses him an M-16 (which Mac, of course, catches with one hand), and says, "Welcome back to the country club." As they walk away, the only affection they allow themselves is to drape their arms over each other's shoulders, with no more emotion than two rugby players forming a scrum.

Heavy, incessant peer pressure forces adolescent boys to measure up to the behaviors of men. Since homosexuality is by social construction the antithesis of maleness, the worst insult that one boy can hurl at another is that he is "queer." Unfortunately, this practice does not go away when American boys reach age nineteen, the average age for infantrymen serving in most of America's wars. In two Vietnam War combat films, *Platoon* (1986) and *Casualties of War* (1989), young American soldiers have convinced themselves that the "Dinks" (Vietnamese) are sufficiently subhuman that they are not worthy of respect as individuals. So when they are angry at the enemy and opportunities present themselves, young soldiers in these two films wantonly rape young Vietnamese girls. In both motion pictures, only one soldier steps in to try to prevent these crimes.

In *Platoon*, Chris Taylor prevents his fellow soldiers from gang raping two little Vietnamese girls. Irritated that Chris has reminded them of how far they have fallen from grace, one soldier retorts, "Are you a homosexual, Taylor?" Another argues, "She's just a fuckin' Dink!" Chris responds by shouting, "She's a fuckin' human being, man! Fuck you!" Another reminds Chris that he has not yet learned the rule of the jungle in Vietnam, spits on Chris, and says, "You're still a fuckin' 'cherry,' pal . . . you don't belong in the 'Nam, man. It's not your place at all." Implicit then, is that real men who find themselves in combat in war zones are permitted to leave their ethics and civilized behavior stateside. In a war zone, men do what men at war have allowed themselves to do since the days of the Neanderthal: conquer a foe, pillage the countryside, and rape his women.

The incident in *Casualties of War* between Sgt. Meserve (Sean Penn) and Cpl. Eriksson (Michael J. Fox) is much more intense, because Meserve and his men, alone on a long-range reconnaissance patrol, kidnap a young, pretty Vietnamese girl for "some portable R and R" (read gang rape). Meserve knows that all must take part in the crime, so after they rape and murder the girl and dispose of her body, none of the five men dare report it to military authorities. So when Eriksson, who objects to the kidnap, refuses to join in the gang rape, Meserve and Cpl. Clark (Don Harvey) attempt to shame him into compliance with typical schoolyard attacks against his manhood:

> SGT. MESERVE: What's the matter? Don't you like girls? Haven't you got a pair? Is that your problem?
>
> CPL. CLARK: Maybe he's queer.
>
> SGT. MESERVE: (repeating himself) Are you a faggot? Is that your goddam problem?
>
> Eriksson looks over and makes eye contact with another soldier, Pvt. Diaz, who also objected to the rape, but when he is confronted by Meserve, he backs down.
>
> SGT. MESERVE: (watching Eriksson look at Diaz) Oh, wait a minute! Maybe he *is* a queer. (Laughingly) Maybe Eriksson's a homosexual (Meserve pretends to perform fellatio on his rifle barrel.) We got us *two* "girls" on our patrol.
>
> Later, Meserve again insists that Eriksson participate in the rape. But Eriksson refuses.
>
> SGT. MESERVE: Maybe when I'm done in there (with the girl), I'm gonna come after you. Maybe when I'm done humping her, I'm gonna come hump you!

Since the U.S. armed services, unlike those of our European allies, remain essentially homophobic institutions, any comedy about gays in war films must be solely at their expense. For example, dialog to the effect of kissing one's sergeant to earn a psychological discharge from the army is added for comic relief, and everybody knows that the speaker is kidding. No one minds a good joke to lighten a war drama, but comedy, as well as drama, teaches young boys lessons about what is permissible and taboo in social constructions. And then, when Cpl. Max Klinger (Jamie Farr), in the long-running TV series *M*A*S*H*, appears in a dress, hoping to earn a "section 8" discharge for being either homosexual or a cross-dresser (Klinger was not that particular), the canned audience laughs.

To the Nazis, homosexuality was an even greater evil and threat to the manhood of the master race than to the homophobic Americans of the 1940s. To Hitler, despite the gay predilections of some of his own SA storm troopers, homosexuality was deemed a capital offense in the German Army. Plus, the Nazis gathered up thousands of homosexuals and sent them away to concentration camps for extermination. *Cross of Iron* (1976) introduces this by implying that the villain of the piece, Capt. Stransky (Maximilian Schell), is a latent homosexual. But true to his dastardly nature, Stransky was also a hypocrite. He deduces that his adjutant, Lt. Triebig, and his orderly, Pvt. Keppler, are having a homosexual affair. Stransky first tricks Triebig into admitting his sexual preference with an all-too-convincing speech in praise of the merits of a soldier's world without the company of women. Then he smiles sadistically and strokes Keppler's cheek, as if in affection, but then turns toward them both, scowling, and sternly warns them that, "If you are caught, you will be hanged . . . slowly."[4]

In *Top Gun* (1986), Lt. Pete "Maverick" Mitchell (Tom Cruise) and Lt. J. G. Nick "Goose" Bradshaw (Anthony Edwards) clown around a little about their close relationship and create some rather gay-sounding moments. But only in as intensely macho an environment as this school for elite naval aviators can men even joke about being a pilot's "rear" (electronic warfare officer who sits in the cockpit directly behind the pilot) and Goose's playing mother hen to Maverick. We won't even speculate here about the symbolic overtones of Maverick's "rear" having the nickname of "Goose." It likely has more to do with Goose's long neck than anything else.

In one scene, Maverick and Goose are diving in their F-14 Tomcat to engage two enemy fighters. Maverick radios his wingman, "Cougar," to say, "You hook 'em." Goose, Maverick's ever-handy helpmate and resident squadron comedian, chimes in, "And I'll clean 'em and fry 'em." In another scene, after almost being ejected from the Top Gun school for buzzing the control tower, Goose insists that Maverick behave himself, reminding him that he (Goose) has a family to support and think about. Maverick says, "You're the only family I've got." When Goose is killed in a training accident, Maverick mourns him. Like a husband grieving for his wife, Maverick is unwilling to be "adulterous" and carry on with another "rear" whom the school has assigned to take Goose's place in the cockpit.

Similar horseplay with a homosexual bent occurs in *Jarhead*, the story of a squad of the most macho marines you could ever encounter, and thoroughly heterosexual, in the Saudi desert during Operation Desert Shield. One minute they're tossing around a football, and the next they're engaging in a "field fuck" to intentionally scandalize a television reporter and her cameraman. This bizarre act begins when their boss, SSgt. Sykes (Jamie Foxx), is doing a PR interview with the reporter and decides he wants to display how his men can work in full chemical gear (suits to protect them from nerve gas). So Sykes orders his squad, who is throwing around a football, to put on these protective suits and play football for real, although the heavy chemical gear—including gas masks—make running around in 110-degree heat unbearable. The men obey their sergeant, until finally they've had enough. One marine, Swofford (Jake Gyllenhaal) shouts, "Field fuck!," and the men begin tearing off their clothes and pretending to have anal and oral sex with each other, hollering and laughing. Horrified, Sykes hurries the reporter and cameraman into a Humvee and carts them away from the men. Cut to the next scene, in the rain that night, as the men, on punishment detail, heft sandbags up a makeshift pyramid, while Sykes sits, drinking coffee, under a shelter nearby. "I don't hear you laughing now," the NCO taunts.

THE MATE

The male stereotype of the mate is similar to the chaste love affair of Jack and David in *Wings*, but without overt, more characteristically male–female signs of affection. It may be two flyers like Maverick and Goose, but more frequently it's two soldiers who work so closely that they appear to be mated. They share a foxhole and sleep together, like the "couples" in *Battleground*: Pop and Rodrigues, Sgt. Walowicz and Hanson, Jarvess and Abner. Or one soldier carries a heavy Browning machine gun, while his mate carries the gun's tripod and thirty-caliber ammunition, like Cpl. Fedderson (George Peppard) and Pvt. Forstman (Harry Guardino) in *Pork Chop Hill* (1959).

But when one man dies, survivors mourn like Maverick for Goose in *Top Gun*. In *Pork Chop Hill*, Forstman completely cracks up, paralyzed by tears and shock, when Fedderson, who was following him to a new location to set up their machine gun, is killed by an artillery shell. Babbling and distraught about Fedderson, who was following him when killed, Forstman yells back at his friend's body like he still can hear him, saying, "I told ya to keep up!" In *Battleground*, when Rodrigues is killed, Pop, as do Jarvess and Hanson when Abner dies and Walowicz is wounded, mourns for his foxhole mate. Along with Maverick, afterward, none of these three seems quite as comfortable with their newly assigned foxhole companions.

Other "mates" until the end are Archy Hamilton (Mark Lee) and Frank Dunne (Mel Gibson) in *Gallipoli* (1981). Although initially they are rivals in the 100-meter sprint, the two become inseparable friends. The dramatic final scene in *Gallipoli* reminds the audience that Hamilton was always a little bit faster sprinter than Dunne, and in the grim finale, those few extra seconds mark the difference between Dunne saving Hamilton's life and arriving too late. Similarly, in *Wake Island* (1942), Pvt. Joe Doyle (Robert Preston) and Pvt. Aloysius K. "Smacksie" Randall (William Bendix) are inseparable buddies who party, brawl with each other, and ultimately die side by side in a trench while fighting the Japanese.

Father figures sometimes have mates. As mentioned earlier in this chapter, in *Saving Private Ryan*, Capt. Miller and Sgt. Horvath were father and mother to their squad. Occasionally, especially when Miller's hand would begin to shake uncontrollably, Horvath would act concerned and ask Miller if he was okay. In *Sands of Iwo Jima*, Pfc. Charlie Bass (James Brown) and Sgt. John Stryker (John Wayne) were as close to being mates as the standoffish Stryker would allow. Stryker is the boss of the squad and thus plays hard to get, but Bass treats him more like a spouse than his sergeant. Every time Stryker goes on liberty, the sergeant gets stumbling drunk, drinking to excess and mourning his failed marriage. Bass tries various arguments to cajole Stryker into not getting drunk again. Stryker jokingly responds, "Can this be love?," implicitly reminding Bass that there is a sexual line that cannot be crossed in relations between men, especially marines. Undeterred, Bass continues to protect his mate, stalking Stryker whenever he goes into town. When Stryker ends up drunk, Bass rescues him. Later, to identify for the audience who is the symbolic male in this relationship, Stryker affectionately remarks, "You got an old maid's failings: You worry." On his next leave, Stryker, for once sober, pops out of a building, only to find Bass waiting for him. "You know you've got a lotta bloodhound in you," Stryker remarks. In the climax of the film, when Stryker is shot and killed by a Japanese sniper, Bass arrives first to shoot the enemy soldier, furiously pumping a half dozen more rounds into him than necessary.

BATTLING BROTHERS

Occasionally, in addition to men made mates by order of the U.S. War Department, screenwriters resort to using characters who are actually related, such as the battling half-brother marines in *Gung Ho!* (1943). Two quite different looking half brothers bicker constantly about everything from whose father was better to who should be first in the chow line. Their disagreements sometimes dissolve into fistfights. They also compete for the same girl. Also, quite typically, screenwriters Joseph Hoffman and Lucien Hubbard use this belligerence to show how marine training can channel unbridled testosterone into honorable warrior male behavior. Throughout the film, one brother, Larry O'Ryan (David Bruce), keeps one-upping his brother, Kurt Richter (Noah Berry Jr.), with the object of their affections, Kathleen Corrigan (Grace McDonald). Kurt even joined the marines, as O'Ryan puts it, "to make a hit with her," so, of course, O'Ryan joined, too. Although his brother is far from a Lothario, Richter tells Corrigan to beware of O'Ryan, whom he calls "that wolf in uniform."

Finally, in battle against the Japanese on Makin Island, brotherly love and esprit de corps trump brotherly competition. A squad of marines is ordered to attack an enemy machine gun nest. Each man has been assigned a turn to assault the Japanese position alone, while the rest fire to provide him cover. Richter's number comes before O'Ryan's. Based on the lack of success of the marine who assaulted the position just before Richter, O'Ryan assumes that Richter, too, will be killed. O'Ryan lies to Richter, admitting that he only pursued Corrigan to irritate him, and then pushes Richter's helmet down in front of his eyes and one-ups him again, jumping up to attack the Japanese position. O'Ryan is killed. Later, as the marines prepare to leave the island, Richter stands over O'Ryan's hastily dug grave and quietly mourns.

Similarly, Richard Jaeckel and William Murphy play Frank and Eddie, the battling Flynn brothers, in *Sands of Iwo Jima*. And, as in *Gung Ho!* and acting like brawling adolescents, the brothers spend their little amount of screen time punching each other and wrestling on the ground. Once again, with the exception of a few wisecracks, this wasted effort disappears in the heat of battle and is redirected at the enemy. Frank is wounded. When Eddie finds out, he braves enemy fire to carry Frank to safety. To keep Eddie from exposing both of them to snipers, Sgt. Stryker trips Eddie, toppling both to the sand. Of course Frank, wounded and now covered with sand, remarks that Eddie is clumsy.

There is also the true story of the five Sullivan brothers and the film, very loosely based on the deaths of these young men, simply titled *The*

Sullivans (1944). The brothers died together when the USS *Juneau* sank during World War II. The heroic pattern of brotherly love in *Sands of Iwo Jima* and *Gung Ho!* continues in the film. The way the movie tells their story, when the *Juneau* is torpedoed, all the brothers but one could have escaped. Instead, all the brothers clamber back down into the bowels of the ship to try to rescue their brother. There they all die when the ship sinks.

In actuality, the ship's demise was much more complicated than in the film. It took two days for the *Juneau* to finally sink. Approximately 100 of the vessel's crew, including two of the Sullivan brothers, survived the last Japanese attack on this light cruiser, but due to communications problems and the presence of Japanese warships in the area, rescuing the sailors took several days. By then, savage shark attacks, wounds, and exhaustion took their toll, and only ten survived, but neither Sullivan. The heroic death of the five brothers made for a great story of love and sacrifice, but not the public relations nightmare for the U.S. War Department that the Sullivans' real deaths would have precipitated. A heroic attempt to rescue their beloved brother made for a much better movie ending, and the navy did little to disabuse the public of 20th Century Fox's considerable use of "poetic license."

THE VIRGIN

Another of the rights of passage from boyhood into manhood is a male's first sexual experience. In countless films, young troops claim to have considerable experience in lovemaking, but in reality, they score with ladies less often than Wolf in *Destination Tokyo*. In these scenes, to again demonstrate male hegemonic values, women are objectified for one purpose only: to assist young men in crossing the bridge to full-fledged manhood. Inexperience in almost any sense is viewed as unmanly, so it's not surprising that new, untested replacement troops are referred to by their fellow soldiers as "cherries," those who are still virgins with respect to combat. There are such occasions as in *Hamburger Hill* (1987), where young troops experience relief and exhilaration after their first firefight, because they have, in the sense of experiencing combat, "popped their cherries." No longer combat virgins, these young men had finally faced death for the first time and survived to brag about it.

There are plenty of virgins, or near virgins, in *Biloxi Blues*, as the dialog below indicates. In the following scene, the boys are on leave and nervously awaiting their turn to cross the divide between virginity and manhood, courtesy of Rowena, the previously discussed Biloxi prostitute:

JEROME (Matthew Broderick): Hey, what if she's ugly? I mean, really ugly.

SELRIDGE (Markus Flanigan): Then you close your eyes and you think of some cheerleader.

JEROME: I don't want to close my eyes: That's the same as doing it to yourself.

SELRIDGE: Not if you're feeling someone underneath you, or on top of you.

JEROME: On top of me? Who would be on top of me?

SELRIDGE: She would. She could be anywhere. Under a table, on a chair, or an ironing board.

JEROME: On an ironing board? What kind of girl is this? I thought we were going to a regular place.

SELRIDGE: Don't you know anything?

JEROME: Maybe not in actual experience, but I have all the information I need.

SELRIDGE: You don't know shit, Jerome. Do you know how many positions there are?

JEROME: American or worldwide?

CARNEY (Casey Siemaszko): (laughs) This guy is a riot.

SELRIDGE: For five bucks, how many positions are there?

JEROME: Let me think.

SELRIDGE: Do you want me to tell you?

JEROME: No.

SELRIDGE: I'm gonna tell you. There are seventeen acceptable positions.

JEROME: Acceptable? What is there, an Olympic committee that votes on positions?

CARNEY: I can't believe this guy is from New York.

JEROME: Besides, you're wrong. There are fifty-two positions.

SELRIDGE: Fifty-two? You're crazy. Where did you ever get that from?

JEROME: I saw a dirty deck of cards once.

SELRIDGE: This jerk is worse than Epstein.

JEROME: You owe me five bucks.

SELRIDGE: Hey, listen, twerp, you're lucky if you do one position.

JEROME: I'm not doing anything if it's on an ironing board.

CARNEY: Why not? You'll get your shirt pressed for free.

Another untested young man is dubbed "Virgil the Virgin" by his fellow bomber crewmen in *Memphis Belle*. In everything other than love, young Virgil (Reed Diamond) seems experienced and mature. He was in the restaurant business before the war and tells his mates about his plans to open a number of franchised restaurants that all serve the same kind of hamburger—a forerunner to McDonald's. But in the romantic arts, Virgil is indeed a "cherry." Although, as discussed earlier, "Rascal" was not successful in seducing that English girl (Jane Horrocks), Virgil somehow manages to convince her to deflower him in—appropriately—the cockpit of his bomber. Virgil becomes very nervous and accidentally drops a heavy wrench on her foot. Sensing how uncomfortable and unsure of himself he is, she asks, "You've never done this before, have you?" Virgil responds, "No. Am I doing something wrong?" Smiling, she simply says, "No." She removes her chewing gum and slowly pulls him down to her.

Not all virgins are deflowered in war films. In *Mister Roberts* (1955), after months at sea, the crew of a cargo ship is finally granted liberty on an idyllic South Seas island. Most of the crew, true to the comedic nature of the film, find outlandish ways to celebrate, including stealing a motorcycle and riding it into the bay, crashing and vandalizing an army party, stealing the army commandant's pet goat, and chasing young women until most ran off, screaming, into the night. But there was one exception in young seaman Bookser (Patrick Wayne). He, too, found a young native girl—but not at a party or bar, at a church meeting. The virginal Bookser reports to Roberts, the ship's exec (Henry Fonda), that the two did stay out for the entire night, but that all they did was hold hands, sit by the seashore, and talk.

THE RAPIST

In man's history, rape and pillage have been—and sadly remain today—traditional spoils of war for soldiers. In ancient times, commanders reduced the cost of paying their men by tacitly or openly including these spoils as part of a soldier's compensation. In the centuries that have followed, more civilized "rules" of war have proscribed most of these activities. And in the twentieth and twenty-first centuries, as women have emerged as rights-holding citizens, rape—including during wartime—has become especially heinous.[5]

Images of males committing rape in American war films often fall into two categories: atrocities (often rape followed by murder) committed by the enemy and acts of rape by Americans, usually portrayed as a lamentable deviation from the norm of "civilized" American soldierly behavior. A propaganda technique used often in American movies during World War II was to portray the enemy as a savage who would stoop to such low crimes as rape. As an example of Nazi depravity, screenwriters Robert Rossen and William Woods used the rape of Karen Stensgard (Ann Sheridan) in *Edge of Darkness* to precipitate the climactic uprising against the Germans in this Norwegian village. In dialog among the Germans, the audience learns that when they arrived to occupy the village, their commander had ordered his men to restrain themselves from their "usual conduct," which included rape and other crimes against the helpless citizenry. But later, the commander wishes to flush out the leaders of the local resistance movement, and decides to precipitate an incident to cause the partisans to show their hand. He allows his soldiers to mistreat the townspeople in the manner they were accustomed to in previous campaigns. This is when Stensgard's rape occurs. Her father revenges himself on the guilty German soldier, and the Germans arrest him, along with all the other suspected resistance leaders. The plan is to have these leaders publicly executed. In his hubris, the commander does not believe that the villagers would rise up as one to try to overthrow the Nazis. But they do, and the townspeople kill every last German soldier.

American propaganda about rape, as portrayed in feature films during World War II, was much harder on the Japanese than the Germans. Screenwriters played the "race card" with this Asian enemy in *China* (1943), as Japanese infantrymen murder a peaceful Chinese farm family, including a baby, but not before raping the women. In righteous anger, the American hero, Mr. Jones (Alan Ladd), machine guns the Japanese soldiers who committed this atrocity.

As introduced earlier, *Cross of Iron* is about war-weary, disillusioned Germans fighting and trying to survive on the Russian front during World War II. At one point, a reconnaissance patrol led by Sergeant Steiner (James Coburn) comes across a farmhouse, capturing a squad of female Russian soldiers billeted inside. At first, Steiner must stop one of his men from raping one of the women. Before the squad's attack, one of the women was outside, taking a bath in a rain barrel. One of Steiner's men joins her inside the barrel, and Steiner makes him get out and take the buxom bather into the farmhouse with the rest of the women.

Next, a particularly odious German soldier—the only true Nazi in the film—along with another of Steiner's men, the youngest and most inexperienced in the squad, are assigned by Steiner to stand guard over the women in the farmhouse. The Nazi flirts with one of these females, but she defiantly spits at him. Determined to establish dominance and rape her, the Nazi leaves the young soldier to guard all the women in the farmhouse and drags the Russian woman to a nearby barn. There, the Nazi forces her to perform fellatio on him. Meanwhile, in the farmhouse, one of the Russian women seductively approaches the young soldier, smiles, and offers him wine. But when he drinks it, she stabs him. In the barn, instead of performing fellatio on the Nazi, the defiant Russian woman bites off his penis. Enraged and in pain, the Nazi kills her, but he is so badly injured that he cannot walk.

Sgt. Steiner discovers both his dead young soldier in the house and the Nazi and the dead Russian woman in the barn. He is so disgusted with the Nazi's actions that he orders all the women into the barn and leaves the Nazi to his fate with the Russian women, whom he leaves behind. Always the pragmatist, Steiner glares at the women's commander and says, "We're even," and as the scene ends, the women surrounding the Nazi close in on him with some sort of savage revenge in mind.

In American films, especially those of earlier wars, any soldier who rapes is demonized. Such is the case in two scenes in *Gone with the Wind* (1939). In the first scene, a Confederate deserter invades Tara and threatens Scarlett, who shoots the attacker. Later in the picture, a homeless former soldier attacks Scarlett in her carriage, but she is rescued by her former slave, Big Sam. Later, the soldier and others are presumably all shot by Scarlett's revengeful husband and his friends. Similarly in *Cold Mountain* (2003), three renegade Yankee soldiers threaten to kill a widow's baby if she won't provide them with food and sex. She swears she has no more livestock for food but offers to let them rape her if they will spare her baby. One of the three soldiers objects to everything the other two are doing, except for stealing her food, but he is outranked. One soldier takes the woman in the house and starts to rape her, but the film's hero, Inman, a runaway Confederate soldier who was hiding inside, kills the man. When the second Yankee enters the house to take his turn with the woman, Inman also kills him. Inman lets the third, more sympathetic Yankee run away, but the woman, like Scarlett, will have none of this. She picks up a gun and shoots him as he runs.

As far back as American silent films about World War I, the "Beast of Berlin" is shown, as American propaganda of the time insisted, to be a villain of the highest order. Such a potential rapist is the Prussian officer in D. W. Griffith's *Hearts of the World* (1918). Of course, as in *Birth of a Nation* (1915), at the last moment the hero saves the heroine's virtue from the would-be rapist. Arab women in *Lawrence of Arabia* (1962) were not so lucky. The Turkish rape and murder of women in an Arab village precipitates a moral crisis for Lawrence, who finally orders no quarter as his men attack the remains of the Turkish Army retreating before him.

Typical of films about the Vietnam War, the elusive Viet Cong (VC) get away with rape and mass murder of noncombatant villagers, as in the opening sequence of *The Siege of Firebase Gloria* (1989) and in *The Green Berets* (1968). But the memory of these atrocities motivates the U.S. troops who discover them to pursue and destroy the enemy.

Those U.S. soldiers who rape are characterized as the lowest of the low, anomalies among "honorable" Americans at war. The squad of rapists in *Casualties of War* consists of two truly odious soldiers (the sergeant

In *Casualties of War*, Sgt. Meserve (Sean Penn), right, argues with Pvt. Eriksson (Michael J. Fox) over the fate of the girl they've captured (Thuy Thu Le). *Columbia Pictures / Photofest © Columbia Pictures Corp.; photographer: Roland Neveu*

in charge and his equally malevolent toady of a corporal), one soldier with a low IQ who seems to have been plucked out of the screenplay for *Deliverance* (1972), plus one more, a newcomer to the squad too afraid to defy the others. Also described earlier, in *Platoon*, these men have just devastated a village, killing at least three innocent villagers. But because they found VC weapons and rice hidden there, the platoon is ordered to burn the village and arrest any suspected VC collaborators. During this scene, soldiers attempt to rape two young girls, prevented only by their fellow soldier, Chris Taylor.

THE WOMAN HATER AND THE PSYCHOPATH

The woman-hating, psychopath murderer suffers from what psychologists today call an antisocial personality disorder. Often abused as children, these men are not capable of forming conventional relationships, especially with women. There is perhaps no more insane psychopathic character in all of America's war films than Pvt. Archer J. Maggott (Telly Savalas) in the World War II film *The Dirty Dozen* (1967). In prison and sentenced to be hanged for the murder of a prostitute, Maggott hears voices that tell him that he is God's avenging angel, and his mission is to slit the throats of prostitutes wherever he finds them. Surprisingly, Maggott makes it through the training program and is allowed to participate in the climactic raid on a mansion full of senior German officers, but when he comes into contact with the girlfriend of one of these officers, he slits her throat, giving away the presence of the American commandos.[6]

Although more capable of coexisting outside the asylum, bomber crew member Capt. Aarfy Aardvark (Charles Grodin), in *Catch-22* (1970), has cracked up and murdered a young woman who lived in the Italian town near the air base. Another crewmember, Capt. John Yossarian (Alan Arkin), finds Aardvark's girlfriend's body on the cobblestones, thrown out a window on the fourth floor of a building. He looks up to find a crazed Aardvark looking down on her from the window. Yossarian runs upstairs to find Aardvark sitting in his underwear in the corner of the room, knees tucked up to his chest, with a blank look on his face. He is obviously suffering a psychotic episode, perhaps due to stress and battle fatigue.

One of *The Dirty Dozen,* Maggott (Telly Savalas), threatens the girlfriend of a German officer (Dora Reisser) with a knife. ***MGM / Photofest © MGM***

YOSSARIAN: You killed her!

AARDVARK: (strangely calm) Well, I had to do that after I raped her. I couldn't let her go around saying bad things about me, could I?

YOSSARIAN: Are you insane? They're gonna throw you in jail. You just killed a girl: You threw her out of the window. She's lying out there in the street!

AARDVARK: (matter-of-factly) She has no right to be there, you know. It's after curfew.

YOSSARIAN: (frustrated) Don't you realize what you've done? You murdered a human being! They're gonna hang you!

AARDVARK: I hardly think they'll do that, not to good old Aarfy. I don't think they'll make such a fuss over one Italian girl when thousands of lives are being lost every day.

Ironically, in this black comedic satire, Aardvark's right. Yossarian tells Aardvark that the MPs are coming to get him, but instead the MPs burst into the room and arrest Yossarian for being absent without leave. Aardvark just sits on the bed and smiles.[7]

Perhaps the treatment of Maggott and Aardvark in these screenplays says something more macho than gentlemanly about American male views regarding wartime rape. After all, the standard rhetoric in the barracks or locker room is that a truly manly man attracts and seduces women with his appearance, personality, and persuasive discourse. The true "stud" is a "chick magnet" and does not need to resort to force to "get the girl." Furthermore, some film scripts maintain that only losers resort to purchasing the services of a prostitute. Like a good huntsman in earlier times, he can stalk and defeat his prey in an honorable, culturally sanctioned fashion. Rape is not honorable, but, of course, as we learned in the behaviors of Buzz Rickson, the pursuit of women as sex objects is acceptable, provided the usual and customary rules of the hunter are observed. Both Maggott and Aardvark are portrayed as crazy losers. Thus screenwriters have made them gross exceptions to the rule that truly manly Americans can hunt their own game, attracting females by their hypermasculinity.

THE FNG

FNG is soldier slang for "fucking new guy." He is often a replacement added to a military unit after the loss of a man due to rotation back to the States, wounds, or death. To make matters more uncomfortable for new men in the unit, the veterans he's joining are often still mourning the loss of the comrade the FNG is replacing. There are many emotions at play in this scenario, but none of them benefit FNGs, who are often inexperienced, anxious "new guys just in from the world," as one soldier in *Platoon* refers to two new replacements in his unit. Screenwriters often use the FNG as a character and story exposition tool, introducing the squad, its characters, its culture, and its mission to the audience.[8]

The addition of a young kid right out of submarine school to the crew allows Delmer Daves's and Albert Maltz's script for *Destination Tokyo* to introduce everything from proper, manly crew decorum while being depth charged to various submariner superstitions. For example, it is taboo to whistle on a submarine, but at least for Tommy Adams, the new "kid" aboard the submarine *Copperfin*, the reception is cordial, friendly, and abounding with new friends who seem to care for the young man. Unlike the reception of most FNGs in later war films, which usually ranges from intolerance to apathy, not one sailor aboard the submarine *Copperfin* is hostile to FNG Tommy. Rarely was such enmity written into screenplays in films made during World War II. It would have been counter to the fictional propaganda message depicting the united, committed military of the time.

After the end of World War II, such as in William Wellman's classic *Battleground*, more realistic relationships between seasoned veterans and

After fighting the Battle of the Bulge, no longer an FNG, Pvt. Layton (Marshall Thompson), second from left, is now a hardened veteran and fits right in with the rest of the squad in *Battleground*. *MGM / Photofest © MGM*

FNGs emerged in American war films. Pfc. Jim Layton (Marshall Thompson) joins the squad as a replacement for a soldier who was killed. In the scene in which he joins the old hands of the squad in the large tent in which they all are billeted, no one talks to him except to tell him that "this bunk is mine." No one teaches him anything or welcomes him to the unit. Only after he proves himself in combat and quietly endures the harsh conditions in the field is Layton, his combat "cherry" now broken, accepted as a full-fledged member of the squad.

Shortly after his arrival, Layton briefly leaves the squad to visit his buddy, Pvt. William Hooper. The two joined the company simultaneously, but Hooper was assigned to another squad. Layton is eager to check in with his friend and see how Hooper's first few days with his squad compare to his own. But when Layton finds Hooper's squad, no one has heard of him. After explaining that Hooper was the new replacement in their squad, they surmise that Hooper must have been the "new guy" who was killed by an artillery shell shortly after he reported in. Not even Hooper's dog tags were found, so no one knew his name. The soldier Layton talks to reports to his sergeant that the dead FNG's name was William Hooper, and the sergeant is somewhat pleased, as he can now complete his daily report, because he can now fill in the name of the deceased. Layton, now alone, returns to the platoon, intent on fitting in, keen on making sure that the soldiers in his squad remember his name.[9]

A generation later, in *Platoon*, nothing much has changed. More experienced soldiers voice many openly hostile comments directed at newcomer Chris Taylor (Charlie Sheen) and the other new replacement, Pvt. Gardner (Bob Orwig), whom one odious squad member refers to only as a "fat fuck." Both were called "lame" and "cheese dicks" because of their lack of experience and poor skills in "humping the boonies," as arduous patrol duty in the jungle is called. Only Sgt. Elias (Willem Dafoe) is kind and helpful to Taylor and Gardner, patiently advising the two FNGs regarding what backpack items they actually need to take with them on long patrols. This will lighten their load considerably, reducing exhaustion and dehydration. Elias even appeals to platoon first sergeant Bob Barnes (Tom Berenger) for Taylor and Gardner, trying to prevent the newcomers being assigned to a hazardous nighttime ambush patrol before they learn enough to survive in a firefight, which is quite likely to occur on this patrol.

But Barnes stubbornly ignores Elias, and on this mission, the inexperienced Gardner makes a rookie mistake in a firefight and is killed. Afterward, Barnes gathers his patrol around him and insists that everyone, "Take a good look at this lump of shit." Barnes says that like Gardner, when "you fuck up in a firefight," a soldier is usually guaranteed a trip out of the bush in a body bag. The general consensus among most of the platoon is that Gardner was lucky to be killed so early in his Vietnam tour. Taylor's voice-over narration explains that the "grunt's" logic is that if you're going to die, it's better to be killed early on, so that the amount of time you suffer is reduced.

An FNG must often endure initiation hazings before he is given full and equal status in the group. For example, in Clint Eastwood's 2006 epic *Flags of Our Fathers*, a FNG is constantly the butt of his buddies' and his sergeant's jokes. Told his "masturbation papers" are not in order, the gullible FNG is told by his sergeant that he must report to the records office to get this straightened out. "Now," says Sgt. Mike (Barry Pepper), "if he calls you an idiot, you take it like a man, okay? Just don't leave without those papers."

In *Hamburger Hill*, a number of fresh-faced replacements are shipped directly to Vietnam from advanced infantry training (AIT) in the United States. At first, these youngsters find it difficult making friends with the veterans, but over time—after they also suffer through combat—the newcomers develop relationships with some of the men. These FNGs make many mistakes, but their platoon sergeant and squad leader, an experienced sergeant, patiently try to teach them the skills they weren't taught in AIT. But in this violent and bloody film, based on a real-life battle, the majority of men in the platoon, experienced men as well as replacements, are wounded or killed assaulting a well-defended hill in the Ashau Valley, a key sector for North Vietnamese infiltration into the South.

FNGs are not always enlisted men. In *84 Charlie Mopic* (1989), for example, a lieutenant/interviewer and an enlisted man/camera operator who work for army public information (read PR) accompany an elite reconnaissance squad on a hazardous patrol. Although some of the troops are initially flattered with the prospect of publicity, the gruff squad leader, simply called "OD" (Richard Brooks), considers the inexperienced officer, whom the men call "L. T." (Jonathan Emerson), a potential hazard to his men's safety. New to the jungle, L. T. makes rookie mistakes related to patrol discipline, and OD, a menacing presence to begin with, often intimidates the officer, once to the point of threatening to kill him.

Some FNG characters are more fully developed than others. In *Full Metal Jacket*, Kevyn Howard is a Vietnam FNG, whose nickname is "Rafterman," looking for adventure and to "bust his cherry" in action against the enemy. In much the same way as a Native American is not designated a full-fledged brave or warrior until he counts coup against an enemy, Rafterman, a marine photographer, considers himself less worthy (read manly) than his buddies, because all he has done so far in his tour of duty in Vietnam is to take ceremonial "grab and grin" handshake pictures back at the base. He yearns to get out in the "bush," fire his rifle a little, face the enemy, and thereby earn a new, more manly designation. Having grown up seeing old John Wayne war movies on television, Rafterman seeks to shuck his FNG status and evolve into a man who exhibits the "stare" of a combat veteran. In barracks discussions, the men who have seen some action in the bush are said to have this look, while wide-eyed innocents like Rafterman do not.

In the big caper war film *Kelly's Heroes* (1970), Don Rickles costars as "Crap Game," a scheming con artist and supply sergeant who joins Kelly's squad to collect on the rich payday that Kelly plans for himself and his men. Rather than for patriotic reasons, Kelly plans to infiltrate enemy lines to steal a treasure, millions of dollars in Nazi gold stashed in a bank in a French town held by the enemy. Crap Game bankrolls the caper and decides to accompany Kelly and his men to protect his investment. But after their armored vehicles are destroyed in an air attack, reality sets in, and FNG Crap Game must become an infantry soldier and carry a heavy machine gun on a forced march. Complaining constantly, Crap Game tries to bribe another soldier to carry his load, to no avail. Only during the climactic fighting at the end of the film does Crap Game step up and truly become a soldier, fighting bravely alongside his comrades.

THE COURAGEOUS BOY

The main ways young boys learn the behaviors expected of them as adults is to observe and imitate their male role models. When war is crashing all around them, young boys, out of necessity, grow up quickly, putting away childish things. In U.S. war movies, boys are generally not pictured in full combat; however, there are examples of actual boys assisting their grown-up role models in dangerous spy work and enabling grown-ups in missions against the enemy.

One of the most courageous boys who comes to mind is Maximo Cuenca (Ducky Louie) in *Back to Bataan* (1945). A few years too young to join the guerilla force led by Col. Madden (John Wayne) and openly fight the Japanese invaders, schoolboy Maximo must content himself with gathering intelligence information on Japanese troop movements and reporting them to Madden. On one occasion, a radio propaganda event staged by the Japanese, Madden plans an ambush, but Maximo inadvertently shows his hand to the enemy by making sure that the Filipino children who were forced to attend this event were not injured when the guerillas attacked. Unfortunately, a Japanese officer spots Maximo leading the children to safety, and the boy is arrested, tortured, and beaten. The Japanese want the child to show them the way to Madden's camp, so Maximo, to avoid further abuse, pretends to acquiesce. Instead, Maximo directs a truck full of Japanese soldiers to a spot on a mountain road where the brave boy suddenly grabs the truck's steering wheel and turns it off the road, sending a truckload of Japanese soldiers—and himself—plummeting over a cliff to their deaths.

Another brave boy-spy is the son of a Dutch underground leader in the World War II epic *A Bridge Too Far* (1977). The Germans unexpectedly move a panzer division into Arnhem, Holland, for what the enemy thinks is a "rest." Unfortunately for the entire operation, the Germans have unwittingly placed this division in the perfect position to confound Allied troops, who are about to stage "Operation Market Garden," a massive Allied attempt to secure three Rhine River bridges in Holland that provide access into Germany.

The boy, credited only as the "underground leader's son" (Erik van't Wout), spots the panzer division commander's vehicle and the tanks and reports this to his father, an underground leader. His father radios the information to Allied headquarters in England. But even after photo reconnaissance confirms that the tanks are in Arnhem, in one of the biggest blunders of the war, British lieutenant general Frederick Browning ignores the evidence and orders the invasion to proceed as scheduled. This and the presence of yet another panzer division wreck any chances for Operation Market Garden to succeed, and Arnhem becomes a killing ground. During the destructive fight for Arnhem, as the boy and his father help rescue wounded civilians and pile the bodies of the dead for disposal, the boy is killed by sniper fire. In a poignant scene, the father picks up and carries his own brave son's limp, lifeless body and places it gently on a pile with the rest of the dead.

The Korean War film *The Steel Helmet* (1951) features a Korean boy who attaches himself to an army sergeant after his family is killed. The name given him by gruff Sgt. Zack (Gene Evans) is "Short Round" (William Chun). Short Round meets Zack when the unconscious sergeant is tied up and left for dead after an enemy bullet pierced Zack's helmet and rendered him unconscious. Luckily for Zack, the bullet rattled around inside the helmet and exited without doing more than rendering him temporarily comatose. Short Round becomes an unofficial member of the squad that Zack encounters and reluctantly joins. Later, wearing "clodhoppers" (boots Zack gave to the barefoot boy) and a U.S. Army steel helmet, Short Round is mistaken for a U.S. soldier and killed by a North Korean sniper.

Like Short Round, many children are left orphaned by wars and quickly learn to fend for themselves like adults. Such was the case of a young Sicilian boy named Matteo (Matteo Zofoli) in *The Big Red One*. Matteo's mother had been killed in the fighting between the invading Americans and the Germans, and he is transporting her body in a push cart when the he meets a squad of U.S. soldiers. One of them, Pvt. Vinci, speaks Italian. With Vinci's translation, the sergeant asks the boy if he knows where the squad's military objective, a hidden German SP (self-propelled cannon) shelling U.S. troops on the beach from a concealed position, is located. The boy says, "Si," he knows where the Germans are, but he won't lead the squad to the SP unless they perform a service for him. Matteo insists on a casket with four handles for his Mama and a proper burial. Frustrated but realizing that Matteo has the Americans over a barrel, Vinci says, "Okay, Jesse James," and agrees to the boy's terms.

Matteo also refuses to leave his mother while he leads the squad to the SP, so the Americans must cart her remains, now malodorous in the hot Sicilian sun, with them. The sergeant, determined to locate the SP, agrees, and the men drag the cart with them, bandanas over their noses to reduce the stench. Later, after the squad successfully takes out the hidden German gun, Matteo gets his coffin and a four-star burial for Mama. Also, when the squad kills the Germans, they free a number of older Sicilian women whom the enemy had coerced into forced labor. The grateful women put on a feast for the squad and, presumably, give Matteo a new home as the squad moves on.

Similar to Short Round, but with the disposition of Matteo, is brave young elephant driver Linh (Dinh Thien Le) in *Operation Dumbo Drop* (1995). At first, Linh is hostile to the Americans, whose artillery may have been responsible for killing his family. But he later becomes attached to the U.S. soldiers and they to him. At one point, Linh does reconnaissance for the Americans and is captured by the enemy, who beat him to find out the location of the troops. Linh lies, sending most of the enemy off in the opposite direction, and the Americans later rescue him. Finally, as with Matteo, the U.S. soldiers provide Linh and the elephant with a new home, kids his own age for friends, and a foster family.

Mikael (Slavko Stimak) is a Russian boy who, despite being about thirteen or fourteen years of age, has been made a soldier manning a Soviet mortar emplacement in Sam Peckinpah's *Cross of Iron*. Although Cpl. Steiner's patrol ambushes and kills all the men in this Russian battery, they spare the youngster. They take him prisoner and bring them back to German lines. Capt. Stransky (Maximilian Schell), citing a directive that they should kill all Russian prisoners, orders Steiner to shoot the child, but the sergeant refuses. Fortunately, a Russian mortar attack interrupts this standoff, and Steiner's men hide the boy in their bunker. For a while, the boy hangs out in Steiner's bunker with the men and is seen more as a child they're protecting than a soldier with whom they are at war. Steiner eventually escorts the boy back across German lines and frees him to rejoin his Russian comrades, but, ironically, as Mikael makes his way back, the Russians mistake him for a German infiltrator and shoot him.[10]

In the Civil War drama *The Horse Soldiers* (1959), a Confederate commander asks the headmaster of Jefferson Military Academy to muster his battalion of schoolboys to attack the battle-hardened veterans of Union colonel John Marlowe's (John Wayne) invading cavalry outfit. The reason is to delay Marlowe's unit until grown-up Confederate cavalry can arrive to engage them. One drummer boy in particular shows great determination to face these fierce Union soldiers. His mother, seeing the boys being marched through their town to what she thinks will be certain death, begs the headmaster to dismiss her son to her care. The headmaster complies, and the mother drags the boy—drum and all—into their home. But the boy escapes his mother, bolts out the back door, and runs to rejoin his regiment. Later, after Marlowe chooses to retreat to avoid having to kill the boys, one of his troopers is seen laughingly giving the drummer boy a spanking.

THE COWARD

"The coward dies a thousand deaths; the brave man only once" is an anonymous saying that informs America's pragmatic assessment of manliness in battle. But in many films, inexperienced soldiers find it especially hard to define cowardice. Does fear of death or injury mean that one is yellow? Many soldiers in war films think that just because they're fearful of the coming engagement with the enemy, they must be cowards, and thus still unworthy of the status of true men.

In these films, there usually is some other, older, wiser character, such as Sgt. Stryker (John Wayne) in *Sands of Iwo Jima*, who is approached by a young soldier for advice about his fear. In this film, Pvt. Fowler (William Self) approaches Stryker as their landing craft moves toward the beach at Iwo Jima. Fowler admits to Stryker that he's scared, but Stryker surprises the youngster by saying, "So am I." "Not you?" the astonished marine says. "Fowler, I'm always scared," the taciturn Stryker replies. In this and other war films, screenwriters always seem to hand the Duke speeches directed at fearful soldiers and sailors, designed to instruct them in Wayne's specialty: the art of manly stoicism. True men must simply swallow their fears, do the soldierly jobs they've been trained to do, and let fate take its course. If it wouldn't have been out of character for the Duke, in some films he might have paraphrased Alfred, Lord Tennyson on the subject: "Ours is not to reason why; ours is but to do and die."[11]

Consider the following from Samuel Stouffer (1976):

> Combat posed a challenge for a man to prove himself to himself and others. Combat was a dare. One never knew that he could take it until he had demonstrated that he could. Most soldiers facing the prospect of combat service had to deal with a heavy charge of anticipatory anxiety. . . . A code as universal as "being a man" is very likely to have been deeply internalized. So fear of failure in the role, as by showing cowardice in battle, could bring not only fear of social censure on their point as such, but also more central and strongly established fears related to sex-typing. To fail to measure up as a soldier in courage and endurance was to risk the charge of not being a man. ("Whatsa matter, Bud—got lace in your drawers?") If one was not socially defined as a man, there was a strong likelihood of being branded as a "woman," a dangerous threat to the contemporary male personality. (180)

As introduced in chapter 2, in Robert Aldrich's gritty World War II film *Attack!* (1956), fear drives company commander Capt. Erskine Cooney (Eddie Albert) to drunkenness and indecision, which indirectly precipitates the deaths of many of his men. A commander in a U.S. National Guard company mobilized during World War II, Cooney received his commission because of local politics rather than his abilities. In character exposition, we learn that Cooney was a victim of his strong-willed father's emotional abuse. Feeling unworthy and unable to perform in a manly fashion, Cooney cracks under the strain of command. When he has this nervous breakdown, director Robert Aldrich enhances the scene by adding childish-sounding music, underscoring Cooney's inability to function as an adult or become the man his father wanted him to be.[12]

Similar to Cooney is First Lt. Norman Dike, one of the very few nonheroic characters in the HBO miniseries *Band of Brothers* (2001). This series dramatically chronicles the true-life story of Easy Company of the 101st Airborne "Screaming Eagles" during World War II, from their advanced paratrooper training to their parachute jump behind the lines on D-Day in Normandy until the defeat of Germany. Dike's ability to disappear when Easy Company was in a desperate situation earned the officer a deservedly bad reputation among the men. Dike was assigned to command Easy Company after its charismatic leader, then-Capt. Richard D. Winters, was promoted and assigned to duty at battalion headquarters.

It's hard to tell from one minute to the next whether "Foxhole Norman," as the men refer to Dike, is really a coward or just a lazy, unconcerned officer who prefers to cull favor with unnamed "big shots" back at battalion and division rather than leading and caring for his men. This task falls to the long-suffering and actual commander of Easy Company, First Sgt. Carwood Lipton (Donnie Wahlberg). When there's a dangerous patrol or German shelling going on, Dike is either nowhere to be found or quickly scuttling toward the rear in the direction of battalion headquarters to "get help." We will discuss Lt. Dike in greater depth in chapter 4, "Manliness and the Burden of Command."

Eddie Albert plays Tom Hughes, a much more sympathetic character, but every bit as fearful, in *Bombardier!* Albert's character, a bombardier in training, is too terrified of falling to his death to parachute from a damaged bomber that is about to crash. Another cadet manages to land the plane, and after a court of investigation, Hughes is given a second chance to prove himself. Later, he gets the opportunity to prove he's no coward. Once again aloft on a training flight, a fellow cadet accidentally falls through the ship's malfunctioning bomb bay and hangs precariously from the bay door. Despite his fears, Hughes summons up all his courage to assist his friend, but while successfully rescuing him, he ironically falls to his death.

In *The Fighting 69th* (1940), James Cagney plays Pvt. Jerry Plunkett, a member of World War I's famous "Rainbow Division." During training in the States, Plunkett brags to all who will listen about how great a soldier he will be and how many medals he'll win. But in the heat of battle in France, with men dying all around him, Plunkett freezes up in fear. Despite his former arrogance and bravado, he acts like a coward. Before Plunkett is led away in disgrace, his commander gives him a second chance to do his duty. But once again, Plunkett proves a coward, but this time his actions cause the deaths of some of his fellow soldiers. Arrested, Plunkett is taken behind the lines to be court-martialed. Artillery shells damage the place where he is being held, and Plunkett is able to escape custody. Likely facing a firing squad, he nonetheless decides to rush back to the front, where he bravely attacks the enemy and is killed. Like so many soldiers before and since, Plunkett's illusions about war—and himself—were vastly different from war's reality of blood, pain, and death. Faced with such reality, Plunkett could not cope. Because his character during most of the movie was also quite belligerent and boastful, his comrades show him very little understanding. Not able to live as the coward he had become, he was willing to die rather than fail as a man.

In *Captain Newman, M.D.* (1963), a World War II-era psychiatrist (Gregory Peck) learns that his patient, Capt. Paul Cabot Winston (Robert Duvall) had been cut off from his unit in a combat area in Europe. Winston hid out in a cellar behind enemy lines for more than a year before it was liberated. But Winston is a blueblood, with a tight-lipped, stuffed-shirt family who he believes would not understand such ungallant, "un-Winstonlike" behavior. Full of survivor guilt about hiding safe in the cellar, he chooses to lapse into narcolepsy and catatonia rather than face the reality of his actions. Especially in his high society circle, Winston's social construction of duty renders his actions taboo, so he chooses to hide in the cellar of his mind rather than face the situation.[13]

In *Captain Newman, M.D.*, Cpl. Jim Tompkins (Bobby Darin) also suffers from survivor guilt. Unlike Winston, Tompkins remains reasonably functional but is clinically depressed, hiding his feelings in a haze of drugs and alcohol. Under the influence of drugs, Tompkins relives the trauma of being shot down and escaping a burning bomber before it exploded, instead of trying to pull his pilot and friend, "Big Jim," out of the wreckage. Only after Tompkins comes to grips with his perceived act of cowardice can he break the depression cycle and begin to heal.

Fear of being killed is not the only kind of cowardice in war films. In *The Caine Mutiny*, Lt. Tom Keefer (Fred MacMurray) is shown to be the only real coward on board the USS *Caine*. The crewmen of the *Caine* give Capt. Queeg (Humphrey Bogart), who visibly suffers from combat fatigue, the nickname "Old Yellow Stain" for supposed cowardice. But

Father Duffy (Pat O'Brien) counsels Private Plunkett (James Cagney) in *The Fighting 69th. Warner Bros. / Photofest © Warner Bros.*

Queeg's suspect actions are not the result of cowardice, but rather a paranoid reaction to the stress of command. But Keefer, trying to avoid blame for the mutiny he inspired, nearly causes the protagonist, Lt. Steve Maryk (Van Johnson), to be convicted. Although he was the principal architect of Maryk's relieving Queeg of command, Keefer lies on the witness stand to avoid being implicated, and in doing so, he puts Maryk's neck potentially into a noose. Fortunately, Maryk has a good lawyer who breaks Queeg on the stand and gets an acquittal. In the end, the quote about a coward dying a thousand deaths seems tailor-made for Keefer.

Apparently suffering from combat fatigue, Pvt. Bettis (Richard Jaeckel) in William Wellman's *Battleground* finally suffers shelling beyond his endurance. During the Battle of the Bulge, a wicked artillery barrage causes Bettis to flee from his foxhole and unit in the Ardennes Forest. Later, some of his buddies discover him working as a cook, safely (he thinks) behind the lines in Bastogne. Nervously, as if out of remorse for his cowardice, Bettis spoils his former buddies with meals of hot food, but, as actually occurred when the Germans totally surrounded the 101st Airborne Division positioned in and around Bastogne, there really was *no* safe, rear area.

Before director Wellman got into the motion picture business, he was the quintessential manly man. A onetime professional hockey player,

Wellman later distinguished himself in World War I flying fighter planes for France in the Lafayette Escadrille, so it is not surprising that in his films a special hell is reserved for soldiers who act unprofessionally and show the white feather. The ironic death Wellman concocts for Bettis occurs when the soldier-cook thinks he is safe behind the lines. The Germans shell Bastogne, and Bettis is killed when the roof in his kitchen collapses on him.

In *Battleground*, some of the actions of Pvt. "Kipp" Kippton (Douglas Fowley) can be seen as cowardly. Army regulations of the time stated that no soldier could serve on the front lines if he didn't have a full set of teeth, and Kippton had an annoying habit of "misplacing" his false teeth whenever it would be advantageous for him to be temporarily moved to the rear. During the Battle of the Bulge, Kippton again "loses" his teeth, but when he learns that the Americans are all cut off from the rear by marauding Germans, and thus there is no chance of his being removed from the fighting, he miraculously finds his teeth. Wellman probably decided that this kind of mischief was malingering, and thus "Kipp" is spared the kind of poetic justice meted out on Bettis. However, Kipp faces the wrath of at least one of his fellow soldiers and at one point pays for his dysfunctional behavior with a sock in the jaw.[14]

Shelling and a Man's Lack of Control

In many war films, submariners (and one marine raider in *Gung Ho!*) have bouts of fear and panic when they are depth charged. In the same fashion as Bettis, some men show great fear and panic when shelled. Perhaps this is because these men realize that when being shelled with either artillery or depth charges, they lose whatever little control over their fates they might have possessed. After all, one of the socially constructed manly virtues is self-control. A true man takes charge, exudes authority, and manages the scariest situations with a John Wayne-like calm. But this is hardest to do during shelling or a depth charge attack, when the men can do nothing but huddle in a foxhole or sit in their bunks on board a submarine and just "take it," when luck is the difference between survival and sudden, violent death or dismemberment.

In submarine films, screenwriters often place one panicky sailor in their crews as the fellow who breaks under the strain. Then, some calm, cool commander or NCO manages to quiet the panicky man's fears by either socking him in the jaw or talking him down. Later, these men mostly apologize to their shipmates, asking for forgiveness for their momentary lack of manliness. Since everyone is afraid during a depth charge attack, shipmates are routinely forgiving. Only in the German-produced submarine epic *Das Boot* (1981) does the captain tell the offending panicky crewman that he will face a court-martial for his momentary panic. Often during shelling or severe machine gun fire, infantrymen like Bettis in *Battleground* want to make a run for safety. Sometimes they try and are killed. Often an NCO like Sgt. Stryker in *Sands of Iwo Jima* prevents them by tackling or tripping them as they flee. Occasionally, as in the story behind the offense committed by the only officer among the convicts in *The Dirty Dozen*, men who run away are shot as deserters by their own commanders.

Capt. Stransky (Maximilian Schell), a German officer in *Cross of Iron*, is a Prussian aristocrat who arrives at the Russian front with only one goal: to win the Iron Cross, a decoration for valor in combat, which he feels he must bring home for reasons of family honor. He states to another officer that he cannot face his family if he does not earn this medal. In a way, like Capt. Winston in *Captain Newman, M.D.*, Stransky must be brave, despite his fears, to live up to the expectations of his aristocratic family. But Stransky is not a brave man, and some of his actions can be termed cowardly, especially during the early days on his new post. Every time a bomb or artillery shell lands nearby, he winces and sometimes ducks, although none of the veteran soldiers around him react at all.

Although any sane person would wince when shells explode around him, director Sam Peckinpah, himself a rowdy, macho man, uses this bit of actor's business to characterize Stransky as less than manly. Initially, the captain is not willing to expose himself to any danger and spends most of his time—especially during attacks—in his bunker. At one point, he even tries to take credit—and earn his coveted Iron Cross—for a deceased officer's heroic actions leading a counterattack against the enemy. But a veteran, Cpl. (later Sgt.) Steiner, who is both disillusioned and stubbornly idealistic, stands in his way, refusing to confirm Stransky's account of the battle required for the awarding of the medal. Finally, at the end of the picture, Stransky gathers up all his manliness and joins Steiner to face the Russians overrunning their position in a final, Peckinpah-style classic gun battle reminiscent of the climactic montage of carnage in *The Wild Bunch* (1969). Steiner tells Stransky, "Follow me, and I will show you where the Iron Crosses grow."

Earlier, we introduced the notion of the difference between fear and cowardice. In *The Hunters* (1958), Lt. Carl Abbott (Lee Philips), a fighter pilot during the Korean War, is, as FDR would say, fearful of fear itself, thinking himself a coward because of how terrified he becomes before each combat mission. Like many other soldiers, sailors, and airmen with problems in these films, he drowns his sorrows in the bottle. To make matters worse, he is the wingman of Maj. Cleve Saville (Robert Mitchum), a flyer nicknamed the "Iceman" for his apparent bravery, masked in a phlegmatic personality and cold-blooded objectivity when in aerial combat. But a fellow fighter pilot, Lt. Corona (John Gabriel), considers Abbott the bravest flyer in the squadron. He tells Maj. Saville the following:

> CORONA: He's got guts. Every time he takes off on a mission, he's scared green but goes anyway.
>
> SAVILLE: Well, that's what counts . . . when they go anyway.
>
> CORONA: Nobody makes you fly. He could dog it, nobody'd care.
>
> SAVILLE: Nobody cares but Abbott.

Later in the picture, Corona dies in a fiery crash, and Abbott continues to drink his troubles into oblivion. Finding Abbott in his bunk in the barracks, Saville confronts him about his fears. Saville says, "Tell me, Abbott, what's it like in that private little hell you've got for yourself?" Abbott responds, "Exclusive. Ain't nobody in there but us little old chickens." Saville silently leaves the room, and Abbott buries his head in his pillow.

The code of bravery required of an F-86 pilot doing combat against Chinese Migs in Korea is implied in a toast. In *The Hunters*, two highly decorated fighter aces hoist glasses of whisky. Their toast to each other is a simple one that only fighter pilots comprehend: "No guts," one says. This phrase is shorthand for the title of a classified air force manual on jet fighter air combat tactics entitled *No Guts, No Glory* that all pilots studied in training. But more than a reference to a textbook, implied in this toast is that bravery is a basic requirement for men in their profession, and that guts is the component that allows them to succeed in their deadly business.

In *The Big Red One*, Pvt. Griff (Mark Hamill) seemingly has earned his badge of manliness before ever facing the enemy. Like the football quarterback, Griff is extraordinarily adept in one of the manly arts: accuracy with his rifle. The men of his squad naturally assume that someone who is the "sharpshooter" of the unit is already in command of all the other manly abilities. Unfortunately for Griff, during his first combat experience, he freezes up and can't fire. Narrator Pvt. Zab (Robert Carradine) says that the next day, "Nobody wanted to use the word coward" in describing Griff's behavior. "At least, not yet."

Adding to the ambiguity of Griff's true motives is a conversation he has with the old Sarge (Lee Marvin) that next day:

> GRIFF: I can't murder anybody.
>
> SARGE: We don't murder, we kill.
>
> GRIFF: (frustrated) It's the same thing!
>
> SARGE: The hell it is, Griff. You don't murder animals, you kill 'em (referring to the Nazis).

Later in the film, the audience learns just how complicated this is: Is failure to kill on order, to do one's duty as a soldier, legitimate conscientious objection? Or is it just fear of the danger of combat? In one scene, the squad is about to be overrun by Germans. To avoid this, the quick-thinking Sarge orders the squad to duck into a cave to hide. Soon, a squadron of German panzers rolls by the cave entrance, followed by their supporting infantry. It appears that it is only a matter of time before the Americans are discovered and likely killed. After the squad discusses the apparently hopeless situation, Griff stands and starts to make for the entrance, as if to make a run for it. Then he stops, turns around, and finds some rocks to hide behind with the rest of the men. Zab's narration says, "We knew he wanted to run for it, and we knew he wouldn't, way before he did. Anyway, the sergeant would have shot him if he tried it." Finally the squad is saved when an offshore U.S. Navy cruiser pummels the panzers and German infantry with artillery fire. After that, Griff pulls his own weight in the squad, shooting at Germans with impunity, and he is involved in no more ambiguous incidents.

In *Pork Chop Hill*, we wonder whether the enigmatic Pvt. Franklin (Woody Strode) is a coward or acting out a past full of racial hatred and discrimination, perhaps just a hardheaded, hateful man. In this Korean War picture, as Lt. Joe Clemens (Gregory Peck) and his company assault the hill, Chinese loudspeakers blare propaganda at them, telling the company that they will die. Franklin doesn't continue up the hill and falls to the dirt to hide. When Clemens spots him, he pretends to have sprained his ankle, but the officer doesn't believe him. He orders Franklin to get on his feet and stay close, so he can be watched. Later, Franklin lags behind again and hits the dirt. Lt. Clemens shouts, "Get up! This'll cost you ten years in Leavenworth. Get up!" Franklin glares at the officer but rises, his rifle pointed in Clemens's general direction. "And don't get any 'funny' ideas [about shooting the officer in the back]. Stay up even with me." Later, Franklin, who is African American, drops out again, trying to escape by escorting a wounded man back down the hill, but Clemens stops him. He assigns another black soldier, Cpl. Jurgens (James Edwards) custody of Franklin, saying, "Don't let him out of your sight."

Later, Jurgens stares disgustedly at Franklin. The subtext here is that it hasn't been that long since President Harry S. Truman issued his order to integrate the U.S. Army. During World War II, despite the heroics of the Tuskegee airmen and personnel in other all-African American units, army generals and some segregationist politicians maintained that blacks made bad combat soldiers, because all were cowardly. (Talk about stereotypes!) So Jurgens glares at Franklin, and Franklin asks why he's staring. Jurgens retorts, "'Cause I got a special interest in everything you do," growls Jurgens, implying that Franklin is a disgrace to all black soldiers.

Later in the film, Franklin gives Jurgens the slip, and Clemens finds him hiding in a shack. Franklin won't move, and he points his rifle at the officer, asking for a nonexistent password. Franklin reasons that if he shoots the officer, there won't be any witnesses for his court-martial. Franklin argues with Clemens, asserting that he won't die for Korea or, for that matter, to protect the United States. Apparently Franklin's circumstances back home aren't worth defending. But considering that Clemens's company is about to be overrun by the enemy, the lieutenant answers, saying the following:

> Chances are you're going to die, like it or not, and so am I, whether you shoot me or not. At least we've got a chance to do it in pretty good company [the few brave men left in Clemens's company]. A lot of men came up here last night, and they don't care any more about Korea than you do; a lot of them had it just as rough at home as you did. They came up and fought. . . . There's about twenty-five of them left . . . a pretty exclusive club. You can still join up if you want to.

Finally, motivated by either esprit de corps or a total lack of better options, Franklin "joins up." Later, the last survivors of the twenty-five are holed up in a bunker, reinforcing the walls with sandbags as Chinese troops assault the bunker with a flamethrower. Clemens suddenly realizes that he's working side by side on the sandbags with Franklin. "Welcome to the club," Clemens jokes. "Some club," Franklin replies, smiling. Reinforcements arrive on time to rescue and relieve Clemens's company, and both the officer and Franklin walk down Pork Chop Hill together.

Franklin, like so many soldiers in these films who initially display cowardice, like Griff in *The Big Red One*, chooses to stand up and fight and survive. But *Pork Chop Hill*, unlike pictures produced during World War II, adds complexity to the otherwise black-and-white issue of bravery versus cowardice: Now the reasons they fight, and whether the cause is worth one's highest sacrifice, complicate the issue. Korea wasn't a declared war. It was a limited war with no greater objective than to interrupt the toppling of one Asian government after another, as described in President Dwight D. Eisenhower's famous domino theory. Probably a draftee, Franklin refused to become cannon fodder for a white government that integrated the military but when he was back home wouldn't let him drink from the same water fountain. To Franklin, this wasn't enough to die for. In the Korean War, and the Vietnam War that followed, the idea of cowardice had become much more complicated.

More Ambiguities

Vietnam War films added yet more ambiguity to masculine notions of bravery versus cowardice. On the one hand, there is a job of work to do, a mission to perform. But the Vietnam War was unlike World War II: Soldiers quickly learned that Vietnam was unwinnable, and perhaps even morally wrong. So the stoically performed manly job of work and duty becomes less important than personal survival. Typical of this situational ethic is voiced by combat veteran Pvt. King (Keith David), as he gives sage advice to his friend Chris Taylor just before the climactic battle in *Platoon*—words in stark contrast to those spoken in America's World War II propaganda films produced in the 1940s. Informed that his combat rotation is over and he is to start his journey back home on the next helicopter, King leaves Taylor with the following simple words of advice:

> Remember now, take it easy. Don't think too much, and don'tcha be no fool. There's no such thing as a coward out here. Don't mean nothin. . . . All you got to do is make it outta here—and it's all gravy. The rest of your life—gravy!

In this statement, there is no thought of mission, no concern with performing manly acts of heroism, winning the war, or doing their patriotic duty. Survival and a ticket "back to the world" will do.

Similarly, the bottom line of all the advice Sgt. Hazard and Sgt. Nelson give young soldier Jackie Willow in *Gardens of Stone* about fighting in Vietnam has little to do with winning the war. It's about survival, and how to get as many nineteen-year-olds as possible through the war alive, so the business of burials at Arlington National Cemetery—to which the two sergeants are reluctantly assigned—becomes less brisk.

Discussions between Sgt. Frantz (Dylan McDermott) and Sgt. Worchester (Steven Weber) in *Hamburger Hill* reveal the frustration with the war in Vietnam, the lack of understanding and support of the American people, and the very personal nature of the combat experience. Talking together after the death of one of their friends, they argue about who/what he died for:

> FRANTZ: Don't tell me he died for God, country, and the 101st Airborne . . .
>
> WORCHESTER: (interrupting) Hey, man, I'd never say that shit to anybody. He didn't die for anybody. He didn't leave his goddamn guts on a goddamn trail in the goddamn Ashau Valley for hometown, a medal, or any of that bullshit. He fired his automatic weapon for you and for third squad. Man, don't give him anything less.

Later, partially in jest, another soldier, frustrated with the waste of human life for "this sorry hill," says that he should have gone to Canada (avoiding the draft, as many did during the 1960s and 1970s) and become an expatriate to avoid prosecution and imprisonment in the United States. But Sgt. Frantz draws his personal "line in the sand" at that and holds forth simply about *his* code of manly service versus cowardice in Vietnam: "All I want from anybody is to get their ass in the grass with the rest of us. You don't have to like it, but you have to show up." As a graphic states at the end of the film, "Hamburger Hill was secured on 20 May 69. The war for hills and trails continued, the places and names forgotten, except by those who were there."

So in Vietnam, neo-macho thinking holds that it is sufficient to show up, do your job, and try to protect your buddies, but it's also okay to find a way to survive. Implied is that in Vietnam films, there is an entirely different male ethic compared to pictures produced during World War II. Influenced by Vietnam, even such World War II films of the modern era as *Saving Private Ryan* value the protection of squad members over mission objectives.

Intentionally Avoiding the Fighting

In a great many war films, a subordinate may wonder when their commanders intentionally avoid a fight. Usually, when commanders do this, they are following orders or employing stealth tactics, avoiding enemy contact and discovery, trying to achieve some greater mission goal. Typical of this conflict between apparent unwillingness to fight and reckless-but-manly aggression is found in the 1960 World War II Roger Corman B-movie *Ski Troop Attack* (1960). A U.S. Army alpine reconnaissance patrol is probing behind German lines during the latter stages of the war in Europe. As the film begins, Sgt. Potter (Frank Wolff) disobeys his orders and attacks a German patrol, killing all the enemy soldiers. Potter is subsequently chewed out by Lt. Factor (Michael Forest) for giving away their position, which violates reconnaissance patrol discipline. Not too intelligent, the macho Potter argues that he's in this war to kill Nazis, but the lieutenant reminds him that stealth is required for scouting behind the lines.

Later, when the squad discovers the beginning of the German advance in what will become known as the Battle of the Bulge, Factor explains to the men that at this point, they have two choices: to find their way back to Bastogne and rejoin their comrades or go on with their stealthy reconnaissance activities and continue feeding headquarters their observations.

Potter, who is disdainful of "ninety-day wonder" officers, disagrees, saying, "I think we oughta go back where the fighting is . . . where any man with guts . . . would wanna be [sarcastically] . . . *sir*." But Factor ignores Potter's implication of cowardice and orders the men to continue their reconnaissance mission.

In *Run Silent, Run Deep* (1958), in a plot reminiscent of *Moby Dick*, Capt. Richardson (Clark Gable) of the U.S. submarine *Nerka*, ignores the orders of Submarine Command Pacific in an obsessive desire to destroy the Japanese destroyer *Akikaze*, which was responsible for sinking the last submarine he commanded, plus three other subs. In doing so, on this mission, Richardson bypasses legitimate targets the *Nerka* could have sunk, so his vessel could approach the waters patrolled by the *Akikaze* undetected. Many of the crew consider the captain's actions strange, and a few accuse him of cowardice. Eventually, however, the captain demonstrates his resolve, and eventually the *Nerka* attacks and sinks the *Akikaze*, plus an additional target, a Japanese submarine. But like Capt. Ahab in Melville's novel, Richardson dies in the attempt. We will revisit this topic in chapter 5, "Courage," which, in the social construction of manliness dating back to the Greek philosophers, is the reverse of cowardice.

THE SISSY

Sadly, it doesn't take little boys long to learn enough about masculine behavior to make fun of a sissy. Sometimes immature, sometimes a dandy, the sissy character is always a fish out of water in the soldier's universe of rough, tough men. There is also the implication that sissies are homosexuals, or at least overly effeminate. Since the male culture classes the feminine as inadequate for the give and take of death in war, the sissy, like the homosexual, becomes a pariah, someone who at the very least cannot be counted on.

In *Glory* (1989), Cpl. Thomas Searles (Andre Braugher) is a highly educated black man who has been raised in the effete, overly polite society of Boston. But Searles is a patriot, and when one of his friends, Col. Robert Gould Shaw (Matthew Broderick), is tapped to command one of the first all-black battalions in the Civil War, Searles decides to enlist. But most of the black men in this battalion are rough, tough, field hands and mostly former slaves. Searles has great difficulty adjusting to military life and training, and the heartless drill instructor makes an example of him more than once. To make matters worse for Searles, he is persecuted by Pvt. Trip (Denzel Washington). Bullied like a boy in prep school, at one point Searles breaks down and cries. But finally, basic training turns Searles into a soldier, who fights and dies, like most of the battalion in this mostly true story, in a vain but courageous attempt to capture Fort Wagner, South Carolina.

In *Full Metal Jacket*, Pvt. Leonard Lawrence (Vincent D'Onofrio) is a full-grown man on the outside, but inside is a little boy who never grew up. He also has a low IQ and/or a learning disability. But now Lawrence finds himself in U.S. Marine Corps boot camp, and his merciless drill instructor (DI), Gunnery Sgt. Hartman (R. Lee Ermey), seems intent on turning him into a man. Hartman nicknames Lawrence "Gomer Pyle," because the recruit always manages to foul up in training. Hartman assigns Pvt. Joker (Matthew Modine) to be Lawrence's personal military tutor in hopes that Joker's intelligence, leadership ability, and charitable nature can help Lawrence become a marine—and a man. Unfortunately, Joker's best efforts with Lawrence fail. Lawrence still commits such childlike infractions as sneaking a jelly doughnut into the barracks, causing the entire company to be punished. This incident motivates his fellow marines to assault him with a "code red" (unauthorized group discipline session) in the dead of night. "Code red" usually consists of a beating or other punishment administered by a group of the offender's fellow marines. In this instance, while two of them held Lawrence down on his bunk, each man in the platoon took a turn hitting him with bars of soap wrapped inside towels. Although Lawrence eventually finds something at which he can excel (he becomes an expert marksman), the code red incident marked the beginning of Leonard's descent into insanity. Finally, on the last night before graduation, he cracks up completely, murders Hartman, and commits suicide.[15]

Some film directors show the male disdain for the female "other" by assigning feminine attributes to characters they hold in contempt. Such an officer is French general George Broulard (Adolph Menjou) in Stanley Kubrick's World War I story of decadent French military officers in *Paths of Glory* (1957). In this film, generals order an impossible attack in which hundreds of soldiers are needlessly killed. Roulade, one of the two villains of the film, reminds viewers more of Louis XIV than a military officer. Always pictured lounging in lush palaces drinking tea or cognac, this sissified general is the antithesis of a rough, tough George Patton or an Omar Bradley, or, for that matter, the hero of the film, the tough and manly Col. Dax (Kirk Douglas). Weaving webs of intrigue, Broulard's schemes are hidden in a mannered, almost feline style. In the end, true to form, Broulard positions himself in such a way that Gen. Mireau (George Macready), the other villain of the film, incurs all the blame.

As mentioned earlier in this chapter, similar to Broulard but far less accomplished, is Cmdr. Neal Owynn (Patrick O'Neal) and his boss, Adm. Broderick (in an atypical role for Dana Andrews), in *In Harm's Way*. Owynn is a slimy politician whose reason for enlisting in the navy is for the votes that a stint in the navy would earn him after the war. Broderick is an incompetent commander who makes lame-sounding excuses for his lack of success in "Operation Skyhook." As previously earlier, both Owynn and Broderick are shown in one key scene as prissy, croquet-playing dandies, in stark contrast to the manly conduct of Adm. Rockwell Torrey (John Wayne), their adversary. Broderick orders Owynn to attach himself to Torrey's staff as his spy, so, as area commander, Broderick will know what Torrey is doing and can reap the glory and publicity. Later, realizing that Owynn is spying for Broderick, Torrey's chief of staff, Capt. Eddington (Kirk Douglas), another tough, manly type, corners Owynn, slaps him in the face, and tells him that if he knows what's good for him he should take the next flight back to the rear and Broderick. Owynn refuses to fight back, and, instead, dandy that he is, can only think to inspect his face in a mirror to see if Eddington's slap left a mark.

THE REMF

U.S. armed services recruitment and public relations people constantly remind us that it takes dozens of support personnel to put a single soldier in the field. They often stress the importance of everyone from cooks to quartermasters to clerk-typists. But there is a reality in the world of men at war that contradicts armed forces public relations, providing a He-man distinction between fighters and clerks. The latter, those who work behind the lines, are as a marine officer in *Full Metal Jacket* sarcastically describes as "in the rear with the gear."

Stouffer (1976), in describing a study he made of World War II combat veterans, explains that to qualify as an authentic combat soldier, there is a definite pecking order to ascend, and, although he is deployed overseas with the front-line soldiers, the REMF ("Rear Echelon Motherfucker"), as Vietnam-era soldiers referred to him, simply did not qualify as a complete man. Stouffer writes the following:

> The man who lived up to the code of the combat soldier had proved his manhood: He could take pride in being a combat man. . . . The pride of the combat man appears in his typical resentment of the rear echelon. This resentment, springing in part from envy of the favored circumstances at the rear, served one function of devaluing what was inaccessible and placing a higher moral value on what had to be put up with [up on the line]. The fact that rear echelon soldiers accepted the lower status made the right to feel this invidious pride a real support for the combat man. (182)

Clearly to combat veterans, as Stouffer puts it, "The final, crushing comment [that] the combat soldier makes is to imply that [a REMF is] not a man, because he is not one of the fraternity of front-line fighters" (183).

In *Hamburger Hill*, Sgt. Frantz (Dylan McDermott) once again makes a clear distinction between those who do manly deeds and those who sit safely by. He considers anyone in the rear echelon—especially the press who cover the war, men not even in uniform—unwelcome on the field of honor when the fighting is over, body bags are filled and zipped up, and the dead are mourned. After a particularly bloody assault on Hamburger Hill, a news reporter arrives to interview his men, but Sgt. Frantz will not abide the reporter's presence:

> NEWSMAN: (trying to interview GIs returning to base after a hard day of fighting) Hey, word down at division is you guys can't take this hill. What do you have to say about that? In fact, Senator Kennedy insists you guys haven't got a chance at all.
>
> FRANTZ: (glares at Newsman for a few seconds) You really like this shit, don't you? It's your job, a story, wait here like a fucking vulture for someone to die so you can take a picture.
>
> NEWSMAN: (becoming angry) It's my job . . .
>
> FRANTZ: I got more respect for those little bastards up on the hill. They take a side, you just take pictures. You probably don't even do your own fucking!
>
> NEWSMAN: What?
>
> FRANTZ: You listen to me. We're gonna take this fucking hill, newsman. And if I catch you on top taking pictures of any of my people, I will blow your fucking head off. You haven't earned a right to be here. You got that?

In the history of American war films, there is probably no better example of the difference between the combat soldier and support personnel than the clerk-typist, fish-out-of-water Cpl. Timothy P. Upham in *Saving Private Ryan*. Because he can speak French and German, Upham (Jeremy Davies) is ordered on a special mission, to join Lt. Miller (Tom Hanks) and six survivors of a battle-weary company that had just been decimated in the horror of D-Day on Omaha Beach. When Miller drops by the command post to meet and pick up Upham, he discovers that the soldier has not fired a rifle since basic training. Upham has to be told to leave his typewriter but take along his helmet. Later, although he has become a member of the squad, subject to all the risks they must take, Upham is treated like an outcast by the men of the squad. They ridicule this REMF for his lack of experience and understanding of patrol discipline.

Later, after a skirmish with Germans that caused the death of a squad member, Upham pleads with Miller not to execute a German soldier they had taken prisoner. Over the revengeful objections of some of his squad, Miller allows the German to run away. Ironically, Upham later learns how savage one must be in war: The same German, now a member of another German outfit, brutally kills a member of Upham's squad. By accident,

Upham captures the German, but this time the REMF has learned his lesson and shoots him. This newcomer has made his bones, is now a bloodied combat vet, and, in the bargain, has been disabused of any notions of chivalry—or humanity—in modern warfare.

Also, as mentioned earlier in this chapter, L. T., the public relations officer tagging along with a recon patrol in *84 Charlie Mopic*, is a REMF. Like Upham, L. T. is neither experienced nor respected by the veterans he accompanies. Military PR people generally are portrayed badly in American war films. Cinematic portrayals of the insensitive, callous REMF publicist in *Memphis Belle* and his counterpart in *Pork Chop Hill* are typical of the disrespect in which they are held by combat flyers and soldiers.

In *Memphis Belle*, John Lithgow's Lt. Col. Derringer (his name is perhaps a subtle reference to the diminutive size of his "gun" in relation to those of fighting men) is assigned the job of press agent for the first American bomber crew to complete their twenty-five-mission tour of duty in Europe. Insensitive, rude, and cynical, Derringer doesn't understand either the men or the group commander's angst, as he loses men and airplanes every day. Only after the commander (David Straithairn) shares his sad correspondence with families of his men who have died in action does Derringer begin to realize how thoughtless and disrespectful he has been—and the huge chasm between REMFs like himself and men bloodied in combat.

In *Pork Chop Hill*, radio communications between the battalion and Lt. Joe Clemens's company have alternately failed and are being jammed by the Chinese. Instead of sending badly needed reinforcements, ammunition, food, and medical supplies, the battalion sends Clemens's beleaguered outfit the division's PR man and a photographer to document a successful "mop up" operation, and this despite the fierce fighting still underway that finds Clemens's company severely depleted and barely holding onto the hill. At first, the PR man appears as callous as Derringer, but when it finally dawns on him that if reinforcements don't arrive soon, the company will be overrun and killed by Chinese troops, the PR man's mood changes. He asks how he can help and even volunteers to stay and lend a hand. But Clemens says that the officer can best serve by reporting what he has seen at the front. Clemens sends him back to battalion headquarters with a handwritten message explaining their dire situation. Thanks to this REMF, reinforcements arrive in the nick of time to rescue Clemens and his remaining men.

In the HBO miniseries *Band of Brothers*, which is based on a true story, Maj. Richard Winters's (Damian Lewis) fervent wish is to go back to commanding his company. Winters had been promoted to a new job at battalion headquarters and hates being a REMF. Having led a platoon and later commanding Easy Company since D-Day and through Operation

Market Garden and the Battle of the Bulge, he feels more and more useless as he continues to be promoted farther away from the actual fighting. His leadership is needed more at headquarters, and before the end of the war, Winters is promoted to battalion commander, but promotions and honors never sit well with him, and he remains uneasy serving behind the lines. Both out of loyalty to the men of Easy Company and his own disdain with the REMF role that has been assigned to him, Winters yearns to return to front-line service.

In another episode in the same miniseries, Pvt. David Webster (Eion Bailey), after recovering from wounds suffered in battle, is treated like a REMF, with no more status than a new replacement, when he returns to Easy Company. Although a veteran of D-Day and Operation Market Garden, Webster was recuperating in the hospital while the rest of the company fought and suffered in the Battle of the Bulge. Now recovered and returned to his unit, he is resented by some Easy Company men, simply because he was lucky enough to have been sleeping on clean sheets in a hospital in Paris while the rest of his company experienced the misery and the carnage in Bastogne. It didn't help Webster's situation when another wounded member of Easy Company slipped away from the hospital right before the fighting in Bastogne, rejoining the company in time to share in the hostilities. Finally, once he again proves himself in new skirmishes with the Germans, the men seem to forgive Webster, and his status as a combat veteran worthy of respect in Easy Company is restored.

REMFs with Dreams of Glory

In war films, some REMFs' greatest desires are to transcend their noncombatant status and, at least for a moment, earn first-class manhood and perhaps a red badge of courage. Typical were a number of faithful support personnel in *Twelve O'Clock High* (1949). Knowing that the next mission was a big one, an important target in Germany, the group's flight surgeon, its chaplain, the adjutant, and various other ground support personnel stow away on the bomber group's B-17s to get in on the action, most serving as machine gunners. Furious with his own chauffer and aide, a sergeant, for stowing away, the group commander, Gen. Savage (Gregory Peck) orders him to "Rip off those chevrons" (insignia of rank for a sergeant). But one of his staff officers advises Savage that if he "busts" the sergeant, he'd have to discipline half the ground support personnel, since so many had sneaked along on this raid. Savage relents, and the stripes stay on.

In *Black Hawk Down*, U.S. Army Ranger specialist John Grimes (Ewan McGregor), a reluctant REMF, is deployed with U.S. Army Rangers and Special Forces in Mogadishu, Somalia. Grimes says that he's itching for action and complains that all he gets to do is work in headquarters and make coffee:

> GRIMES: I mean, you're looking at the guy that believed the commercials about "Be all that you can be." I made coffee through Desert Storm. I made coffee through Panama while everyone else got to fight . . . got to be a Ranger. Now it's "Grimsey black, one sugar," or "Grimsey, got a powder anywhere?"

He spots Spec. John Thomas (Tac Fitzgerald) trying to scratch an itch inside a new, white cast on his wrist and hand.

> GRIMES: What happened to you?
>
> THOMAS: Ping pong accident. So guess what? Your wish has been granted. You're going today [on the big raid into Mogadishu].
>
> GRIMES: You're fuckin' me!
>
> THOMAS: You're taking my place, assisting the 60 gunner. Sgt. Eversmann said to get your stuff and get ready.

Grimes stands mute in amazement, not sure how to feel, elated over achieving his goal or fearful as he faces a crucial test of his mettle. The battle-tested Thomas, sensing Grimes's conflict, allows himself a wry grin. Thomas says, "It's what you wanted, isn't it?" Suddenly aware that his trepidation may be showing and intent on not displaying any unmanly fear, Grimes replies, "Oh, yeah. Oh, yeah."

Later, Sgt. Eversmann (Josh Hartnett) holds a meeting with his squad and has special instructions for his FNG. Regardless of the fact that Grimes has been with the unit for a long time, in combat, Grimes is new and untested. Eversmann instructs Grimes, declaring, "Grimsey, I want you to stick with Waddell [the sixty-millimeter gunner] and give him ammo when he needs it." As his buddies give Grimes more advice regarding what gear to take and what to leave at base camp for this raid, Eversmann sums up all the important advice for this FNG. Eversmann states, "Just remember, when everybody else is shooting, shoot in the same direction." Grimes later finds himself in the thick of a desperate battle and distinguishes himself as a man and as a newly battle-tested combat soldier.

In *The Fighting Seabees* (1944), John Wayne plays Wedge Donovan, the civilian boss of a construction company who builds airstrips and other projects for the navy. These jobs are performed in hazardous conditions in forward areas, and his men are sometimes shot at and even killed. So the next time Donovan and his men go out on a project, he secretly brings along rifles and ammunition for them. The Japanese attack, and Donovan's untrained, undisciplined civilians try to counterattack, but many are killed and wounded. This debacle spurs the creation of the Seabees, a naval construction battalion. The civilian construction workers enlist and become navy personnel, and they are trained to, as their anthem says, "Build and we can fight. We'll build our way to victory, and guard it day and night." And in the next deployment, on a Pacific island, the Seabees, led by Donovan, demonstrate their newly learned military skills in repelling a Japanese attack.

In the HBO miniseries *Vietnam War Story* (1987), in an episode called "The Pass," inspired by a true event, a REMF named McReady (Tony Becker) meets two new friends, French (Wendell Pierce) and Siska (Meritt Buttrick), veteran combat soldiers on passes, in the town of Qui Nhon. By day this town is held by the Americans, but by night the VC take over. Drinking with his newfound buddies in a Vietnamese bar/whorehouse that caters to Americans by day and the VC by night, McReady, a clerk-typist, pretends to also be a combat soldier, an advisor to South Vietnamese troops. But a fellow REMF who knows McReady encounters the three men, and McReady's deception is inadvertently revealed. Siska is incensed by this dishonesty:

> SISKA: Rough, buff, adviser, eh, McReady? You lyin' little prick! Us grunts are mighty sensitive about rear echelon motherfuckers like you playing G.I. Joe! I'm gonna kick your ass up around your ears!
>
> FRENCH: Leave it be, Siska.
>
> SISKA: Fuck you, too!

The two scuffle on the floor, and, amazingly, the REMF does the ass-kicking and must be pulled off of Siska. But they are still Americans, and they resolve their differences by buying each other drinks. Many libations later, McReady tries to explain himself, saying the following:

> MCREADY: I put in for the field, but my top sergeant and my XO [executive officer] won't approve it.
>
> FRENCH: You ain't missin' one thing, believe me, and you're an asshole for wantin' it.
>
> MCREADY: I'm bored outta my mind: All day long, the same damn forms, the same Mickey Mouse routine!
>
> SISKA: Bored? Bored? I spend every life-sucking day in a steel coffin. . . . I can't see, I can't hear, I don't know where I've been or where I'm goin', and if Charlie hits, you're just a pin cushion for B-40s [rockets]. Bored! You really are a stupid asshole!
>
> MCREADY: (insistent) But you get action!
>
> FRENCH: It ain't something you look forward to.
>
> SISKA: Amen to that.

Later, thoroughly drunk, the three sum up the dilemma of the combat soldier in this ditty, sung sarcastically to the tune of *O Tannenbaum* (in a drunken version):

We like it here, we like it here
Yo, fuckin' A, we like it here.
Although we have malaria,
we still maintain our area.
We like it here, we like it here
Yo, fuckin' A, we like it here.

Finally, French gets too drunk and refuses to leave the bar, although it's sundown and off-limits at night, because of the VC. Siska leaves, but McReady won't leave his new buddy, French, who hides in the bar's storeroom. The VC arrive and partake of alcohol and prostitutes. McReady and French try to escape, but a firefight ensues, in which McReady is killed. Ironically, REMF McReady's body will be shipped home along with a Purple Heart medal, as he was killed in armed action against the enemy.

In *Hanover Street* (1979), a REMF British intelligence officer trains deep cover agents to infiltrate the Nazi military. An Oxford professor turned intelligence guru, Paul Sellinger (Christopher Plummer) realizes that he trains men to do heroic deeds but never gets to do any himself. Most of this movie is about a frothy, illicit romance between an American bomber pilot, David Halloran (Harrison Ford), and Margaret, Sellinger's wife (Leslie-Anne Down). But in terms of our discussion of manliness, heroics, and the REMF with aspirations for glory and recognition, the interesting part of this film is the way Sellinger beats himself up over his blandness and status in the rear of the rear echelon.

This is also an important film, because it is a study of real and perceived courage. The flyer, Halloran, is just the kind of man Sellinger has been competing with (or, more to the point, failing to compete with) his whole life: fearless and resourceful in the performance of his heroic duties (read the "captain of the football team" versus the "president of the chess club"). But after Halloran falls in love with Margaret, he loses his heroic edge and becomes the opposite: cautious and second-guessing himself and much less effective as the commander of a bomber flying combat missions over Germany. One exercise in caution causes him to abort a bombing mission, because he imagines he hears trouble in one of his engines. Later, his commander, who dislikes Halloran for his insubordinate attitude, implies that his engine failure might have been imagined or fabricated. The vindictive commander assigns Halloran and his crew to a hazardous mission to drop a spy into occupied France. Meanwhile, although Margaret gives her husband no hint of her infidelities, Sellinger still feels inadequate as a man, having not been tested in combat, and thus unworthy of his beautiful, charming wife. Instead of assigning one of the agents he has trained for the spy mission to France, Sellinger substitutes himself, never suspecting that the pilot assigned to drop him into France is his wife's lover. As fate and screenwriting would stage it, Halloran's plane is shot down, and only Halloran and Sellinger parachute to safety. For various reasons, the two complete the spy mission together.

The following conversation between Sellinger and Halloran typifies Sellinger's male angst about his status as a REMF. He tries to explain to Halloran why he decided to go on this mission himself:

> SELLINGER: All my life, no matter what I did, I've always been the same thing: pleasant. I'm pleasant. I was a teacher; that's a pleasant profession. I'm rather pleasant-looking, if I do say so myself. If anyone was asked to describe me, they'd say I'm . . . pleasant. Now, I never minded it that much before, except now . . . it's beginning to hurt! More than I thought anything could hurt.
>
> HALLORAN: I don't know what you mean.
>
> SELLINGER: Well, take a good look at yourself, and you'll see a hero.
>
> HALLORAN: That's a lotta crap. I don't want to be one.
>
> SELLINGER: Even if you don't want to be one, you are. You can't help it. You're the one who's ice skating on the lake when the little boy falls into the freezing water, and you save him. I'm the one who gives you my coat to wrap him in. When it's all over, you're on the front page of all the newspapers, saying it was really nothing . . . and I have a wet coat.

From conversations during their mission, Halloran deduces that Sellinger is Margaret's husband, so it is ironic that Halloran ends up heroically saving the life of his wounded rival, assuring that Sellinger will live to return to his wife. Again, the wounded Sellinger plays second fiddle to a hero, but, in the end, it is he who collects the reward: Margaret. During the time that Halloran and Sellinger's plane was listed as missing, Margaret realizes how much she really loves her husband. So in the climax, she gives Halloran a "Dear John" speech, telling him that their affair is over.

Veterans with Dreams of Becoming REMFs

In terms of changing roles in war films, it is not always the REMF trying to change his status to something more heroic. Sometimes it is exactly the opposite: a man who already has his combat infantryman's badge of courage, and now, experienced, exhausted, and disillusioned, wants nothing more than to get back home alive. So he applies for a transfer to a REMF job to assure his survival. Like Bettis in *Battleground*, more than one man in *Platoon* yearns to be reassigned to jobs far back in the rear in Saigon, away from the jungle and the constant threat of death. One soldier, "Big Harold" (Forest Whitaker), tries to get away from the bush to do a REMF job back in Saigon. To Big Harold, it doesn't matter how menial the job—in this case, laundry—because to this combat veteran, serving behind the lines means that he would be much less likely to go home in a body bag. But conversations among the "brothers," as the black soldiers of this platoon call themselves, demonstrate that they are convinced that REMF jobs only go to privileged white soldiers. In this scene, two black soldiers, Big Harold and Junior (Reggie Johnson), start out arguing about some particularly bad-tasting rations, but the conversation eventually turns toward the laundry job:

> BIG HAROLD: Tricky bitch, 'reason you gimme dat turkey loaf is nobody else can eat that shit 'cept me, so don't start your game-playing with me, Junior.
>
> JUNIOR: You a pig, man. I hope Manny [another black soldier in the platoon] get dat laundry gig 'for you do.
>
> BIG HAROLD: The fool think he's gonna get it, but he ain't known for his thinking.
>
> JUNIOR: He's a fool, all right, but you a bigger fool [implying from their earlier conversations that black soldiers don't get transfers out of the bush. Instead, in Junior's thinking, they are victims of racial politics].
>
> JUNIOR: It's politics, man, just politics . . .

In *The Big Red One*, Pvt. Vinci (Bobby DiCicco) is another combat veteran who wants a REMF job, but he's not really asking to be transferred. He just doesn't like to be the soldier on point, walking ahead of the others in the squad, perhaps drawing gunfire. Earlier, when Vinci smarted off to the sergeant (Lee Marvin), he was assigned point duty. Now, after a skirmish with the Germans, Vinci asks the sarge if he can be "transferred back to the rear echelon."

One sailor in *The Enemy Below* (1957) thought that the new skipper of his destroyer (Robert Mitchum) was what he referred to as a "feather merchant," because before the war the captain had been in the merchant marine. This means that the sailor was convinced that his skipper was too inexperienced (read REMF) for a combat job. Actually, the captain was thoroughly combat tested. Later, in a game of wits against a German submarine, the skipper shows his skill and cunning, and the sailor recants, admitting to his shipmates how wrong he was.

Both Lt. Hearn (Cliff Robertson) and Gen. Cummings (Raymond Massey) are REMFs for different reasons in *The Naked and the Dead*. To his men, Cummings, a corps commander in the Pacific Theater of Operations, is the worst kind of officer, concerned only about results, not human losses. Besides being insensitive to his high casualty rates, Cummings is not the slightest bit concerned about the welfare of his men. The antithesis of Col. Chamberlain in *Gettysburg*, Cummings sets up his headquarters far behind the lines, where he lives in relative luxury, indulging himself in the best food and drink available. An elitist, Cummings shares no amenities with the enlisted men on the front line, only with his officers. His aide-de-camp, Hearn, had earlier distinguished himself in combat, but he readily agrees to take the job of working in the rear echelon so that he has a better chance of surviving the war. In civilian life, Hearn is a rich, dissolute playboy, so the life of a general's aide appeals to him. But Cummings's snobbery and lack of concern for his men annoys Hearn, who finally becomes insubordinate enough to anger the general, who reassigns him to a combat unit.

Similar to Cummings is another REMF-like officer, the unseen colonel, identified only as "Blackjack," in *Hamburger Hill*. Flying around in a helicopter, barking orders but sharing none of the risk, Blackjack tells his men down below to take Hamburger Hill no matter what the cost. Appraised of the shocking casualties his men are suffering in this frontal attack, Blackjack insists on sacrificing wave after wave of his men. The men quietly resent Blackjack's lack of personal leadership, safe above them in a helicopter. But they have their orders.

Similarly, in *Catch-22*, Col. Cathcart (Martin Balsam) and Lt. Col. Korn (Buck Henry), commander and executive officer, respectively, of a bomb wing stationed in Italy during World War II, spend the entire film sending other men to their deaths on bombing raids but never fly combat missions themselves. They also spend most of their time conspiring with Lt. Milo Minderbinder (Jon Voight) in black market war profiteering. At one point, they make a deal with the Germans to bomb their own airfield in return for a commodities trade.

To the men, REMF officers like Cummings, Blackjack, and Cathcart are the worst kind of leaders, the antithesis of Col. Hal Moore (Mel Gibson) in *We Were Soldiers* (2002), who leads from the front. As the army airborne commander tells his soldiers, "When we go into battle, I will be the first to set foot on the field, I will be the last to step off. And I will leave no one behind."

THE HERO

This stereotype cuts across all the others, because someone has to be the protagonist of a screenplay, pursue the quest, and defeat the antagonist. John Wayne in *Flying Tigers* (1951) or *Flying Leathernecks* (1942) and Cary

Grant in *Destination Tokyo* come to mind. There are also reluctant heroes, like Gary Cooper as Alvin York in *Sergeant York* (1941) and James Garner as Charley Madison in *The Americanization of Emily*, and such true-to-life heroes as Damian Lewis playing Maj. Richard D. Winters in the HBO miniseries *Band of Brothers*. In war, the stereotype of the hero is among the most influential and potentially dangerous for impressionable young boys. In their fantasies, boys see themselves as men serving with distinction, bravely assaulting the enemy's bastion, saving their comrades, and winning the day, just like those media models on the screen. In the last chapter of this book, "Why Men Fight," we will discuss other aspects of the male need to distinguish himself in combat, but here we discuss the idea of heroes.

This is difficult, because most heroes don't consider themselves that special. In *Flags of Our Fathers*, three marines are honored across the United States as the nation's great heroes. They were the three survivors of the squad of marines who raised the American flag over Mount Suribachi on Iwo Jima. But these young men didn't consider themselves either heroic or brave: "They just tried not to get shot" and helped their buddies survive the carnage of that desperate fight against Japanese soldiers under orders to kill as many Americans as they could and never surrender. These three (John "Doc" Bradley [Ryan Phillippe], Rene Gagnon [Jesse Bradford], and Ira Hayes [Adam Beach]) believed that there was no such thing as a hero. Instead, the young men are convinced that heroes are created by the folks back home, "because they need them." People who do things that seem heroic are just doing their jobs, and some trick of fate casts what they did as heroic.

In *Flags of Our Fathers*, three heroes—Bradley (Ryan Phillippe), Gagnon (Jesse Bradford), and Hayes (Adam Beach)—are being honored. *DreamWorks / Photofest © DreamWorks; photographer: Merie W. Wallace*

But movies, like those about the United States during World War II, require heroes, so Hollywood creates them for us. No wonder kids misunderstand. Even the most realistic films—and not all of them are realistic—show regular guys doing their jobs, trying to avoid being killed, fatalistically pursuing the task at hand: killing the enemy while achieving their military objectives. They become heroes by accident.

Believe it or not, the ridiculous macho slogan, "A man's gotta do what he's gotta do" was actually a line in a war movie. It was coined by screenwriter Art Cohn for a character in *Men of the Fighting Lady* (1954). Why did pilot Lt. Cmdr. Ted Dodson (Keenan Wynn) return to a flak-filled enemy position to help another pilot who was in trouble? "Because he thought he could help," replied another pilot. Dodson died protecting his buddy. This was just something extraordinary that circumstances dictated that these men must do. They can barely articulate why. They say they're just doing their jobs.

In *Battleground*, Pfc. Holley (Van Johnson) shows that the difference between heroism and cowardice often hinges on circumstance. During a firefight with the Germans, the normally brave Holley experiences a moment of fright and panic, and he flees. Pvt. Layton (Marshall Thompson), a green replacement, follows Holley, assuming that the more experienced soldier was executing a flanking maneuver. Not wanting Layton to discover his true intentions, Holley leads Layton on a real flanking maneuver, killing and capturing many Germans. As often happens in combat, fate turns a cowardly act into a heroic gesture. He'll probably earn a medal.

Sometimes, heroism comes down to the simplicity of obeying orders. As in the protagonists' brave attempts to hold back the invading Japanese in such films as *Bataan* (1943) and *Wake Island*, Tennyson's adage that "Ours is not to question why; ours is but to do and die" again becomes the mantra of heroes.

Perhaps it's in the way one approaches this stoic acceptance of duty that makes heroes. In *A Bridge Too Far*, from the planning stages of Operation Market Garden, Field Marshal Montgomery's daring strategy to "end the war by Christmas" was greeted with great skepticism by many of his subordinate generals. As Lt. Gen. Frederick Browning (Dirk Bogarde) explains the details of Market Garden to a group of these commanders, Polish major general Stanislaw F. Sosabowski (Gene Hackman) becomes convinced that the plan won't work and that he and his men are likely to be killed. The taciturn Sosabowski tells Browning that he has considered asking for a letter verifying that he was forced to act on orders, "in case my men are massacred." Taken aback, Browning asks if Sosabowski is officially requesting such a letter. "No," he replies. As a fatalist, he reasons, "In the case of a massacre, what difference would it make?" Sosabowski is greatly concerned for his men and suspicious of Montgomery's strategic competence. But, like other commanders, he knows that the show will go on with or without him, and the manly thing to do is to endure the outcome—even if it means his death—along with the men of his brigade. Experience has shown Sosabowski that there will always be stupid, poorly considered orders to obey and that his duty as a soldier and a man is to do and die.

Equally doubtful, British lieutenant general Brian Horrocks (Edward Fox) takes another approach. Unlike the soft-spoken Sosabowski, Horrocks is a type-A personality and jokester, with a one-liner for every occasion. Regardless of his serious doubts whether his 30 Corps can keep to Montgomery's unrealistic timetable, which could cause disaster for the entire operation, he has confided his misgivings to only a few senior commanders. To the rest, he's 30 Corps' biggest cheerleader. Both Horrocks and Sosabowski heroically lead their men into the valley of death, one with gritted teeth, and the other with a grin.

As mentioned earlier, Gary Cooper's character Alvin York in *Sergeant York* and James Garner's Charley Madison in *The Americanization of Emily* are accidental, reluctant, and quite unorthodox heroes. *Sergeant York* chronicles the real-life Tennessee farmer Alvin York, who, although a violent, rowdy drunkard in his youth, converts to a fundamentalist Christian denomination and reforms his life. This new, Christian ethic includes no drinking, assiduously turning the other cheek, and foreswearing all violence or killing. When he is drafted into the army in World War I, York initially files for conscientious objector status.

But Jack Warner produced this film at the behest of the U.S. War Department. Anticipating the many thousands of religious men who would soon be drafted into the army to fight in World War II, the U.S. Office of War Information wanted to use York's experience as an example of why Christians should kill their fellow men. Their goal was to show audiences that York—a Medal of Honor winner for courage and bravery in battle—was "rendering unto Caesar the things that are Caesar's," as the Bible would say, and defending his Christian nation against an evil enemy. After a moral wrestling match with his ethics, York agrees to fight and does so brilliantly: In one battle, York, an extraordinary marksman, kills 20 Germans and captures 132 prisoners. But York's rationale for performing this heroic feat is not at all like some of the others previously mentioned, as this postbattle dialog with an officer investigating the incident explains. When asked why he, a pacifist, could kill all those Germans, York says the following:

> YORK: I'm as much agin' killin' as ever, sir, but it was this way, colonel. . . . When I heard them machine guns and all them fellers a droppin' around me, well, I figured that them [German machine] guns was killin' hundreds, maybe

thousands, and there weren't anything anybody could do but to stop them guns. And that's what I done.

OFFICER: You mean to tell me you did it to *save* lives?

YORK: Yessir. That was why.

OFFICER: Well, York, what you just told me was the most extraordinary thing of all.

York performed his heroic acts intentionally. This was certainly not the case with the reluctant hero, navy commander Shears (William Holden), in *The Bridge on the River Kwai* (1957). Having barely escaped with his life from a Japanese POW labor camp in the Burmese jungle, and masquerading as an officer to get higher-class treatment in a military hospital, Cmdr. Shears hopes to be transported home and out of harm's way when he recovers from his injuries. Instead, the British "borrow" him from the navy and ask him to return to the labor camp along with British commando raiders and blow up the bridge his comrades are building across the Kwai River. The furthest thing imaginable from a heroic type, Shears thinks he won't have to go on this commando raid if he tells the truth and confesses to impersonating an officer, but the British already know about it. Trapped, Shears "volunteers."

Like a fish out of water, Shears finds himself surrounded by British heroic types, especially Maj. Warden (Jack Hawkins), already decorated for bravery for other bridge demolition jobs against the Japanese. Shears is told that if someone is injured while on the mission to blow up the bridge, the others will have to just leave him behind. A wounded man may even have to take an "L" pill ("L" for lethal) to commit suicide rather than be taken prisoner. British colonel Green (Andre Morell), in charge of the commandos, says, "The objective comes first in our work." This is just the opposite of Shears's hedonist, humanist ethic.

Later, in the jungle, things have gone poorly. One commando is killed during the initial parachute jump. Then Warden is injured during a chance encounter with a Japanese patrol. Warden is wounded, so he insists that the commando group leave him in the jungle. By then, Shears is sick and tired of all these heroics and sounds off, saying the following:

> You make me sick with your heroics. There's a stench of death about you. You carry it in your pack like the plague. Explosions and L pills, they go well together, don't they? And with you there's just one thing or the other, destroy a bridge or destroy yourself. This is just a game, this war . . . you're crazy with courage . . . for what? How to die like a gentleman, how to die by the rules! When the only important thing is how to *live* like a human being! I'm not gonna leave you to die, Warden . . . because I don't care about your bridge, and I don't care about your rules. If we go on, we go on together.

So Shears and the others fashion a litter and carry the protesting Warden through the jungle to the site of the nearly completed bridge. Warden, still injured, is unable to help mine the bridge and must observe from atop a nearby hill. Shears is stuck with accompanying another commando, Lt. Joyce, to set the explosives and—in the hope of also destroying a train full of Japanese officials—manually set off the charges later. Unfortunately, at the last minute, they are discovered, and Shears dies trying to save Joyce and blow up the bridge. Shears does everything he can to avoid heroics, but at the last minute, with the mission and protecting another commando on the line, he abandons his principles and does his lethal job—a truly reluctant hero.

James Garner's Charley Madison in *The Americanization of Emily* is yet another unorthodox kind of hero: a self-admitted coward made into a hero by sheer accident. Having served in the marines at Guadalcanal, Madison suddenly realizes that a "man could get killed out here." Since he was a successful and popular Washington, D.C., hotel concierge before the war, Madison calls a few high-placed friends at the Pentagon and is transferred from the marines to the navy, given a commission, and retasked as a navy admiral's "dog robber," a personal aide to a high-ranking officer whose responsibility it was to see to the admiral's every need and want. Happy to serve in this new, noncombatant role, Madison plans to sit out the war providing gourmet meals, vintage wines, and even women to the admiral and his fellow senior officers.

But fate steps in, when, due to stress, the admiral (Melvyn Douglas) becomes delusional for a time and orders Charley and his fellow dog-robbers to make a film about the landings on D-Day on Omaha Beach and make sure that they document that the "first man to die on Omaha Beach is a sailor." Through a series of mix-ups, Charley ends up amidst the mayhem and explosions on Omaha Beach. At first, the admiral and his staff think that Charley is the first navy man killed, but he turns out to be only slightly wounded. At the end of the picture, Charley, as his girlfriend Emily laughingly puts it, "craven to the end," ends up a hero, immortalized on a bronze statue and publicized as one of the heroes of D-Day.

PR nonsense aside, are there real heroes today? In an interview with Richard Schickel in *Time* magazine (2006), Clint Eastwood, who has played many heroes, is relatively convinced there aren't:

> SCHICKEL: So, is there any conceivable possibility in the modern world for assertion of conventional heroism?
>
> EASTWOOD: I don't see it right now. I certainly don't see any politician that's a hero in any party anywhere. I think John McCain did something that I don't know if I could do, and I don't think many men can look in the mirror and say they'd do: give up a chance to get out of prison because his dad was an admiral

> and the [North] Vietnamese were going to let him go. I mean that took cojones, donating another three and a half to four years of his life to stay in prison rather than be the one guy who gets to walk away: "Hey, fellas. I'll say hello to everybody." Pat Tillman, giving up his NFL career to fight—and die—for his country is like that for me, too. But most of the political structure I get so disappointed at. We're reduced to a society that is sitting here, arguing about who used the "N" word thirty years ago. You see grown men doing this stuff in order to get into a power position, and it's really kind of disgraceful. (81)

In chapter 4, we'll discuss a theme we have already introduced, but because it runs like a river through so many combat films, masculinity and the burden command places on men deserve special mention.

NOTES

1. Albert, portrayed as a mama's boy, is controlled by his fears. He has never completed the necessary psychological development in which he was to have individuated from his mother. Margaret Mahler, Fred Pine, and Anni Bergman's (1975) research into the mother who interferes with the child's innate searching for his own individuation from her sheds light on the characters of Albert and his mother. Mahler says that when individuation is hindered—in Albert's case by his fearful, clinging mother—the "development of the child's full awareness of self is retarded" (4). Albert was not able to emerge from his symbiotic fusion with his mother and assimilate the achievements that would mark his own individual characteristics. Controlled by his insecurities, he has not individuated from his mother to the point that he can make his own decision to do something about his sympathies for the French Resistance.

2. The mentoring relationships as seen in *A Rumor of War* and *Platoon Leader* reflect a study by Hilary Weiner (1990) about a soldier's motivation. She found that perceived leader support was the strongest predictor of performance motivation. Job-related self-esteem and personal adjustment were also affected by perceived leader support. Lt. Caputo and Lt. Knight soon realize the importance of leader support in their combat performance and ultimately in their own survival.

3. The description of Ethel S. Person, Arnold M. Cooper, and Glen O. Gabbard (2005) of Sigmund Freud's concept of the need for approval by the father is reflected by Pfc. Conway's conflict. But this need for paternal approval is necessary for instilling self-assertion in the son. The world is then rendered manageable for a male. Throughout the son's lifetime, the son–father relationship affects the son's self-image, as well as his view of the world. A deep and lasting bond is established between a father and son as the son seeks the father's approval and praise. A son may rebel against his father, as did young Conway, but eventually the child is pulled out of the "symbiotic orbit" he inhabits with his mother. Conway's more feminine, humanistic philosophy, associated with the "symbiotic orbit," is replaced with the shared maleness of his father later in the film, as Conway accepts his father's values. In essence, the function of the father is to be the bridge between

the symbiotic internal world with the mother to the father's external world of reality. The need for a father's protection and approval was viewed by Freud as one of the strongest needs in childhood.

4. Davis Richards, in his book, *Identity and the Case for Gay Rights: Race, Gender, Religion as Analogies* (1999), gives an analogy of homophobia and anti-Semitism. He refers to Sigmund Freud's observation of anti-Semitism as an irrational thought that was rooted in the exaggerating of small, morally irrelevant differences into stereotypical truths. Richards then proposes that the homophobia of the military builds upon similar small, morally irrelevant differences. He maintains that the military portrays these differences as rendering the homosexual soldier as incapable of exercising the duties of military service. Capt. Stransky provides us with this take on this phenomenon.

5. Rape in war is often confused with sex, rather than its most dominant motivating factor, power. Nicholas Groth, in *Men Who Rape: The Psychology of the Offender* (2001), reports that power often motivates the rapist. In a desire to possess his victim sexually, this sexuality often becomes a means of compensating for his underlying feelings of inadequacy. The soldier often feels helpless as a pawn of unseen generals and politicians. In committing a rape, the soldier uses physical aggression to overpower his victim, thus achieving a kind of power over another that he does not currently possess over his own life and body. In the surreal phenomenon of war, soldiers who feel powerlessness were often susceptible to committing rape as a means of falsely achieving a warped sense of power.

6. Pvt. Maggot epitomizes the diagnosis of the antisocial personality disorder. Additionally, the stress of combat has produced a state of delusional thought in which Maggot has auditory hallucinations that command him to be God's avenging angel. He appears to feel no remorse while violating the rights of others as he kills prostitutes. In fact, his delusional thinking helps him rationalize his behaviors by thinking that he is acting as the avenging hand of God. In discussing the antisocial personality disorder, Donald Black, in his book *Bad Boys, Bad Men: Confronting Antisocial Personality Disorder* (1999), first defers to how the American Psychiatric Association's *Diagnostic and Statistical Manual of Mental Disorders* describes this condition, and then discusses it, saying the following:

> [The Antisocial Personality Disorder is] an established pattern of behaviors and attitudes that deny or violate the rights of others, including crime and other violations of social norms, deceit, impulsivity, aggressions, recklessness, irresponsibility and lack of remorse. Often adults diagnosed with Antisocial Personality Disorder have a history of Conduct Disorder in childhood. Like Antisocial Personality Disorder, Conduct Disorder occurs mostly in males. These children often show aggression and cruelty toward people and animals, are destructive of property, show deceitfulness or thievery, and exhibit serious violations of the rules. Violence is a common part of the lives of these children, both in their environment and their families. Furthermore, these children tend to come from environments where adult supervision is minimal and where physical discipline (often abusive) teaches 'might makes right.'" (17, 21, 36)

7. Aardvark, sitting with a blank stare in a fetal position after throwing his girlfriend out the window to her death, clearly represents psychotic behaviors associated with combat stress (post-traumatic stress disorder [PTSD]). Michael

Roy (2006) writes that 80 percent of soldiers who meet PTSD criteria also have at least one other psychiatric diagnosis. This dual condition is called comorbidity. Frequently, PTSD's related comorbid diagnoses include depression, anxiety, substance abuse, disassociation, and various personality disorders. Up to 40 percent of these soldiers have comorbid psychotic features. Aardvark appears to reflect the avoidance symptoms of PTSD. A detachment from others and a restricted range of affect resembling schizophrenia can be seen in his behavior. Interestingly enough, combat soldiers suffering from PTSD score highest on the clinical scale of schizophrenia on the Minnesota Multiphasic Personality Inventory (MMPI). Scores on this MMPI scale suggest symptoms of thought disorders and psychosis. Soldiers suffering symptoms of PTSD with psychotic features exhibited at least moderate severity in "delusional thinking, conceptual disorganization, hallucinatory behavior, suspiciousness, paranoia, and persecutory thoughts" (43). When Aardvark becomes paranoid about what his girlfriend is going to tell others about him after her rapes her, he shows delusional thinking and conceptual disorganization symptoms related to PTSD with psychotic features.

8. In *Flashback: Post-Traumatic Stress Disorder, Suicide, and the Lessons of War* (2007), Penny Coleman discusses the FNG as someone soldiers do not trust. She describes the FNG as an unknown quantity whose lack of experience can be a threat to survival to his comrades. Furthermore, the FNG often is replacing a "buddy" who has died or has left the unit because his tour was over and he was rotated back to the States. Regardless, the dynamic is that the FNG ends up paying the dues for someone he has never met. His fellow soldiers' anger and resentment over the death or absence of a close friend are projected onto the new recruit.

Initially, the FNG is often shunned, because a newcomer to the war is much more likely to get himself killed, and in doing so, endangers others around him. As E. Tayloe Wise reports in *Eleven Bravo: A Skytrooper Memoir of War in Vietnam* (2004), the shorter the time a soldier had spent in Vietnam, the more likely he was to die. Wise found that during a twelve-month tour, 40 percent of soldiers who had been in-country in Vietnam for less than three months were killed. In comparison, only 6 percent of soldiers died during their last three months. These statistics explain the reluctance of the soldiers who are "short," that is, getting close to their departure dates, to associate with FNGs. The "short-timer," slang for a soldier who has only a little time left on his tour of duty, shuns the FNG simply to increase the odds of making it home alive.

From the time an FNG first arrives in Vietnam until he rotates "back to the world" a year later, he goes through five stages of development. Bruce W. Tuckman's famous five stages of group development—forming, storming, norming, performing, and adjourning—can be adapted to the FNG experience (Smith, 2005). Initially, when he arrives in Vietnam, the FNG is in the forming stage. The newcomer, trying to become oriented to his new milieu, tries to get to know his fellow soldiers. This stage is often characterized by a great deal of tension, made worse for the FNG as many of his fellow soldiers shun him. Group members are also often on guard and reluctant to share relevant information during this initial stage.

If the FNG survives, group tension lessens, and fellow soldiers begin to exchange more information, increasing interdependence among the soldiers. This takes them into the second stage of group development, called storming. During storming, conflicts arise among the group members, promoting group unity and cohesion. This takes the newcomer into the third stage, called norming, in which he feels a sense of belonging and identification with the unit. Such was the case in *Platoon*, after newcomer Chris Taylor has been slightly wounded in a firefight and is subsequently accepted by the "heads" (marijuana smokers) of the platoon as a full-fledged member of their fraternity. The fourth stage of group development is the performing stage, in which the team of soldiers matures as a group and works at their highest potential. This stage occurs after the newcomer has become a veteran and even becomes a "short timer." The final stage of group development is adjourning, in which our veteran finishes his tour of duty, is rotated out of the unit, returns home, and his absence is mourned by his buddies (69).

9. Development of esprit de corps (a common spirit of comradeship, enthusiasm, and devotion to a cause amongst the members of a group, according to the American Heritage Dictionary) is a leadership goal in military units. Mutual trust creates cohesion among unit members, as discussed by the U.S. Department of the Army in their *U.S. Army Combat Stress Control Handbook*; however, it is esprit de corps that keeps individual soldiers dedicated to the greater mission of patriotic duty. In creating these highly cohesive units, a drawback is that cohesion can also create a sense of macho superiority over new, inexperienced unit members. In *Battleground*, after FNG Layton's comrades initially shun him, he proves himself in combat, overcoming harsh conditions and the fearsome German onslaught during the Battle of the Bulge. Thus, he demonstrates his abilities and is relatively quickly accepted as a full-fledged and bloodied member of the platoon.

10. The Russian boy-soldier, taken prisoner by Steiner's patrol, is treated as a child, rather than a prisoner of war. This phenomenon exemplifies the Stockholm Syndrome, as described by Frank Parkinson in his book *Post-Traumatic Stress Disorder/Prevention* (2000). Steiner's men appear to develop characteristics of this syndrome as they exhibit close feelings of attachment to the boy. The prisoner often develops feelings of sympathy and empathy toward those who are holding them captive. Despite the fact that the boy may end up at the other end of a rifle sight from him, Steiner still escorts the boy back to the Soviet lines so he can rejoin his comrades. Although the boy dies before rejoining his fellow soldiers, Parkinson reports that after a captive is repatriated, the way the former captive thinks and feels about himself, his country, his captors, and his homeland changes.

11. In *The Anxiety and Phobia Workbook* (2005), Edmund Bourne defines anticipatory anxiety as an "anxiety that has a tendency to build up gradually in response to encountering a threatening situation" (3). Sgt. Stryker advises his younger, more inexperienced soldiers that he, too, feels fear when he thinks about an upcoming engagement with the enemy. His men are surprised that this apparently stoic man also experiences anxiety as he anticipates confrontation with the enemy, thus anticipatory anxiety.

12. A victim of childhood emotional abuse by his father, Cooney is a constant threat to the safety of the men that he commands. In dysfunctional families where there is abuse, the abused suffer feelings of helplessness. Triggered by the stress of combat, the fearful Cooney sees himself as helpless and unable to exercise the brave and manly duties of war, and he relives the episodes when his father verbally abused him. His subordinate officers have no respect for him, so he

can't turn to them for advice or solace. In *The Abuse of Men: Trauma Begets Trauma* (2001), Barbara Jo Brothers reports that soldiers who admit to needing psychological help are often shunned by their comrades. Such displays are a "sign of physical, moral, and emotional weakness" (36). As the man in charge, Cooney feels that he can't turn to anyone to confide his self-doubt. His superior is no help, either. Cooney's battalion commander, Lt. Col. Clyde Bartlett, comes from the same town. In a way, reminding Cooney of his situation back home, Bartlett serves as a surrogate abusive father. Bartlett knows Cooney is incompetent and cowardly but hopes to curry favor with his rich, influential father after the war. Instead of relieving him of command, Bartlett tells Cooney, in modern slang, to "man up," swallow his fears, and do his job. But once again, Cooney fails, and another officer shoots him to protect the rest of the company.

13. Winston displays a dissociative state as a way of dealing with his guilt after hiding from combat in a cellar for more than a year. In *The Trauma Spectrum: Hidden Words and Human Resiliency* (2005), Robert Scaer links the state of disassociation with what he refers to as the "freeze response." Scaer reports that an analgesia is produced as a reaction to an intensely stressful situation. This state of analgesia allows the individual to maintain immobility. The effects are similar to a narcotic in that they "alter the individual's perception and impair cognitive functioning" (181). Winston battles the innate messages from his childhood that place honor and courage above all else. His hiding in the cellar has caused an inner cognitive conflict that he is unable to reconcile psychologically. The only plausible psychological escape from his emotional conflict and pain is for his brain to stifle his intrusive thoughts by dulling his awareness. Chemicals from his brain create a dissociative state in which his emotional pain is numbed.

14. Malingerers are defined by the U.S. Department of the Army in *U.S. Army Combat Stress Control Handbook* (2003) as "those few soldiers who, in an effort to avoid duty, deliberately and willfully fake illness, physical disablement, mental lapse, or derangement, including battle fatigue" (69). Kipp's "misplacing" his teeth to keep from serving at the front during the Battle of the Bulge would fall into the army's definition of malingering. The act of finding his teeth when he finally realizes that he doesn't have a chance of withdrawing from the fighting only verifies the fact that Kipp is a malingerer. In the handbook, the offense of malingering is considered a form of misconduct, when the physical or mental symptoms are under the voluntary control of the soldier.

15. Lawrence exhibits characteristics of learned helplessness associated with both his persecution by the DI and the ridicule and beatings administered by his fellow marines. Learned helplessness can be best explained using the example of a dog who is constantly beaten. Fear and an inability to defend himself emerges. This learned helplessness is exacerbated for Lawrence, as he also has low intellectual functioning. This makes it difficult for him to comprehend what is expected of him as a soldier. Helplessness often leads to depression. As Aphrodite Matsakis writes in *Back from the Front: Combat, Trauma, Love, and the Family* (2007), believing you are helpless or ineffectual causes negative thinking and irrational thought that can subsequently result in negative events. The depressed soldier can distort his view of the world, his surroundings, and himself. Individuals who do not know how to express anger appropriately can "turn their anger inward" (100). In his *Handbook of*

Psychobiography (2005), William Schultz says that Sigmund Freud described suicide as a situation in which an individual sees himself as an object of hate that needs to be killed. The primary goal for suicide, then, is "murder of self" (162). So Freud believed that someone who commits suicide "doesn't quite want to die. He wants rather to kill" (162). In Lawrence's murder/suicide, then, Freud would say that Lawrence was actually killing two objects of hate: his DI and himself.

4

Manliness and the Burden of Command

American war films stipulate that when it comes to command, only real men need apply. Only real men have the credentials (anatomically and otherwise) to lead real men. This chapter examines the usual and customary issues American war films introduce to dramatize how manliness and the burden of command interconnect.

SURVIVOR GUILT

Guilt, especially survivor guilt, plagues most commanders, from the squad leader in charge of a squad that encounters a Japanese ambush in *Windtalkers* (2002) to the U.S. Army Air Corps general in *Command Decision* (1948) who must reconcile sending hundreds of airmen to their deaths to achieve a strategic objective. Even when a commander leads by example, as Col. Moore (Mel Gibson) in *We Were Soldiers* (2002) or Brig. Gen. Frank Savage (Gregory Peck) in *Twelve O'Clock High* (1949), the leader's actions can have unexpected deadly consequences. Because of the nature of war and the nature of men, even when providing the manly, brave role model for their men, commanders can inadvertently cause men to die. As quoted at the end of the last chapter, Moore, commander of the newly formed 7th Cavalry, vows to be the first soldier to step off onto the landing zone and the last to leave, and he says that will see to it that no man is left behind. These noble words sound inspiring on the parade ground, but later, in combat, when one of Moore's young officers is killed carrying a wounded man back to the American lines, Moore is troubled. "He died keeping my promise," Moore says, and the macho commander cries.

Later, surrounded and outnumbered, with no chance to retreat, Moore once again has cause to wonder if his hubris has caused the repeat of the tragedy that once befell the original 7th Cavalry. To his crusty, no-nonsense sergeant major and personal confessor, Basil Plumley, Moore remarks in despair, "I wonder what was going through Custer's mind when he realized he'd led his men into a slaughter?" In typical macho fashion, Plumley barks his response: "Sir, Custer was a pussy! You ain't." There, in the midst of all the blood and devastation of battle, Moore looks at Plumley and smiles and laughs, exclaiming, "Goddamn!" This electric moment wakes Moore from self-pity, an emotion clearly not allowed in the commander's manual of acceptable manly behaviors. Moore immediately turns to tactical planning and formulates a bold reaction to repel the enemy's final assault. Unlike Custer, who gathered his men into a circle, dismounted, and allowed the Sioux to surround and slaughter every man under his command, Moore conceives of a wild sortie right down the middle of the onrushing enemy, which results in winning the battle.[1]

Likewise, in *Twelve O'Clock High*, Brig. Gen. Frank Savage leads by example and is intolerant of any officer who doesn't. Although he would be within his rights to detail subordinate officers to lead the hazardous B-17 bombing raids over Germany that he orders, Savage instead flies these missions alongside his men. When Col. Davenport (Gary Merrill), the commander of a "hard luck" bombing group assigned to hazardous raids over heavily defended German targets, cracks up under pressure, Savage is put in temporary command and ordered to shape up the group.

Savage feels that Davenport has become too "buddy-buddy" with his men. Given the group's mediocre flying record, he decides that harsh discipline is the way to shape up the group. The shock treatment begins as soon as he arrives, as Savage begins strictly enforcing all regulations: He will run the group "by the book." Used to much more lax leadership, his men cringe.

Savage soon finds an ideal scapegoat for his new, harsh style of discipline, when he reads the personal record of the group's executive officer. Savage discovers that the exec, Lt. Col. Gately (Hugh Marlowe), has been ducking flight duty and has only logged three combat missions in the months he has been there. Savage considers Gately's actions a gross dereliction of duty. He summons Gately to his office, puts the officer at attention, and reads him the riot act. He notes that Gately has "more four-engine time than any man in the group." He continues saying, "For those reasons, you could've done more than anyone to take the load off Col. Davenport." Savage blames Gately for Davenport's breakdown, reasoning that only a total lack of support could bring such an outstanding commander to the point of mental exhaustion. But rather than transfer Gately out of the group, Savage decides to make an example of him, to demonstrate to his men that the craven still must stand with the real men and take their chances in combat. Savage states the following:

> Gately, as far as I'm concerned, you're yellow, a traitor to yourself, to this group, and to the uniform you wear. . . . I hate a man like you so much that I'm going to get your head down in the mud and trample it. I'm going to make you wish you'd never been born. . . . You're going to stay right here and get a bellyful of flying. You're going to make every mission . . . and I want you to paint this name on the nose of your ship: *Leper Colony*. Because in it, you're gonna get every deadbeat in the outfit, every man with a penchant for head colds; if there's a bombardier who can't hit his plate with his fork, you get him; if there's a navigator who can't find the men's room, you get him because you rate him.

Mortified, Gately changes almost overnight from a gold brick to the perfect, tough-as-nails commander Savage demands. He flies every mission, distinguishes himself in combat, and even continues flying after suffering a painful spinal fracture. Eventually, when Gately's back injury results in his hospitalization, Savage is told of Gately's injury and his fortitude. The doctor tells Savage that the officer's broken back must have caused him excruciating pain, but Gately kept flying. Gately had learned his lesson, and, as discussed in chapter 2, stayed in the game and played hurt. Realizing that Gately has become an exemplary officer, Savage visits him in the hospital and, in his own, terse, manly way, shows his concern for Gately. The unmanly officer has redeemed himself and re-joined the fraternity of men. As Savage exits the hospital room, Gately, relieved that he has once again become a full-fledged member of the fraternity, turns his head away from the door and cries.

But all is not going as well for Frank Savage the man. He may be manly and rough on the outside, but inside is a different story. Savage, too, succumbs to the fatal flaw that these kinds of war movies present in almost an identical manner: the standoffish commander begins to care too deeply for the men he leads into battle, reducing his ability to dispassionately make the hard decisions that send these young men to their deaths. As in most war films, this simple human emotion in a commander is portrayed as a character flaw, a chink in his manly armor. Caring for his men too deeply is why Davenport had his emotional breakdown in the first place. And now, Savage's growing affection for his men and his increasing guilt as many of them die leads to his own breakdown. It comes to a head after his exec, Maj. Joe Cobb (John Kellogg), whom Savage has come to admire deeply, is killed leading a mission. Ready to command another mission himself, Savage finally loses it: He can't even manage to hoist himself up

Gen. Savage (Gregory Peck) issues orders to his adjutant (Dean Jagger) in *Twelve O'Clock High. 20th Century Fox / Photofest © 20th Century Fox*

into the cockpit of his B-17. The general mentally and physically collapses on the spot. Gately, of all people, his spinal fracture now healed, steps in to fly the lead bomber in the mission, and other staff officers help Savage back to his quarters. There, virtually catatonic, Savage sits like a stone during the entire mission. Only when his bombers return and land does he come out of his stupor, allowing himself to sleep.[2]

Another U.S. Army Air Corps general faces many similar problems in a similar film, *Command Decision*. General K. C. Dennis (Clark Gable) is also trying to win the war in Europe via daylight strategic bombing missions over Germany. Trying to destroy Germany's aircraft factories before they can rush their new, deadly jet fighters into production—a move that could overturn Allied air supremacy—is costing heavy losses in aircrews and planes. Dennis is under terrible political pressure from Washington to curtail losses, but he considers the mission to be crucial and more important than the losses of planes and men. Throughout most of the film, Dennis seems to ignore the cost in human life, but in his deepest inner feelings, each death affects him. We find this out only after politics causes Dennis to be fired, and he still urges the general who replaces him to launch one last mission to finish the job of destroying the German jet fighter factories.

Dennis's replacement, Gen. Clifton Garnet (Brian Donlevy), is unsure about spending more lives, concerned about the military and congressional politics that caused Dennis to lose his job. But Dennis lectures Garnet about doing his job, even if it means having to live with the number of men killed. Dennis says, "Make every one of [these missions] count. See that they're not used up for nothing." So Garnet makes the "right call" and orders up the maximum effort against the German factories that Dennis wanted destroyed. This time, the aircrews succeed in their mission.

Dennis, expecting to be shipped home to the United States to some "doghouse assignment" in a training command, is instead ordered to take over a bigger, more hazardous command in the Pacific, in charge of a new B-29 bomber group. But Dennis is not happy, because instead of heading home to a stateside assignment and a reunion with his family, he'll once again have to order young men to their deaths. Dennis is as committed to doing his job as much as Savage or Davenport in *Twelve O'Clock High*, and—perhaps because he's the unflappable, ultra manly Clark Gable—he manages to do it without a nervous breakdown. Although Dennis remains conflicted and guilty about "killing" his young flyers, he doesn't let it show or unduly influence his decisions.[3]

These films demonstrate that Hollywood's model of unemotionally bearing up under the weight of this conflict between duty and humanity is the stated job of the commander, the man, the leader. The story in *Command Decision* demonstrates that unlike Savage and Davenport, the two more fallible group commanders of *Twelve O'Clock High*, the manliest men can and should complete their assigned jobs—no matter how difficult—without cracking up under the strain. Even in the top echelons of command, perhaps especially at the highest level, there is a pecking order between the military's Übermenchen and the rest.

DUTY OF LEADERSHIP VERSUS HUMANITY

Some films of recent years delve much further into the depths of these questions than some of the melodramas of the past, and they provide fascinating dialectics on duty versus humanity for audiences to ponder. Such a picture is Terrence Malick's visual delight, *The Thin Red Line* (1998). In this film, the commander is no Übermensch, nor is he a man of good character. Lt. Col. Tall (Nick Nolte) is a career officer, and although he's a West Point graduate, he has twice been passed over for promotion to full colonel. He watches the war enable younger men to pass him by and ascend to the ranks of general officers, while he languishes. Although he hates himself for "brown-nosing generals to curry favor," Tall still does it, and he sees his present situation commanding a battalion charged with clearing away the Japanese from entrenched positions on the strategically and politically important Pacific island of Guadalcanal as his last, best chance for career advancement.

In other films we've discussed in this context, internal conflicts between duty and humanity trouble such commanders as Davenport, Savage, and Dennis. In *The Thin Red Line,* two officers personify the internal conflict between concern for their men versus the need to complete the mission for personal gain. Tall is not at all troubled by the prospect of sending his men to their deaths, if their deaths serve his career purposes. Completing the mission and thus servicing his ambitions are all that matter. Capt. Staros (Elias Koteas) leads one of Tall's companies. Although a competent officer and leader, Staros is, first and foremost, a humanist. He's reasonably committed to the mission but not at all devoted to completing it at any cost, much less to advance Tall's career at the expense of his men.

Tall won't even stop his battalion's advance against the Japanese long enough for food and water and other supplies to catch up with them. Instead, over the radio, Tall orders Staros's company to perform a suicidal frontal attack on a Japanese position, a move that will undoubtedly result in heavy losses. Staros favors a safer flanking maneuver to the frontal attack, but flanking takes much longer, and Tall wants to impress his general with speedy results. Before the attack, Staros prays that he will not betray either himself or his men, saying, "In you I place my trust." But when the attack begins, the Japanese cut down his men in a bloodbath. When the remains of his company return back down the hill, Staros reports to Tall that the frontal attack won't work and requests permission to outflank the Japanese. Now literally frothing at the mouth, Tall says he won't authorize a flanking movement "just to avoid a fight!"

Staros refuses. He knows another frontal attack is the equivalent of a Japanese "banzai" suicide charge and won't sacrifice his men on the altar of Tall's ambition. One of Staros's subordinate officers cautions him to follow Tall's orders, saying, "It's not your fault, Jim. He's ordering you to." But in Staros's mind, hiding behind the safety of "obeying orders" isn't sufficient reason to permit his men to be slaughtered. A lawyer in civilian life, Staros asks Tall to note the time and the names of the witnesses to their conversation, assuming that the impasse between them will result in a court-martial. Tall, taken aback, begins to wonder if the fallout from this incident might be worse for his flagging career than not taking the hill expeditiously. But he just repeats his command. Staros refuses again, explaining that, "I have lived with these men for two and a half years, and I will not order them to their deaths."

The next day, a reconnaissance patrol finds a blind spot in the Japanese defenses, and the hill is taken. Tall orders Staros to accompany him as they walk and talk. Having no understanding or empathy for Staros's devotion to his men, Tall simplistically assumes that Staros doesn't have the "stomach" to sacrifice men's lives for a military objective. He equates the captain's humanism with an unmanly lack of fortitude and courage. Tall relieves Staros of his command, stating, "I don't think you're tough enough. You're just too soft. You're too softhearted. You're not tough fibered enough" (read "you're too much like a woman").

To avoid the questions that would arise in a court-martial, Tall doesn't file charges against Staros. Instead, he buys him off with a transfer to Washington to serve in the Judge Advocate Corps, along with a few decorations, including a Silver Star and a Purple Heart. As the captain prepares to leave, Staros's men thank him for refusing his commander's order, saving their lives. Staros reveals his feelings, saying that these young men were like his sons. In a voice-over as he is transported back to the States, Staros says, "You are my sons. You live inside me now. I'll carry you wherever I go."

Staros portrays another, less artificial form of manliness: The fiercely protective love of a father for his children is the emotion that guides his behavior, not a lack of virility, as Tall maintains. This ethic rejects the false, macho, selfish manhood of his commander for something too often sacrificed on the altar of military ambition: affection and respect for one's fellow man.

AVOIDING RESPONSIBILITY

The conflict between men who agonize over duty versus their responsibility to retain their humanity is heavily debated in *The Guns of Navarone* (1961). Capt. Keith Mallory (Gregory Peck) is in constant personal conflict with Cpl. Miller (David Niven) over the same issue: devotion to the dictates of the mission, which often override a concern for the welfare of his men. But unlike Tall, Mallory has no ambitions, no personal agenda for advancement. But to Mallory, the mission is paramount, and in this case, he sees no problem in sacrificing members of his small commando force for the greater good. Mallory's team has been ordered to destroy a vital German big gun emplacement that threatens Allied warships and thousands of troops near Crete in the Eastern Mediterranean. Mallory is no-nonsense, somewhat gruff, and totally task oriented, certainly as tough as any of John Wayne's characters. The story constantly tasks Mallory with making difficult choices that put good people in harm's way.

Miller, on the other hand, refuses to take any responsibility for decision making, and thus, in his rationalization of his role in the war, he is not culpable for the death, horrors, and destruction that he precipitates. A genius with explosives, Miller does what he's told and leaves it at that. But, for the sake of the conflict that powers this screenplay, Miller can't keep his feelings to himself. He constantly acts as Mallory's vocal conscience, often arguing for humanitarian concerns over military expediency. In the following scene, they have just discovered that one of the Greek partisans, Anna, an attractive young woman with whom they have been teamed throughout most of this adventure, is actually a double agent and has been spying on them for the Germans. Some in Mallory's group are squeamish about killing her, but they can't just tie her up and take the chance that she will get loose and reveal their plan to blow up the German guns. Miller, sarcastically pressing his criticism of Mallory, says that logically, Anna must be shot.

Mallory: We've no time for this!

Miller: Now just a minute! If we're going to get this job done, she has got to be killed! And we all know how keen you are about getting the job done! Now I can't speak for the others, but I've never killed a woman, traitor or not, and I'm finicky! So why don't you do it? Let us off for once! Go on, be a pal, be a father to your men! Climb down off that cross of yours, close your eyes, think of England, and pull the trigger! What do you say, sir?

Mallory: (angrily) Well, if you're so anxious to kill her, go ahead!

Miller: I'm not anxious to kill her, I'm not anxious to kill anyone. You see, I'm not a born soldier. I was trapped. You may find me facetious from time to time, but if I didn't make some rather bad jokes, I'd go out of my mind. No, I prefer to leave the killing to someone like you, an officer and a gentleman, a leader of men.

Mallory: If you think I wanted this, any of this, you're out of your mind. I was trapped like you, just like anyone who put on the uniform!

Miller: Of course you wanted it, you're an officer, aren't you? I never let them make *me* an officer! I don't want the responsibility!

Mallory: (now growling) So you've had a free ride all this time! Someone's got to take responsibility if the job's going to get done! You think that's easy?

Miller: (shouts) I don't know! I'm not even sure who really is responsible anymore.

Anna is suddenly shot—killed, ironically, by the other Greek woman in their group. Then everyone else exits. Mallory turns to Miller, still holding his gun.

Mallory: You think you've been getting away with it all this time, standing by. Well, son, your bystanding days are *over*! You're in it now, up to your neck! They told me that you're a genius with explosives. (raising his voice and emotional level as only Gregory Peck can do) Start proving it! You got

> me in the mood to use this thing [his pistol], and (shouting) by God, if you don't think of something, I'll use it on you! I mean it!

Miller avoids responsibility for killing by refusing to be commissioned an officer. In effect, he demasculinizes himself for the sake of his humanistic feelings and would prefer to be considered just a weapon of mass destruction, turned first on one enemy and then on another. Then, as the National Rifle Association (NRA) says today, "Guns don't kill people: People kill people." Mallory, channeling the NRA, reminds Miller that manliness is more than exercising force and killing people: It's making difficult decisions and taking responsibility.[4]

OBEYING ORDERS (DOING ONE'S JOB) VERSUS HUMANITY

In Hollywood's often retold renditions of this dilemma, not all enlisted men can hide behind so effective a facade of scruples as Cpl. Miller in *The Guns of Navarone*. In these kinds of films, such enlisted men as Sgt. Joe Enders (Nicolas Cage) in *Windtalkers* and Sgt. Eddie Porter (Herbert Rudley) in *A Walk in the Sun* (1945) are deeply troubled by such concerns, because unlike Miller, they're in charge, so they can't dodge them. Attrition in the ranks has put Enders and Porter in charge, and now their decisions are final and potentially deadly to their men if they choose poorly. In *Windtalkers*, Enders, wracked with guilt over the deaths his orders have caused—orders given because he's done his duty and followed orders explicitly—wonders if doing one's duty rather than judging the situation at hand is wrong. Does a man's duty—his personal job of work—trump *all* other concerns? Can he use it as an effective rationalization, smoothing over the flashback horror of men dying at his orders? If a man doesn't do his job, his manly duty, by the book, can he hold his head up? Is there ever a time for compromise, and if one does, is a man any less a man for trying to find a middle ground?

In the jungles of what is likely Guadalcanal (all that's conveyed in the movie about the location is that it's in the Solomon Islands), Enders leads what's left of his squad. He became acting squad leader when all his superiors were killed. Strictly following his orders has resulted in the squad becoming nearly surrounded by the Japanese, who appear from all directions out of the jungle. Enders's men urge him to call a retreat before all are killed. Instead, Enders replies, "No, we got orders" (to hold their position). Because of his resolute adherence to orders, all of his men are killed. As the last man dies in his arms, he mutters, "Goddam you, Joe Enders." Then, after a Japanese grenade explodes close by, Enders is left wounded and unconscious, left for dead by the Japanese.

Later, however, he is found and rescued. He receives a Purple Heart for the wounds that damaged his hearing and balance, plus a Silver Star, as he interprets it, "for not dying. The fifteen men who fought with me got decorated, too . . . for dying."

In a hospital back in Hawaii, Enders recovers some of his hearing, enough to fake a medical test so he can return to action, but he remains wounded physically and psychologically, suffering from post-traumatic stress disorder and deep survivor guilt. At points throughout the film, he suffers flashbacks to that day on Guadalcanal to the cries of his men, and especially the soldier who cursed him. Enders indeed feels damned, or at least in some kind of fighting man's limbo, neither dead nor alive. Righting this perceived wrong, finding redemption for himself, perhaps to die as he thinks he should have along with his buddies on Guadalcanal is what motivates Enders volunteer to return to duty. He could easily obtain a medical discharge and return to New York, his hometown, a decorated hero. All requirements of a man have been met, and Enders has the scars and medals to prove it. But guilt, the great equalizer, propels him back into the maelstrom. Survivor guilt prompts a man to ask if it's unmanly, even cowardly, to return home alive when everyone else dies. Enders begins to doubt that unbendingly obeying orders was the only correct option, so guilt motivates him to return to the battlefield.

Sgt. Enders (Nicolas Cage), left, under fire, tries to decide what to do next in *Windtalkers. MGM / Photofest © MGM*

He volunteers for special duty, as an escort or protector (referred to in the film as being either a bodyguard or babysitter) for what the marines call a "code talker." This is a marine of Navajo Indian descent, a radio man who uses a special code, spoken in his Native American tongue, to transmit vital tactical information without fear of Japanese interception. For example, the code word for "tank" is the Navajo word for "turtle." In real life, this code befuddled the Japanese, who listened in on the marines' radio traffic but could understand nothing. So the enemy desperately wanted to capture a code talker, whom the Navajos call a "windtalker" (the word in their language for talking on the radio), so they could torture the code out of him.

In real life, the Japanese were never successful. This is the fictional account of a newly promoted sergeant, Enders, who is assigned to make sure that his code talker is protected as much as possible in combat and that he never falls into the hands of the Japanese. His strict orders—the orders that he comes to question later in the film—were to "protect the code—at all costs," meaning that if he was sure the Navajo was about to be taken prisoner by the Japanese, Enders must kill him.

Of course, believing that he was responsible for the deaths of his squad on Guadalcanal, Enders is not happy with this part of his assignment. He had hoped to draw a regular combat job, but the medals he earned singled him out for promotion and this special duty. In effect, in Enders's thinking, being a "damn good marine" and getting his men killed has ironically put him in the position of perhaps having to kill a marine in cold blood himself.

Although it takes Enders some time to warm up to his new Indian companion, Pfc. Ben Yazi (Adam Beach), he eventually does. After a terrible battle in which Enders's brave actions earn him yet a second Silver Star, he and Yazi are drinking sake. Yazi asks Enders how he earned his first medal:

> ENDERS: Orders were to hold some shitty swamp marsh on the ass end of nowhere. And I did. All of the men under my command—men who trusted me—begged me to pull back. Not one of 'em made it. Just one stupid asshole. And for that, they gave me the Silver Star.
>
> YAZI: It wasn't your fault, Joe. You were just following orders.
>
> ENDERS: (sarcastically) Yeah. I'm a good fucking marine.

Despite Yazi's attempts to use chants from his Navajo religion to exorcise the demons that bedevil Enders, the burden remains heavy on Enders's shoulders. Doing what is required of a squad leader—strict adherence to orders—got his men killed. But in the marines, if you don't obey your orders, what are you?

Like the bomber commanders who grew to care too much for their subordinates, Enders soon begins to admire Yazi. He later decides that it's likely he won't be able to pull the trigger if the time came when he had to kill his assigned code talker. Enders tries to explain this to the top sergeant of his company and asks to be relieved of his special duty. Gunnery Sgt. Hjelmstad (Peter Stormare) won't transfer Enders, saying, "You're saving a lot of marines protecting the code talker." A tough old marine, Hjelmstad reminds Enders of his responsibilities as a man, which include internalizing his emotions and making his personal problems and scruples secondary to the good of the U.S. Marine Corps: "There's a war going on worldwide, and it ain't being waged on your wants and wishes," growls Hjelmstad. But Enders, like Griff in *Flying Leathernecks* (1951), just can't turn off his humanity. Although he has no trouble shooting the enemy, he can't bring himself to kill a marine, much less his friend Yazi, no matter how important a duty it is.

But later, just to give Enders more to agonize about, cruel fate forces him to intentionally kill another marine. One of the men in his squad carries a flamethrower. This is a very dangerous job, since the tank he carries is full of combustible fuel (the man calls it a giant Zippo lighter), and if it's hit by a bullet, the marine carrying the tank will burn to death. The Americans are being overrun by Japanese when the flamethrower operator's tank is hit, and the marine writhes in agony on the ground, covered in flames and screaming. Enders mercifully shoots the man, ending his suffering.

As the Japanese attack continues, another code talker, Pvt. Charlie White Horse, is captured. By this time, Enders has run out of all his ammunition, so he can't shoot the enemy soldiers who have captured White Horse. All he has left is a grenade. Enders makes eye contact with Charlie for a second, and the code talker nods his assent. Enders tosses the grenade, and all six Japanese, along with Charlie, die. Enders is beside himself. In one battle, the man who is plagued with guilt for the deaths he caused back on Guadalcanal has become responsible for the deaths of two more of his fellow marines.

Later, when a shocked Enders curtly tells Yazi that he killed Charlie, the code talker is furious, draws a pistol, and is ready to shoot him. Yazi doesn't know the secret that has been kept from him, that Enders's prime directive is to protect the code at all costs. Enders is so miserable that he urges Yazi to pull the trigger, but the young code talker doesn't. Enders later explains the details of his secret, and Yazi forgives him for killing his best friend.

On their next and final patrol, to locate a Japanese gun emplacement and use Yazi's code talker skills to call in an air strike, the marines are once again under heavy enemy attack. History seems to be repeating itself: Hjelmstad is killed, and Enders once again finds himself in command. At one point, surrounded and short on ammunition, his men turn to him: Should they retreat? The Guadalcanal incident is replaying itself. But they see that the enemy gun emplacement—the object of their patrol—is already hurling deadly fire on a column of fellow marines, killing many. They can't retreat; they have a mission and orders. Enders stubbornly yells, "We're gonna make it, we're not gonna die," and he presses on.

As the battle worsens for the marines, once again surrounded by Japanese, and ammunition supplies become more critical, Enders realizes that he may have to have to shoot Yazi. But this is where he draws his own personal line: Enders decides that manly, soldierly duty or not, he can't kill his friend. "No one else is gonna die, Ben," Enders tells Yazi. But the two simultaneously seem to decide to go down trying to call in that air strike on the Japanese. Yazi is wounded in the leg, but he manages to direct the strike onto the target, destroying the Japanese guns; however, while covering Yazi so he could do his duty, Enders is fatally wounded. He dies in Yazi's arms, finally catching up with the men of his squad he lost back on Guadalcanal. Later, discharged from the service, Yazi tells his young son stories of his brave friend Joe Enders, a "great warrior."

THE BURDEN OVERCOMES THE MAN

In *Windtalkers*, Enders succeeds in both saving Yazi and successfully completing his mission. Sgt. Porter (Herbert Rudley), in *A Walk in the Sun*, succeeds only in driving himself into a mental breakdown. Much of this film documents Porter's descent from a competent and experienced but tightly strung NCO to a man lying sobbing on the ground, unable to perform either his function as a leader or his perceived manly role as a soldier doing his job. In the unusual opening to the film, a voice-over narrator awkwardly introduces most of the major characters of this Texas Division platoon. The V/Os for most of the men describe some personal or idiosyncratic characteristic, such as, "he speaks two languages, Italian and Brooklyn." About Porter, the V/O says simply, prophetically, and with some hesitation not found in the other character descriptions, "Well, he has a lot of his mind, a lot on his mind." The film follows this platoon from their landing at Salerno to the completion of their military objective—attacking and taking a strategically located farmhouse six miles inland.

From the outset, seeing and hearing his uneasiness with the nervous humor of the other soldiers on board the landing craft, we immediately sense that Porter has been in one battle too many. At one point, Pvt. Rivera (Richard Conte) jokes that the artillery shelling of the landing craft here at Salerno are inaccurate. He uses a baseball pitching metaphor, saying that here the Germans have "no control," but that when they landed at Messina, the Germans "pitched some strikes." Obviously still suffering from PTSD over Messina, Porter nervously interrupts Rivera, saying, "What's so funny about Messina? We lost a lotta good Joes there." But Sgt. Bill Tyne (Dana Andrews), Porter's direct subordinate, will have none of Porter's nonsense. Remembering the manly code that prohibits men from dwelling too long on the honored dead, he criticizes Porter, saying, "Whaddya want us to do, *cry* about it?" Tyne knows the male code, and as they prepare to land on a hostile beach, he doesn't want the men to think too much or remember fallen comrades. And certainly, in Tyne's thinking, the fighting edge of his men will suffer if they become emotional about death and dying. Porter responds to Tyne by muttering, "That's a lotta cocky chatter." "It's better than having the jitters," Tyne retorts. "Would it make you feel better if we told you *we* had the jitters?" he asks Porter. "Yeah, it would," says Porter, momentarily relieved. "Well," says Tyne, "We got 'em."

But the difference between the two sergeants is that Tyne knows what the manly code requires of a commander in this situation: He must keep his feelings and worries to himself. He knows that the men are closely watching their leaders for cues about how to act and that unnecessary emotion—or the hint of fear—gives them the wrong message. If a commander doesn't appear to his men to have an air of cool decisiveness about him, the men have little confidence in the orders he gives them. And if the men start second-guessing his orders, discipline breaks down and the mission may fail. Then more men could die.

From the start of this enterprise, Porter exudes just the opposite of what a leader of men must be: He radiates a sense of fear and crippling indecision. This is evidenced by Porter's next revealing line. He tells Tyne that he's worried how the platoon's newly assigned, young lieutenant will handle his first landing. Porter says, "Boy, I wouldn't want his job for anything." Tyne, reminding Porter of his subservient role in the platoon's hierarchy (he is junior in rank to the lieutenant and lower in enlisted man's seniority to the platoon's first sergeant), flicks the edge of Porter's chevrons on his sleeve with his fingers, smiles, and says, "Nobody's giving it to you." But a few moments later, Porter is one heartbeat away from command: The lieutenant is mortally wounded by a German artillery shell that explodes next to the landing craft.

Sgt. Pete Halverson (Matt Willis) takes command, and the platoon lands on the Salerno beachhead. Halverson decides to go find the captain, their company commander, and tell him about the fate of their lieutenant, and he tells Porter to lead the platoon 100 yards onto the beach, dig in, and wait for him to return. Porter doesn't even want to assume this much

In his first meeting as squad leader, Eversmann does not try to imitate his commander, Capt. Steele (Jason Isaacs), who stiffly spouts army slogans and sports metaphors. Eversmann is from the ranks, and the men's respect for him—and his authority—is based on having trained and soldiered beside them. So, in his mission briefing, Eversmann begins by admitting that it's the first time he's led an assault, but he then stresses the fact that they have served on missions together before and that professionalism is the key to success: Each man knows and does his job. To Eversmann, still new to command, all that has to happen is for a man to do the job he's trained for and success must follow. In the next two days, he'll learn that there's much more to it.

Eversmann's squad will helicopter to the hotel and establish a base of fire on an important street corner next to the building, helping to set up a perimeter of safety and permitting the Deltas to capture and transport the insurgent leaders back to the U.S. base. Although he is concerned enough to give extra instructions regarding duties and responsibilities to a troop who is new to the squad and combat, Eversmann is privately a little worried about himself, whether he will do his own job right. In a conversation with an older, highly experienced Delta nicknamed "Hoot" (Eric Bana), Eversmann reveals his insecurity. Stoically, knowing that combat will quickly teach the young sergeant what only experience can, the Delta gives Eversmann the same simplistic speech the young NCO gave his own men: Know the job and do it right. In this case, Hoot says, "Just watch your corner and get your men back alive."

The mission goes badly: Unexpectedly, resourceful Somalis manage to shoot down a Black Hawk helicopter. Eversmann's squad is ordered to leave their post at the hotel and rush some blocks away to the crash site to provide protection for the downed copter's crew. To continue to help with the main mission, to support the arrest of the insurgent leaders, Eversmann orders two of his men to remain at the hotel to provide cover for the evacuation of the Deltas and the captured insurgents. One of the men Eversmann leaves behind—perhaps questioning his new leader's judgment—complains. "Why me?" he asks. Instead of using an empty sports metaphor, Eversmann gives the man a backhanded compliment, saying, "Because you're reliable." Satisfied but still not ready to stop griping, the soldier carps, "I hate being reliable."

Later, as one of his men lies wounded and dying, the man apologizes to Eversmann, presumably for getting shot and becoming a burden on the rest of the squad. Eversmann, falling back on his "good training equals success" philosophy, assures the man that he has discharged a man's duty in a professional way, and thus he has nothing to be sorry

Sgt. Eversmann (Josh Hartnett) gets his first command in *Black Hawk Down. Columbia Pictures Corporation / Photofest © Columbia Pictures Corporation*

for: "You did your job—the way you were trained," he explains. Nothing more needs be said, since in war, a man doing his job as trained is all that's expected.

But later, Eversmann confides in Hoot that he has things he's sorry for, namely the loss of some of his men. The Delta now explains to Eversmann what the young man needed to learn for himself, that this is war, and that no commander—and no amount of training—can control bad luck. "Sergeant, you got your men this far. You did it right today. Now you gotta start thinking about getting them out of here." Hearing that he did his job right, Eversmann is at least temporarily mollified, and he turns his attention toward his new task. The burden of command still rests heavily on Eversmann, but for now, he continues to think clearly and make important decisions by repeating the mantra that doing his manly job efficiently is all that counts, since, he reasons, this is really the only thing a soldier in the field can control.

FEAR OF COMMAND

In Sam Fuller's Korean War drama *Fixed Bayonets* (1951), an enlisted man, Cpl. Denno (Richard Basehart), has another kind of problem: Similar to Cpl. Miller in *Navarone*, he's afraid to lead. It isn't because Denno is a coward, and it isn't because he suffers from self-doubt and battle fatigue like Sgt. Porter. In this film, he shows he's as brave as anyone else in his platoon. But before coming to Korea, Denno lost all his self-confidence because he washed out of Officer Candidate School. There he realized that he could take an order, but he couldn't give one, especially an order that could cause men to suffer injury or death. Denno explains the following to his squad leader, the appropriately named Sgt. Rock (Gene Evans):

> Some men are afraid of high places; some are afraid of water. And some are afraid to be responsible for the deaths of a lot of other guys. That's me, Rock. I don't want to carry that load.

The tough and gruff Sgt. Rock tells Denno that there's very little chance he'll have to give any orders, since the platoon has a lieutenant, a platoon sergeant, and Rock himself above him in rank. But, like *A Walk in the Sun*, director Samuel Fuller's story kills off the lieutenant, the platoon sergeant, and finally Rock. Denno and one other corporal are next in line of succession, but before his death, Rock had anointed Denno next in command.

Denno's dilemma, like Sgt. Enders's in *Windtalkers*, is whether to continue the mission they were ordered to perform as a rear guard for their regiment, holding a mountain pass against the North Koreans long enough for the regiment to retreat across a river and blow the bridge behind them. Orders are to hold until 9 a.m. to allow the regiment time to cross the river. The other corporal wants to cut and run an hour earlier, knowing that he and the remainder of the platoon will then have a much better chance to survive. The longer they wait, the more likely it is that the enemy will attack them in great numbers and possibly with tanks. But Denno, channeling his mentor, Sgt. Rock, finally grows some backbone and learns how to make decisions. He orders the men to stay and fight. Some die, but the regiment makes it safely across the river, and Denno and most of his men escape, catch up, and rejoin the regiment.

Perhaps the decision for a small group of soldiers to risk their lives so a larger number of men can live on was an easier, more logical decision for Denno. In a way, he was *saving* lives—a great many lives—by ordering his few men to hold their ground against the North Koreans. The humanistic side of Denno—the side that prevented him from issuing orders that put men in danger—was satisfied by this logical sacrifice of a few to save hundreds.

Is there always a possibility that doing one's manly duty and following orders leads to a greater good? Can this be enough to quiet a thoughtful commander's anxiety over the deaths his orders precipitate? Is manliness somehow diminished, even feminized, in a manly soldier's eyes, if achieving a tactical objective in war takes second place to human feeling, to bringing your men back alive? These anxious, contentious themes are often found among the dramatic problems screenplay writers introduce into U.S. war film screenplays.

INADEQUACY AND THE BURDEN OF COMMAND

Most war films portray American officers as relatively adequate to the task and well-trained, thoughtful, capable soldiers. Occasionally, as with West Point-educated Lt. Col. Tall in *The Thin Red Line*, although he knows his job inside and out, blind ambition causes him to needlessly order his men to their deaths. But what about a man who is promoted only because of political influence, like Capt. Cooney in *Attack!* (1956), rather than for his skill or ability—a man advanced much too far beyond his Peter Principle? (Peter and Hull [1970] write, "In a hierarchy, every employee tends to rise to his level of incompetence" [158]. In Cooney's case, he has risen far beyond his own capabilities. So in addition to his own personal anxieties, Cooney knows for sure that he can't do the job.) A commander such as this, inadequate both as a leader and as a man, makes either no decisions or bad ones and can precipitate the pointless casualties. As we will discover here and in other films discussed later in this chapter, "I don't know" is a phrase that destroys Porter, and if voiced by any commander, it can get men killed. But why wouldn't a commander know what to do? It's not because he hasn't been trained. Perhaps it's because some films posit that in the blood and explosions of a battle, lesser, inadequate men just can't think straight, while real men, according to Rudyard Kipling (1914), "can keep their heads when men all around them are losing theirs."

Mentioned briefly in chapter 3, in two episodes of the HBO miniseries *Band of Brothers* (2001), Lt. Norman Dike (Peter O'Meara) is commander of Easy Company of the 101st Airborne Screaming Eagles, fighting desperate battles against the Germans during World War II. Well educated at Yale and trained in military tactics like any other reserve officer, Dike doesn't know what to do because he is afraid, not only of being killed but of making the wrong—or any—decision, and it has little to do with worrying about his men. Crippled by self-doubt, Dike is depicted as an unmanly soldier, because under the stress of combat, he can't make calm, reasoned decisions. And, as is discussed here, Dike, by his sudden absences when the going gets tough, avoids doing almost anything. Finally, forced by circumstances to lead an important attack on a heavily defended town, he must make hard decisions, whether he's ready or not.

At first, in episode 6 of this miniseries, we find Dike to be an enigma. Is "Foxhole Norman," as the men of Easy Company sarcastically refer to their commander, really a coward, or just a lazy, unconcerned, incompetent officer who prefers to slip away to cull favor with unnamed "big shots" back at battalion and division rather than leading and caring for the men of his company? As mentioned in chapter 3, the task of leading and caring for Easy Company falls to its long-suffering first sergeant,

Carwood Lipton (Donnie Wahlberg). When there's a dangerous patrol or German shelling going on, Dike is either nowhere to be found or seen quickly scuttling toward the rear in the direction of battalion headquarters to "get help."

Dike was assigned to command Easy Company after its charismatic leader, then-captain Richard D. Winters (Damian Lewis), was promoted and assigned to duty at battalion headquarters. Winters quickly sizes up Dike and sees that the lieutenant isn't up to the task of efficiently leading the company that he led from D-Day until his recent promotion. But Winters also can't do anything about it, because Dike is too well connected with the top brass. It is assumed that he's being "groomed for oak leaf clusters" and some staff job and was only assigned to command Easy Company to get combat experience.

In episode 6, we first meet Dike as he returns from one of his frequent "walks," during which no one in the company knows where he is. His only question upon his return is to Sgt. Lipton, and all he wants to know is, "Where's my foxhole?," hence the nickname. In this episode of the miniseries, which chronicles part of Easy Company's role in the Battle of the Bulge and is simply titled "Bastogne," the story is seen through the eyes of senior company medic, Eugene Roe (Shane Taylor). Since the Germans have cut them off from the rest of the Allied expeditionary forces, and because the weather has so far prevented airdrops, Roe is almost completely out of medical supplies. He goes around from soldier to soldier looking for bandages and other first aid supplies the men carry, especially the special aid kits they were issued when they parachuted into Holland during Operation Market Garden. He is huddling around a fire with a few men when Lt. Buck Compton (Neal McDonough) asks them where Dike is. One says, almost sarcastically, "Try battalion CP, sir." When the officer is out of earshot, another soldier jokes to the medic, "Hey, Eugene, Lt. Dike's got a full aid kit. Try him," implying that when Dike's around, which isn't often, he is fully supplied, probably due to his frequent visits far behind the lines. Also, although the men have been shelled relentlessly and almost everyone has suffered small wounds, Dike doesn't have a scratch, hence there is no need for him to open his aid kit.

Later, when Roe finally catches up with Dike, he's sleeping in his foxhole, and it's daytime. When he asks Dike for his aid kit, the officer at first isn't sure what it looks like. Finally he finds his, but before he hands it to Roe, he asks, "What happens if I get hit?" Eugene, a mild-mannered fellow, for the first and only time in the miniseries, tensely and tersely replies, "I'll be there." Then, in a telling statement, Dike responds, "I don't plan on getting hit." This implies that the officer has done considerable thinking about how to avoid injury while on his current assignment.

Many of the soldiers of Easy Company in *Band of Brothers*: Top (left to right): Sgt. Sisk (Philip Barantini), Cpl. Liebgott (Ross McCall). Bottom (left to right): C. Lipton (Donnie Wahlberg), TSgt. Malarkey (Scott Grimes), SSgt. Toye (Kirk Acevedo), 1st Lt. Buck Compton (Neal McDonough), Pvt. Petty (Adam James), SSgt. Guarnere (Frank Don Hughes). *HBO / Photofest © HBO*

Both the script and the actor's performance show Dike to be a loner, aloof and disconnected with both the officers and men of Easy Company, perhaps because he resents the current assignment that has put him so close to the shooting, or, more likely, because he realizes he's not up to the manly task that the other officers and Sgt. Lipton seem to take in stride. On one atypical occasion, when once again delegating more of his duties to Lipton, Dike actually inquires about Lipton's background and hometown. Lipton, looking away as if to visualize his West Virginia hometown, tells him, but when he's finished, he looks back toward Dike, only to see that the officer has already walked away, once again in the direction of battalion headquarters. Lipton just shakes his head in disappointment.[7]

Later, when Dike and a platoon from his company are ordered to go on a reconnaissance patrol, one soldier is unconvinced that he has the right leader. To Roe and others, he gripes, "The asshole [Dike] couldn't find a snowball in a blizzard." Roe understands the soldier and probably agrees, since the night before he had to instruct Dike in basic cold weather foot care to avoid contracting trench feet.

Roe, ordered not to accompany the men on this recon mission, waits for the platoon to return. He *really* begins to doubt Dike when he hears firing from the direction Dike's men have gone and sees Dike hightailing it in the opposite direction. His men are a few thousand yards behind Dike, some wounded, firing at the enemy. But Dike, on his way speedily to the rear, says, "We're pulling back. We made contact. I gotta get back to the CP." Roe, a polite Louisiana Cajun boy, doesn't voice the unstated question, "But what about your men?"

In episode 8, Easy Company continues with the intention of pushing back the German bulge. Lipton must report the death of a soldier who accidentally shot and killed himself with a Luger handgun he retrieved from a German he killed. Lipton reports this to Winters back at battalion headquarters. The captain asks, "Where's Dike? I expected to get this kind of news from him." Later, in a voice-over, we hear Lipton say the following:

> "Where's Dike?" I probably heard that question a thousand times. I probably asked it a few times myself. There were long stretches where we didn't know where Lt. Dike was. He'd disappear, go off on these walks for hours at a time. Wouldn't have been so bad if he was just one the guys in the company. But Lt. Dike was supposed to be *leading* the company! Capt. Winters was a CO [commanding officer] we could all respect. . . . Dike wasn't a bad leader because he made bad decisions. He was a bad leader because he made no decisions. Dike was a favorite of somebody at division. He'd been sent down to Easy Company to get some combat experience. Sometimes we got the feeling Easy Company was an annoyance to him . . . something he had to get through before he could continue his march up the ladder.

The men agree:

> SOLDIER #1: I'm tellin' you, boys, we're screwed [having Dike to lead the company].
>
> SOLDIER #2: If you ask me, I'm *glad* Lt. Dike's never around.
>
> SOLDIER #3: Hey, you know what? We're doing all right, even with "Foxhole Norman."
>
> SOLDIER #1: We're doin' all right *now*, but in case you ain't noticed, there's a town down the hill over there, and in that town are these guys, and these guys are called Germans. And these Germans got tanks . . . and *our* side wants to go into that town. You wanna take one guess at who they gonna want to go knockin' on their goddam door? Jesus Christ! We got all this, and we got a CO who's got his head so far up his fuckin' ass that that lump in his throat is his goddam nose!

Lipton approaches the soldiers, and the diatribe ends. He asks the men what's going on. A soldier says, "You know, sittin' around, freezin' our asses off, singin' Dike's praises."

They approach their next objective, the village of Foy, occupied by the Germans with tanks that the soldier mentioned in his diatribe earlier. Knowing that German 88-millimeter cannons were soon to open fire on their position, Buck orders the NCOs to make sure the men fortify their cover (foxholes) in preparation. He yells over to his superior, Dike, to approve these orders. All he gets in return is a distracted, "Yeah," from Dike. "You all take care of it. I gotta go talk to regiment." And once more, with a severe German artillery barrage about to burst over his men, Dike is nowhere to be found.

Later, after the bombardment and Dike's return, another shelling takes place. The men are taking a terrible beating in this attack. Lipton is in his foxhole when Dike suddenly appears. Wide eyed, he yells at Lipton, "You get things organized here. I'm going to go for help!" And Dike is off again. All the men around Lipton are aghast. Later, cursing, the men mock their commander. The officer appears to possess no manly virtues, no ability to command. He's a terrible liability.

Finally, during the assault on Foy, although Winters had given Dike explicit, repeated instructions, Dike disregards them and holds up the company's attack, cowering behind a haystack and giving the Germans time to zero their mortars in on the company's position. Under heavy fire, some of his men huddle around Dike and beg him to make a decision. "What's the plan?" they implore. "I don't know, I don't know!" he screams. Lipton shouts at Dike, "Sir, we're sitting ducks out here! We have to keep moving!" Meanwhile, since Dike won't answer his radio, he doesn't hear that this is the same message Winters is shouting uselessly across the noisy battlefield. Restrained from running out and rescuing Easy Company himself, he orders another officer, Lt. Ronald Speirs, to relieve Dike. Speirs does so and carries the attack successfully to the enemy. Fortunately for all concerned, Dike is killed by the German artillery.

After Foy is secured and a few more battles won, Winters secures a battlefield commission for Lipton. He'd earned it for effectively commanding Easy Company during the time Dike was in charge. Paralyzed with fear of his own frightful and unmanly incompetence, Dike's performance clearly draws out the negative traits that a leader—and a man—must avoid if he is given the mantle of commander.

ORDERS, HUMANITY, AND THE FUBAR MISSION

In *Saving Private Ryan* (1998), Tom Hanks's character, Capt. John Miller, shares much of the same post-traumatic stress as does Sgt. Enders in *Windtalkers* and Sgt. Porter in *A Walk in the Sun*. Miller had led his men through battles dating back to the U.S. campaigns in North Africa, Sicily, and Italy, and he and his company have just survived the carnage of Omaha Beach at Normandy. Not surprisingly, Miller has the shakes. He has ordered so many men to die to achieve various military objectives, both good and bad. Now he finds himself ordered to risk more men's lives on an operation that everyone describes as truly "FUBAR," an acronym for "fucked up beyond all recognition."

An entire squad is being sent to risk their lives to search for an army private, the last surviving son of a widowed mother who has just been notified that her three other sons have been killed in action. Miller's squad, including Pvt. Reiben (Edward Burns), T-5 Medic Wade (Giovanni Ribisi), Cpl. Upham (Jeremy Davies), and Pvt. Mellish (Adam Goldberg), complains that they are mother's sons, too, and how is it logical for them to risk their lives for Pvt. Ryan? Why are they suddenly diverted from their usual job of killing Germans to a sappy, humanitarian mission that could get them killed even faster? To find Ryan, they must venture behind the fluid enemy lines in Normandy, a few days after D-Day, looking for a paratrooper who could be anywhere or already dead. Many in Ryan's airborne unit were killed jumping behind German lines the night before D-Day. Discussing his mission with his men, Miller describes their mission as trying to find a "needle in a stack of needles."

REIBEN: You wanna explain the math of this to me? I mean, where's the sense of riskin' the lives of the eight of us to save one guy?

MILLER: Anybody wanna answer that?

WADE: Reiben, think about the poor bastard's mother.

REIBEN: Hey, Doc, I got a mother, all right? I mean, you got a mother. Sarge's got a mother. I mean, shit, I bet even the captain's got a mother. [he turns and looks at Miller, who has a bemused expression on his face] Well, maybe not the captain, but the rest of us got mothers.

UPHAM: Theirs not to reason why, theirs but to do and die.

MELLISH: La-la, la-la, la-la, la-la, la-la, la-la, la-la, la-la. What the fuck is that supposed to mean, corporal, huh? We're all supposed to die, is that it?

MILLER: Upham's talking about our duty as soldiers.

UPHAM: Yes, sir.

MILLER: We all have orders, and we have to follow 'em. That supersedes everything, including your mothers.

UPHAM: Yes, sir. Thank you sir.

REIBEN: Even if you think the mission's FUBAR, sir?

MILLER: *Especially* if you think the mission's FUBAR.

At first, the stoic Miller tries to gloss over the men's griping with wit and wisecracks, but as the mission continues and some of his men die, finding and saving Ryan becomes more problematic, and serious thought is given to forgetting the whole thing. Miller's shakes continue, and his anxiety worsens over the idea of sacrificing all his men to save Ryan. Always the good officer, Miller confides in private conversations with his father confessor figure, Sgt. Horvath (Tom Sizemore):

> MILLER: You see, when . . . when you end up killing one of your men [here he's referring to ordering men to their deaths], you see, you tell yourself it happened so you could save the lives of two or three or ten others. Maybe a hundred others. Do you know how many men I've lost under my command?

Capt. Miller (Tom Hanks) with Sgt. Horvath (Tom Sizemore) in Spielberg's *Saving Private Ryan*. *DreamWorks / Photofest © DreamWorks*

> HORVATH: How many?
>
> MILLER: Ninety-four. But that means I've saved the lives of ten times that many, doesn't it? Maybe even twenty, right? Twenty times as many? And that's how simple it is. That's how you . . . that's how you rationalize making the choice between the mission and the man.

Horvath later reminds Miller that part of the uniqueness of this mission is that "This time, the mission *is* the man."

Miller sees nothing socially or personally redeeming about war. He doesn't buy into any part of the macho warrior ethic. Instead, this former high school English teacher, a humanist, hates all the killing, not just this particular assignment, but the entire war. At one point, Miller deals with a squad member who wants to forget about the mission and just go kill Germans. That makes sense to the soldier, but saving Ryan doesn't. Miller disagrees and says the following:

> You want to leave? You want to go off and fight the war? Alright. Alright. I won't stop you. I'll even put in the paperwork. I just know that every man I kill, the farther away from home I feel.

When Miller's squad finally finds Pvt. Ryan, the object of their mission also disagrees with the idea of sending a patrol just to save him and send him home.

> RYAN: Hell, these guys [the members of Ryan's squad] deserve to go home as much as I do. They've fought just as hard.
>
> MILLER: Is that what I'm supposed to tell your mother when she gets another folded American flag?
>
> RYAN: You can tell her that when you found me, I was with the only brothers I had left. And that there was no way I was deserting them. I think she'd understand that.

This creates even more confusion in Miller's mind. Part of what's wrong with the war for Miller is that there seems to be nothing good, nothing honorable about all this killing. But finally, Miller, with the help of Sgt. Horvath, who helps him articulate it, finds a logic, a harmony with the state of affairs that allows him to follow orders, and thus do his job and his duty, and still not feel like he wasted his men on a FUBAR operation. Horvath helps Miller articulate that harmony when he says the following:

> I don't know. Part of me thinks the kid's right. He asks what he's done to deserve this. He wants to stay here, fine. Let's leave him and go home. But then another part of me thinks, what if by some miracle we stay [and help Ryan and his shorthanded squad defend the bridge that they've been ordered to hold], then actually make it out of here. Someday we might look back on

this and decide that saving Private Ryan was the one decent thing we were able to pull out of this whole god-awful, shitty mess. Like you said, captain, maybe we do that, we all earn the right to go home.

NCOs in the Vietnam War films *Gardens of Stone* (1987), *Platoon* (1986), and *Platoon Leader* (1988) are similarly conflicted. None are under the illusion that their generation's war is anything like World War II. Because of their horrifying experiences in Vietnam, these NCOs—Sgt. Hazard (James Caan) and Sgt. Nelson (James Earl Jones) in *Gardens of Stone*, Sgt. Elias (Willem Dafoe) in *Platoon*, and Sgt. McNamara (Robert Lyons) in *Platoon Leader*—know that winning their war is unlikely; however, all are career NCOs, and all must find a way to do their duty—their jobs—while acknowledging that their entire mission, like Capt. Miller's, seems to be FUBAR. So to these sergeants, the number one task—as in *Saving Private Ryan*, is not the mission. The number one task for NCOs in Vietnam is to try to accomplish whatever parts of their mission they can while protecting the young men under their command. Humanitarian concerns are not secondary to mission goals for these commanders: Like Miller, their overall mission becomes *the men*. They find nothing inconsistent with manly duty in this, no dereliction of duty. They can perform their duty, and thus conduct themselves as men, by redefining their duty as the saving of their young troops from needless death.

In *Gardens of Stone*, Sgt. Hazard and Sgt. Nelson have served tours in Vietnam and have the ribbons to prove it. Hazard is especially conflicted with their present assignment: They are NCOs in the U.S. Army's "Old Guard" company, an elite unit responsible for providing honor guard details for funerals at Arlington National Cemetery. Hazard can't abide this duty, since activity "in the garden," as they refer to the cemetery, is brisk, as this story occurs during the height of the Vietnam War. Hazard wants a transfer to some training base, so he can teach young soldiers how to survive in the jungles of Vietnam, but his hardheaded commander refuses to transfer him. At the end of the picture, Hazard instead wangles himself a transfer back to Vietnam, where he says he at least can be of some good.

In Oliver Stone's *Platoon*, Sgt. Elias leads a squad in Vietnam and often argues with the unit's top NCO, Sgt. Barnes (Tom Berenger), and the topkick's sycophant, Sgt. O'Neill (John C. McGinley), about putting new replacement troops "just in from the world" in harm's way before he has time to teach them how to survive in the jungle:

ELIAS: They don't know shit, Barnes, and chances are we're gonna run into something. Think about it.

O'NEILL: That's just great, Bob. Whadda you want me to do? Send one of my guys out to get zapped so some lame ass just in from the world can get his beauty sleep? Nah!

> ELIAS: Hey O'Neill, take a break! You don't have to be a prick every day of your life, you know.

It's hard for Elias to think of anything but getting his men home in one piece, because he too understands that Vietnam is not like World War II. It's not winnable:

> ELIAS: What happened today was just the beginning. We're gonna lose this war.
>
> PVT. CHRIS TAYLOR: Come on! You really think so? Us?
>
> ELIAS: We've been kicking other people's asses for so long I figured it's time we got ours kicked.

In *Platoon Leader*, Sgt. McNamara also knows that the war is lost: He's seen it firsthand in the villages. He knows the Viet Cong and North Vietnamese have the population by the throat and that the Americans can never win the fight for the hearts and minds of the Vietnamese people. McNamara sees his job as being to save men's lives in an indirect way. He has been saddled with a new, idealistic young second lieutenant (sarcastically named Lt. Knight), just in from the United States. Of course, the officer thinks he knows what he's doing, but if McNamara doesn't intercede, Knight (Michael Dudikoff) will get them all killed. So McNamara patiently schools the young officer in the skills they don't teach young lieutenants in advanced infantry training. Knight learns quickly, so more of McNamara's men survive.

Nothing much changes when Hollywood fast-forwards to the wars in Iraq and Afghanistan. *Stop-Loss* (2008) is the story of a young army NCO, SSgt. Brandon King (Ryan Phillippe), who returns from tours in Iraq and Afghanistan a decorated hero but with post-traumatic stress and a belly full of war. King's enlistment is up, and he's ready to separate from the service and return to civilian life; however, the army invokes their infamous stop-loss order, forcing him to remain in the service against his will. Worse yet, after a few weeks, he is ordered to ship out to Iraq again.

Trying to explain to a sympathetic friend (Abbie Cornish) why he can't return to the war, King says that he thought he was going to Iraq to protect his country and his family and possibly to deliver some payback for 9/11:

> But when you get there, you realize the war wasn't about any of that. The enemy ain't out in the desert: They're in the hallways and rooftops, living rooms, kitchens. Everybody's got a weapon. Everybody. Nobody knows who's who. The only thing you can believe in is surviving, protecting the guy to your left and the guy to your right. Side by side, willing to die for each other. By the time you start seeing your friends' bodies held together by a belt after a car bomb, you [get] a "kill or be killed" mentality.

Then, through a flashback, King tells the story of his last mission, in which he has to lead his men into a hazardous alley, where some of them were killed. In a desperate firefight, weaving in and out of Iraqi houses, King was helping a wounded buddy to safety, but, in doing so, he had to kill a child. He had no choice, because the child's father—a militant—was holding up the youngster as a shield while shooting at King and his buddy. King explains that he opened up with a burst of automatic rifle fire, killing both the father and the son but allowing him and his buddy to survive. Then King picks up his monologue, saying, "I'm done with killing, and I ain't leading any more men into a slaughter."

ORDERS, HUMANITY, AND THE RIGHTEOUS MISSION

Unlike Vietnam, earlier American war films depicted the mission as thoroughly righteous, presenting a different set of problems for commanders. There are two 1950s-era prototypes for how Hollywood routinely dealt with the clash between finding a way to uphold one's manly responsibilities to duty while not becoming totally insensitive to human suffering. These model films both feature John Wayne, as the aforementioned Sgt. Stryker in *Sands of Iwo Jima* (1949), and Maj. Daniel X. Kirby in *Flying Leathernecks*. These performances are thematically similar to Gen. Savage's in *Twelve O'Clock High*, discussed earlier in this chapter: The commander must be tough as nails, stay relatively aloof from his men, and ride them hard if they are to be successful in their various combat missions. If they talked about such things, and these macho 1950s characters probably wouldn't, Stryker and Kirby might admit that humanism and sentiment are fine, even for men, during peacetime, and when one is on leave romancing women, but not while doing a man's work. Wayne's portrayal of Stryker and Kirby as tough-as-nails leaders exude a prototypical Protestant work ethic. Getting this unpleasant job of work done efficiently, and with as little sentiment as possible, is the correct and only manly attitude for a wartime commander.

Although *Sands of Iwo Jima* is important, we have already discussed it in earlier chapters. So we choose here to spend more time here dissecting *Flying Leathernecks*, because it more directly deals with this chapter's topic. *Leathernecks* is, simply put, the prototype of prototypes when it comes to manliness and the burden of command. Our instruction in the manly art of command begins as the newly assigned marine fighter squadron commander Maj. Kirby discusses squadron personnel with his executive officer, Capt. Carl "Griff" Griffin (Robert Ryan). Kirby has taken over the squadron just before they are scheduled to ship out for duty in the Pacific and fight in the battle of Guadalcanal. He wants

Kirby (John Wayne) disagrees with Griff (Robert Ryan) in *Flying Leathernecks. RKO Radio Pictures / Photofest © RKO Radio Pictures*

to know if the previous commander personally disliked Griff, since he did not do what is customary and recommend his exec for promotion to commander of the squadron. "I don't think he ever in his life acted on an emotion of any kind," Griff responds. "I think it was his cold, honest opinion that I wasn't up to command." As it turns out, Griff is truly *not* ready for command: He had set no boundaries in his cordial relationships with the men of the squadron and conducts himself more as a mother hen or older brother than a rough, tough commander. This was obvious to Griff's former boss, who reasoned that the officer was not ready to make hard, marinelike choices when men's lives were at stake.

Kirby soon finds this out for himself: One of his young pilots, Lt. Simmons, breaks formation to go flying off after Japanese planes on his own. He runs out of fuel and crashes but parachutes to safety. Kirby grounds Simmons and tells the young pilot he'll face a court-martial for his failure to follow orders. Griff tries to intervene for Simmons, but Kirby is adamant that discipline must be maintained. Kirby is also irked that Griff would try to "square things" with the CO over so flagrant an abuse of orders.

This is not to say that Griff fails to grasp the importance of discipline, which makes his buddy-buddy relations with the men all the more curious. Griff overhears his men griping about what Kirby did to Simmons, and he tells them that Kirby was right to do what he did. One pilot says he hopes that Kirby will eventually become softhearted and relent. Another pilot sarcastically disagrees, saying, "Softhearted? Don't you know a heart is strictly nonregulation equipment for a professional soldier? And Kirby's a professional soldier." Griff, who is also a career marine and supposed to be one of those professionals, takes offense and walks away. The pilot is surprised that Griff is offended.

Being friendly with the men, drinking with them, sharing their concerns, and "holding their hands" is how Griff has approached his job as executive officer, but his actions appear "unprofessional" to the men. The other pilots in the squadron, who came from civilian occupations and plan on returning to them after the war, don't want to live by the military code. They're just helping out their country during a time of crisis. They leave military thinking and military actions to their professional soldier superiors. The crux of the problem for Griff is that the men of the squadron don't see Griff *acting* like a professional soldier, so the pilot who made that remark didn't think for a minute that Griff would consider it an insult.

When a pilot is killed during a Japanese artillery barrage, Griff mourns for him, telling Kirby that the pilot was the "nicest guy in the squadron." Then, realizing that Kirby didn't know the pilot, Griff starts to say, "Of course, you didn't get to know him, but," Kirby interrupts Griff and tells him to go get some sleep. Later, Kirby allows himself to vent his displeasure to the wise old squadron doctor, who serves as both doctor and psychologist/counselor to Kirby. He says that he knew a "whole squadron full of nice guys at Midway," implying that they, too, were all dead, and that a commander can't afford to get emotional and mourn the deaths of these fine young men. If he did, a commander couldn't function as dispassionately as required. Kirby may mourn privately and even beef about it to the "Doc," but he can't let himself appear "weak" to his men. Both his stature as commander and a manly marine dictate this behavior.

So Kirby goes to extraordinary lengths to present a cold, hard, manly persona to his subordinates. When another pilot also fails to follow orders and flies off on his own like Simmons, he is killed. Coldly, Kirby orders all the men of the squadron to go look at the pilot's body. When they've all left but Griff, Kirby explains to his subordinate that this new casualty is a better object lesson than Simmons, and since they're running short on pilots, he'll relent on the court-martial orders and return Simmons to flying status. But Kirby doesn't want Griff to credit him with this decision, and instead he orders Griff to tell the men that he talked Kirby into dropping the charges against Simmons. Kirby believes that he can't get the by-the-book obedience in combat he desires if the men think he's at all wishy-washy about the consequences of noncompliance.

Griff's failure to assume the disciplinarian role with the men continues to eat at Kirby. When a pilot nicknamed "Cowboy" wisecracks at an important briefing, a unprofessional thing to do, he is given a punishment detail. Later, Griff gripes to Kirby about Cowboy's remarks, saying, "I'll eat him out later about this." But Kirby jumps all over Griff, saying,

> KIRBY: Well, ya should: It's your fault he's acting the way he is. This "come bring your troubles to Papa" attitude is makin' 'em all act like a bunch of college kids.
>
> GRIFF: (defensively) Well, that's what they are.
>
> KIRBY: Not out here, they aren't. This is where we separate the men from the boys.

Professionalism must be maintained. Marine discipline and the dictates of manliness in doing the job and accomplishing their mission means that weak, laissez-faire leadership cannot be tolerated. If Kirby was a religious man, he might quote a phrase from the Bible here, saying that part of the rite of passage from boys to men is to "set aside childish things."

Later, we are again shown that the stress of command weighs hard on Kirby, but all a tough, he-man will do about it is to complain privately to his father confessor, Doc. He hates that he must write entirely too many letters to dead pilots' families, and when Lt. Castle is killed in action, Griff criticizes Kirby for scheduling Castle, who was ill, to fly. Kirby, more irritated than ever with Griff's immaturity and lack of professionalism, sounds off. He complains that although his entire squadron suffers from jungle nausea and malaria, he must continue to order them to fly missions. Griff doesn't yet understand, but Kirby knows that the squadron's mission requires him to schedule pilots to fly who should be grounded until they feel better. That's the dedication to duty required of a marine and a professional. Or, as we discussed in chapter 2 about the analysis of sports metaphors, Kirby would maintain that the men, to be men, must all "play hurt." Kirby secretly visits men when they're wounded and recuperating in the base's hospital, smiles, and asks them if there's anything he can do/get for them, but he doesn't want the others to know about this. The divide between Griff and Kirby widens.

This conflict comes to a head when they must split up the squadron to fly two simultaneous missions. One is a relatively easy job, flying escort for bombers, while the other, a ground strike, is a hazardous, low-flying mission that requires precision bombing and strafing work. Missions in close air support of ground forces have cost the squadron many casualties, because the pilots must hit their targets while flying through murderous ground fire. Griff complains that Kirby has scheduled his most experienced men for the hazardous mission and ordered relatively inexperienced pilots to fly the "milk run" (easier mission). Griff wants to give the more experienced pilots, the ones he has a stronger attachment to, a break. Kirby explains that instead, he is giving the newer pilots more experience before they must fly more hazardous missions.

But, seeing an opportunity to give Griff more practice in command, Kirby instructs Griff to schedule himself to lead the milk run and reassign one of the newer pilots to the more hazardous mission. Griff is suddenly quite conflicted with this request, not knowing which of the new pilots has the most air-to-ground attack training. Griff doesn't want to be the one to decide which new pilot to order into harm's way, and he solves his dilemma by urging Kirby to leave the schedule the way it is, with himself flying the ground strike and all the newer pilots assigned to the milk run. Kirby explodes:

> KIRBY: (sarcastically) Sure, you'll fly the ground strike with us. You beef at the decisions I make, but you're too soft to make them yourself. You can't bring yourself to point your finger at a guy and say, "Go get killed."
>
> GRIFF: (finally frustrated enough to become insubordinate, he closes the tent flap for some privacy for what he's about to say) I've got a bellyful of you. And I'm not buying the bill of goods you're selling. In my book, it's easy to be a turtle . . . put a shell between yourself and the rest of humanity. Maybe I'm not making my point clear: Four hundred years ago, a poet said it better than I ever could: "No man is an island." When the funeral bell rings, it's not just for the dead guy, it's a little bit for all of us. Each man's suffering belongs to everyone, or else, why are we shooting off these guns? And I don't know what your reaction's gonna be, but here's what I hope it is.

He challenges Kirby to a fistfight, but before they get to it, the call comes in to report to their commander for another mission. Afterward, Kirby receives orders to immediately go stateside. Before he leaves, he has some "plain English" for Griff. He tells him that he didn't recommend his exec to take over the squadron. Griff interrupts and won't let him explain why, but after some time back home, a new squadron is formed with Kirby in command and Griff again slated to be Kirby's exec. Most of Kirby's original squadron flyers are also assigned to this new unit, but in the interim, Griff has done some soul-searching, since two commanders in a row have considered him unfit to lead. Slowly, we see Griff try to become more like Kirby. Finally, they fly a mission in which Cowboy (Don Taylor), who is also Griff's brother-in-law, becomes separated from the rest of the squadron when his plane develops a failing engine and is under attack by Japanese fighters. But the squadron has just been ordered to discontinue their assigned mission and rush to repel a Japanese kamikaze attack on the fleet. Although some of the other pilots beg Griff to allow them to rush to Cowboy's aid, Griff realizes that protecting the fleet takes priority and refuses. Cowboy is shot down and killed, but Griff has finally "toughened up"—in Kirby's words—enough to make a commander's hard decisions.

In this, their final mission together, Kirby is wounded and is to be flown stateside for treatment. This time Kirby recommends that Griff take over the squadron. With his broken shoulder in a cast, he climbs into the transport plane headed for the States, and Griff approaches. He says,

> GRIFF: "I didn't think I'd get the squadron on your recommendation. I thought you were a heel.
>
> KIRBY: I was, and *you're* going to be. I didn't do you any favors, Griff. I'm sorry about Cowboy. I know how tough it was to make a decision like that. You're gonna wind up staggerin' into your bunk every night with your hip pockets [read "ass"] draggin', and you'll lay there and look at the ceiling while your stomach turns over, and you'll hope to God you called every shot right during the day. The next morning, you'll wake up, wishing you were a flight lieutenant again, so all you have to do is what the man told you. And you'll get bad-tempered and snarly, just like me. And you'll probably wind up, just like me, climbing into an aircraft with your hip pockets draggin', to go back to some desk job. Brother, I didn't do you any favors.

Then, with no hugs or close handshakes, they exchange a manly warrior's farewell:

> GRIFF: I'm going to say something dizzy. If and when we meet stateside, will you get drunk with me as my guest?
>
> KIRBY: I'll be happy to come aboard. So long.
>
> GRIFF: So long. I'll try to call the plays right. I had a good coach.

Then, after Kirby's plane takes off, the first thing Griff does is gruffly bark orders to his new executive officer, channeling Kirby as Pfc. Conway did after Sgt. Stryker's death in *Sands of Iwo Jima*. There is no place for a humanist who spouts poetry in warfare—sports metaphors, perhaps, but none of the mushy stuff. Griff finally realizes this, does a military about-face, and becomes a complete man and commander.[8]

Conway and Griff have the same problem: Their humanism does not equip them to make the tough, manly decisions as leaders in warfare. But in the 1950s, never fear, John Wayne was here. But were these sentiments a product only of an earlier time? Were there films made in the twenty-first century with the same manly themes?

John Wayne's 1950s code of command is clearly restated in the twenty-first-century war picture *U-571* (2000), a slam-bang adventure film and also—unfortunately—an absurdly untruthful revisionist history of how the Allies in World War II came into position of a codebook and the German Enigma decoder machine. In real history, this knowledge, once obtained, allowed the British and Allied navies to intercept and decode the German Kriegsmarine dispatches, turning the tide of naval warfare in the North Atlantic. But in this picture, the Americans did all the heavy lifting. In reality, heroic action by members of the British Navy was responsible for obtaining those codebooks and Enigma machines; however, the real story wouldn't have made a very good Hollywood war film, nor be a great star vehicle for leading man Matthew McConaughey.

This, then, is the story of the coming-of-age of young lieutenant Andy Tyler (McConaughey), channeling all the major manly themes of *Flying Leathernecks* in a twenty-first-century war film of highly doubtful historical—and, as we shall see, technical—accuracy. As the picture opens, Tyler, like Griff, is the executive officer of an American fighting unit, in Tyler's case, U.S. Navy submarine *S-33*. Tyler is friendly—too much so—with the enlisted men of the *S-33*, even to the point of sitting down with the boys and hoisting a few beers. Tyler is distressed to learn that, again like Griff at the outset of *Flying Leathernecks*, his captain, Mike Dahlgren (Bill Paxton), has not recommended him to command his own sub. Simply put, Dahlgren tells Tyler, "I don't think you're ready to take on a command of your own." This distresses Tyler, as this gossip makes its way around the crew and back to him. He's embarrassed and frustrated, because his ratings in all areas of submarine operations are tops. Yet Dahlgren senses that there's a piece missing in Tyler that must be remedied before he's ready to become a real leader of men. Crewmen are too familiar with Tyler, and he with them. Dahlgren knows that an officer whose presence doesn't elicit respect and instant obedience lacks the ethos to command. And, more importantly, he's not sure that Tyler can coldly and unhesitatingly order men to their deaths for the good of the mission.

As in *Flying Leathernecks*, there is a father confessor whom Tyler seeks out for advice. This time, it's the wise older chief of the boat, Chief Petty Officer Henry Klough (Harvey Keitel), known simply to all on the *S-33* as the "Chief." The Chief understands why Tyler has been passed over: He recognizes the difference between the boyish way that Tyler behaves, thinks, and speaks around the men, as opposed to the way captains conduct themselves. When Tyler asks why the Chief didn't warn him that this disgrace was coming, the wise CPO wisely says, "Ain't my place, sir." But later in the picture, when the mission and the men are at risk, the Chief steps in to dole out advice.

Tyler's weakness for coddling his men and not appearing to be a firm leader can be seen from the outset, when the men complain to him when their shore leaves are cancelled. They don't know it yet, but the reason for the change was because they have been ordered on a special operation. With the crew at attention, the captain stands aloof and gives orders so the sub can quickly put to sea. As soon as the crew is dismissed, a gaggle of sailors heads straight for Tyler to ask what's going on and complain that their shore leave was ended so quickly. They would never think of displaying this kind of behavior around the captain, but they felt secure in going to their "buddy," Mr. Tyler. Instead of telling the men that they'll find out soon enough and in the meantime they should just do their jobs, Tyler goes running to Dahlgren for an explanation. Then the audience is shown the correct behavior for a commander: The captain tells Tyler that *he'll* find out in due time, and in the meantime *he* should just do his job.

And the job is a tough one: The Americans have detected a German U-boat, *U-571*, having mechanical trouble, and it's adrift in the Atlantic. The American plan is to get their hands on an enemy Enigma decoder by posing as the German supply sub dispatched to assist in repairing the ailing U-boat. They even weld some metal to the visible portions of the *S-33* to make its silhouette look more like a German sub. They hope to board the enemy sub and kill or capture its crew before being detected as Americans. Two of the U.S. boarding party speak fluent German.

Later, in a briefing conducted by marine major Coonan (David Keith), who has been assigned to the sub to lead the assault, Tyler, not yet grasping the importance of the mission over the men, complains that his crewmen are "just sailors, not combat marines." Maj. Coonan replies that the German submariners are also "just sailors" and that he will train Tyler's men himself. Somewhat embarrassed by Tyler's misgivings, Capt. Dahlgren chimes in, "You've come to the right boat." Obviously, to a mature commander, Tyler's behavior is additional evidence that his executive officer has not yet evolved into the steely eyed, crusty officer ethos required of a candidate for captain.

The mission begins well. The boarding party captures the *U-571* with little difficulty, and they're in the middle of transferring German prisoners to the *S-33* when a German rescue sub arrives and torpedoes the *S-33*, killing Dahlgren, the prisoners, and all but one crewman on board the American sub. Tyler and the American boarding party dive the U-boat and manage to get it working well enough to (amazingly) torpedo and sink the German rescue sub. Surfacing afterward to look for survivors, they pick up only one *S-33* crewman and one German prisoner.

With the captain gone, Tyler is in command. He holds a meeting to discuss the situation with the boarding party, made up of a handful of crewmen and the Chief. In light of all this tragedy, some of the men want to forget about the mission and send out an SOS for the nearest American rescue ship. The *U-571* is damaged and barely able to make headway on only one of its two propellers. But if the Americans sound an SOS from this location, the Germans will assume the enemy has the Enigma and change their codes, and all the lives lost on the mission will be wasted. One vocal and disrespectful crewman, Mazzola (Eric Palladino), is especially forceful as he votes for using the radio. Just as forcefully, the Chief reminds Mazzola that he has no vote in this. While Tyler looks on helplessly, Mazzola responds that he thinks radioing for help is what the captain would do, but the Chief interrupts again, asserting simply, "Captain's dead."

This is a telling remark: The Chief didn't say, "The captain's dead: Lt. Tyler is in complete command now." Perhaps it was writer/director Jonathan Mostow's approach to keep the old Chief speaking in terse phrases, or perhaps it was his way to say that the Chief hadn't made up his mind whether Tyler was ready for the job of command. Mazzola, thinking along the same lines, confronts the Chief again, ignorantly maintaining that the Enigma mission wasn't worth their lives. He disrespects Tyler, incorrectly quoting crew gossip that Tyler wasn't just passed over for command of his own boat, but that he was being kicked out of the navy for incompetence. He wants the Chief to take over. The Chief disabuses Mazzola of this false rumor, roughly grabbing the crewman by the shirt and saying, "Lt. Tyler is your commanding officer, and you will respect him as such."

But the Chief is also displeased with Tyler, who so far shows no indication that other than his competent submarine skills, the young lieutenant is capable of commanding grown men. During the earlier meeting, when asked what he'll do, Tyler honestly responds, "I don't know." Later, over coffee, the Chief privately and forcefully gives Tyler a quick but effective lesson in the manliness of the submarine commander when he states the following:

> This here's the navy, where a commanding officer's a mighty and terrible thing . . . a man to be feared and respected . . . all-knowing, all-powerful.

> Don't you *dare* say what you said to the boys back there again . . . "I don't know." . . . Those three words will kill a crew dead as a depth charge. You're the skipper now, and the skipper *always* knows what to do, if he knows or not.

After this trip to the woodshed with the Chief, Tyler stiffens up and assumes a tougher, more resolute stance with the men. When the *U-571* is buzzed by a German reconnaissance plane, Mazzola argues that they should try to shoot it down. Of course, it's unlikely they would knock a plane down, and more probable that the pilot would radio to headquarters that a German sub has been captured by the enemy. The Kriegsmarine would know that the Enigma codes were compromised, and the mission would fail. Of course, the not-too-bright Mazzola disagrees with Tyler and yells at the sailors manning the antiaircraft gun to shoot at the German plane. Tyler countermands that order, and a shouting match of "shoot" versus "don't shoot" ensues. Finally, when the plane flies off, Tyler socks Mazzola in the jaw and yells, "Whaddya think you're doing? This ain't no goddamn democracy!" John Wayne would be proud.

Then, as screenwriter Mostow piles on the plot complications, the *U-571* encounters a German destroyer that assumes that the vessel is manned by Germans. The destroyer sends over a motor launch with an officer, presumably to confer with the sub captain. Realizing that within a few moments the mission would again be in danger of being compromised, Tyler orders his crew to fire the deck gun to blow away the German vessel's radio tower. With one amazingly accurate shot, they completely destroy the destroyer's radio communications. The *U-571* submerges and tries to escape the destroyer, which pursues them, engaging in a depth charge attack. The sub is hit, and their remaining torpedo tube's pneumatic firing ability is damaged.

Tyler must order one of his men, nicknamed "Trigger," to make a hazardous and likely fatal dive into the sub's bilges to repair the damaged pneumatic line. Trigger bravely makes the dive without benefit of aqualung and makes the repairs but drowns in the process. Like Griff, who makes the hard decision to sacrifice one of his best friends for the sake of the mission, Tyler has finally made the tough call in sending young Trigger to his death.

The sub resurfaces, fires its torpedo, and in an amazing bow shot (the second in the movie—they also destroyed the German rescue sub with such a low percentage tactic), blows up the destroyer, rescuing the mission; however, the *U-571* is mortally wounded and will soon sink. Tyler and his men abandon ship, watch it sink, and are soon rescued by fellow Americans. The mission has been accomplished, and this new, mature commander shows that he has the right stuff. As evidence that Tyler has passed into manhood and command capability, the Chief announces, "Mr. Tyler, if you ever need a chief, I'll go to sea with you any time."

Tyler, a commander who was too friendly and sociable with his men, had the difficult task of replacing a commander whom the men found cold and antisocial, but in whom they had confidence and loyalty. In the World War II story *The Frogmen* (1951), the opposite occurs. Lt. Cmdr. John Lawrence (Richard Widmark) is assigned to command Underwater Demolition Team (UDT) 4, whose charismatic commander was recently killed. The men, still mourning their deceased "skipper," Cmdr. Cassidy, would resent anyone who replaced him, but they especially dislike Lawrence, whose personality is just the opposite of the flamboyant, affiliative Cassidy: stiff, analytical, and all business when he addresses the men.

On their first mission together, beachhead reconnaissance for the assault on a Japanese-held island scheduled for the following day, the men dislike a decision Lawrence makes. After his squad is picked up, he chooses not to circle back to the beach to pick up a few UDT divers who had just survived a direct artillery hit on their boat. But for sound tactical purposes, and to assure that the rest of his team survives to complete their more important mission the following day, Lawrence orders his boat not to pick them up. He orders another boat from their mother ship to rescue the divers. But the men, who figure that their late team leader Cassidy would have called it differently, comment and wonder if Lawrence was just too scared to return for the men. To make matters worse for Lawrence, on this day's mission, he scrapes his leg on an escarpment of coral and comes down with what the ship's doctor calls "coral poisoning," so he must order Chief Petty Officer Jake Flannigan (Dana Andrews), one of Lawrence's harshest critics, to lead the UDT's mission the next day. "Coral poisoning, my eye," carps one sailor. "He's got beachitis."

With two strikes against him, there's more trouble between Lawrence and the men: He must discipline CPO Flannigan, portrayed as a very unprofessional man for a senior NCO, for a stunt he pulled during the mission the next day. As a joke, Flannigan and another sailor, "Pappy" Creighton (Jeffrey Hunter), rigged a sign to give a welcome from UDT 4 to the marines who would assault the beach that day. But in planting the sign, Pappy is badly wounded. Lawrence is furious with Flannigan for jeopardizing his life and the lives of his men and tells him he plans to bust him in rank.

Needless to say, this goes down poorly with the men, who en masse request a transfer. But the men soon begin to doubt their assessment of Lawrence when the officer volunteers to disarm a "dud" Japanese torpedo that has struck their ship. Finally, on their next mission, to destroy a Japanese submarine pen, Lawrence stays behind to set off the explosive charges. He is stabbed in an underwater battle with Japanese frogmen, and when members of his team come to his rescue, he orders them to leave him and save themselves. Of course they refuse and bring Lawrence back. Later, as Lawrence lies in sick bay opposite Pappy, the men finally decide he is worthy of their loyalty and accept him as their leader.

Add to Lawrence such stern commander types as Jeff Chandler's tough but ultimately beloved father figures, for example, Capt. Jebediah S. Hawks in *Away All Boats* (1956) and Brig. Gen. Frank Merrill in *Merrill's Marauders* (1962), and one can find many additional examples of this same portrait of the tough, crusty, Übermensch commander. Chandler's two characters demand much of their men and at times seem harsh and unreasonable, but both of Chandler's characters care deeply for their men and think of them as if they were their sons. Like Stryker, both Hawks and Merrill die at the end of these films, but they ultimately create the circumstances necessary to achieve their mission.

Command can stress a person in many different ways. In *Sink the Bismarck!* (1960), Capt. Jonathan Shepherd (Kenneth Moore) appears to all as an emotionless, all-business type of officer who efficiently does his job as director of naval operations during World War II. But Shepherd, who lost his wife to a German bomb in the blitz, is really quite capable of deep feeling. To pursue and sink the indomitable German battleship *Bismarck*, he sees that he must order the aircraft carrier *Ark Royal* into the battle. There's only one problem: His son is serving on board the *Ark Royal* as an aircraft gunner and would surely be hurled into harm's way in a sea battle against the *Bismarck*, the pride of the German fleet. Pragmatism says that the *Ark Royal* and its battle group must be ordered into the fight, but the audience can see the conflict of the father concerned for his son on Shepherd's face.

Later, Shepherd learns that in one of the air sorties of *Ark Royal* against the Bismarck, his son's plane ran out of fuel and ditched in the ocean. Terrified that he would lose both his wife *and* his son, and that this time it would be *his* order that sent the youngster to his death, Shepherd is beside himself with worry and fear. But, ever the stiff-upper-lip British officer, he internalizes his concern and does his job, the only manly thing to do. Later, after being notified that his son and his aircrew had been rescued, Shepherd goes to his office and privately has a good cry.

As we have learned about such leaders as Gen. Savage and Sgt. Porter, the burden of command can simply overwhelm some men. And what if they entered into combat already psychologically handicapped? In Humphrey Bogart's Oscar-nominated role as Capt. Queeg in *The Caine Mutiny* (1954), he arrived on board to assume command suffering from combat fatigue. Then his personality drifts away from sanity into deep paranoia, forcing the men to mutiny against him to save their ship.[9]

It's not easy being in charge: Only real men need apply. Layered over all the breakdowns and the emotions we've reviewed in this chapter is the nagging problem of male value systems regarding mental stability. Does our culture say that "real men don't crack up," that the truly manly can avoid falling into mental illnesses?[10] In the next chapter, we venture further into the nature of men in war films when we dissect the virtue of courage—or lack thereof—in war and manliness.

NOTES

1. Moore depicts the dangers of self-pity in a combat situation. When comparing himself to Custer and the original 7th Calvary, Moore temporarily loses his ability to lead, along with his self-confidence. When individuals allow self-pity to overwhelm their decision making, they become paralyzed both emotionally and psychologically. For this reason, self-pity is neither an acceptable nor manly behavior on the battlefield. Once Moore puts this aside and returns to the here and now, he is able to make a confident, well-devised plan that wins the battle.
2. After Cobb is killed, Savage retreats into what appears to be a catatonic stupor, and he remains that way until the bombers return. Savage most likely suffered from what is called a brief psychotic episode, in which, according to Ebert, Loosen, and Nurcombe (2000), the individual goes into a "grossly disorganized or catatonic behavior. . . . This disorder may occur after the death of a loved one during combat . . . and while experiencing a stressor in the war zone" (284).
3. Unlike Savage and Davenport, Dennis is able to command and excel in leadership ability, although still feeling a conflict between his duty as a commander and his level of feeling as a human being. He is able to block out his feelings for his young fliers when he must make life-and-death decisions. Dennis appears to be able to compartmentalize his feelings for the men under his command and not allow such feelings to cloud his decisions. Compartmentalization is not an easy psychological technique to learn when a military leader cares about the people under his command, but it is a technique that is vital when making decisions that will ultimately affect these young men's lives. Dennis appears to be one of those military leaders who has learned the invaluable tool of placing his feelings for his men away when making these decisions, focusing only on the best possible military strategy.
4. Miller gives us a perfect example of how a soldier is able to rationalize the horrors of war and the death and destruction for which he has been personally responsible. He projects all blame onto his commanders, thus absolving himself of any responsibility for his part in the war. If he is able to keep his culpability at a minimum by rationalizing his behaviors, he is able to prevent any guilt or shame from emerging. Guilt and shame can only materialize when an individual takes responsibility for their actions. Miller has found a way to protect himself from this guilt by projecting blame onto others.

5. Inheriting a command position after the lieutenant and Halverson are killed creates a personal Peter Principle for Porter (Peter and Hull, 1970). Porter has reached his level of incompetence by being placed into a leadership position for which he believes he is not qualified. Being promoted beyond one's level of incompetence in a military command situation is dangerous. Many lives can be lost due to such a man's inadequacy, lack of self-confidence, and absence of leadership abilities. So often in the backstory of a person with low self-confidence and self-esteem, we find a child who could never live up to parents' high expectations and thus never gained parental approval. Porter's ineffective and incompetent leadership may, in fact, be related to a life of never believing in his potential and having parents who never believed in him. With such a background, because he was placed in a position of authority that was above his capabilities—or at least his perceived level of capabilities—Porter was destined to fail and suffer a mental collapse. He did not have the necessary psychological tools and techniques to fall back on when the horrors of war overwhelmed him. Feelings of helplessness, hopelessness, and lack of self-worth, characteristic of a major depressive disorder, appeared in evidence. Finally, Porter withdrew into his inner self as a way to escape the reality of his failure and the horrors of war surrounding him.

6. After Warnicki returns from a horrific patrol in which only he returns alive, he is finally able to hear his son's voice on phonograph. His son's voice causes him to be triggered into, in computer terms, an endless loop of incongruity between the horrors of war and his life waiting for him at home. Finally, delusional thinking emerges; Warnicki irrationally believes that he can escape the trauma around him and earn his reward—going home to his son—if he can single-handedly kill all the remaining German soldiers. He has experienced a psychotic break: His ultimate disassociation from concrete reality is reflected by his continuous repetition of the phrase spoken by his son in the recording.

7. To the viewer Dike appears to be an individual who is void of emotion and aloof. He isolates himself and has poor interpersonal relationships. This is characteristic of a schizoid personality disorder. This disorder renders individuals like Dike unable to connect with other human beings. They are unable to interact with those around them in an effective manner and choose to be loners. Those afflicted with this disorder are unable to elicit appropriate social cues when dealing with others. Social skills are nonexistent. So in communicating with other military personnel, schizoid individuals would be ineffective. Thus was the case with Dike.

8. Kirby reassures Griff that despite the consequences (his brother-in-law's death), his subordinate had made the militarily correct decision. Throughout the movie, Kirby's job was to separate the boys from the men. He had modeled and reinforced the acceptable manly behaviors expected of someone man enough to command a U.S. Marine Corps squadron. Role modeling is the strongest component in learning. This concept of learning theory is often employed by the military while in combat to teach leadership to their subordinates. In the end, Kirby realized that Griff was ready to take on the role of a squadron leader. Griff had successfully learned to imitate Kirby's cold, calculated decision making and had collated out the weaker humanistic characteristics that had become obstacles to his growth. Griff had finally become the military man that Kirby had modeled for him.

9. Queeg was already the victim of combat fatigue and his own paranoid delusions before he assumed command of the USS *Caine*. Delusions of paranoia are frightening but all-too-real fears that make the sufferer perceive the world as a place where everyone and everything conspires against them. Worn out from combat duty in the Atlantic before he set foot on the *Caine*, Queeg succumbed to these paranoid delusions, making him ineffectual in his command and finally causing his men to effectively make a mutiny to save their ship and themselves.

10. Unfortunately, in our society, mental illness and accepting help from mental health professionals is still, as a John Wayne character might say, a "sign of weakness." For men in general, and more specifically for men in the military, it is unmanly to ask for or receive psychological treatment for any mental disorders. Men are often "help rejecters" and are resistant to psychological intervention. Interestingly, however, in my own psychological practice, once some men have been encouraged or forced into therapy by their wives or significant others, they are often the ones who continue the therapeutic involvement on their own, even after their partner has completed their treatment. It is initially difficult for the male to break through the emotional wall that they have created early in their development, permitting them to share their inner pain, but once these stoic men break through their psychological barriers, the inner self that they have been internalizing throughout their life emerges, causing cathartic relief.

5

Courage

It's difficult for men to consider themselves manly if, like the Cowardly Lion in *The Wizard of Oz*, they are convinced that they are cowards. Inevitably, in countless films, especially those starring John Wayne, there is a scene in which some young soldier approaches the Duke and confesses that he's frightened. Since the indomitable Wayne (different movies, same character) does not appear afraid, the young, anxious soldier—usually about to experience combat for the first time—assumes that he's not. Wayne's character sets the kid straight, telling him not to worry, because everyone, including himself, is frightened before a battle. In one film, Wayne adds a caveat: He advises that the youngster stay away from anyone who says he's not scared, "because he's an idiot." In scenes like this, the young soldier appears to feel better, knowing that even his rough, tough commander is fearful. The only difference is that Wayne's characters display no outward symptoms of fear. The message, then, for young men viewing these films, is that real men internalize everything, keeping their fears and misgivings to themselves; however, even Wayne occasionally feels the need to vent his misgivings.

As discussed in chapter 4, in *Flying Leathernecks* (1951), as the commander of a squadron of marine pilots, Wayne vents his frustrations and concerns to his designated "father confessor," the squadron's flight surgeon. As also discussed in the previous chapter, the burdensome tasks of a leader include trying to look like you know what you're doing, even when you don't, and providing an effective role model regardless of how you really feel. In *Flying Leathernecks*, Wayne is a courageous man: He never admits he's scared of being killed or wounded, but he shows uncharacteristic angst over sending so many young men to their deaths. His job doesn't allow him to show or share his concerns with his men, so the flight surgeon at least allows Wayne's character to act a little more human.

GREEK COURAGE

Courage as a requisite quality of manliness is nothing new. Discussed as far back as Aristotle, in the Greek language, the word for manliness, *andreia*, is synonymous with courage. As a gendering activity, the value of the virtue of courage is taught to, and experienced by, young boys early on. Boys are told that to differentiate themselves from girls they must put away fear and at least appear to be courageous. When girls cower and scream and stand on a chair when a mouse is discovered in the kitchen, boys are basically told that they must come to the rescue, fearlessly chasing the rodent with a broom, mayhem in mind.

Fear—the opposite of courage—is for sissies, boys are told. The Cowardly Lion knows that, and because he occasionally experiences fear, he has a self-image problem. At one point, the Lion even calls *himself* a sissy, as do boys who take Wayne's style of manly behavior too much to heart. In *The Red Badge of Courage*, John Huston's 1951 film adaptation of Stephen Crane's classic novel, young Henry Fleming (Audie Murphy) has a similar conflict with his self-image. Young Henry is a soldier in the Union Army in 1862. His company has not yet experienced battle, but the chance to fight will be upon them in a day or two, and only Fleming seems worried about it. Unfamiliar with the true horrors of war, Fleming's comrades have convinced themselves that they will soundly defeat any Confederate force displayed against them. These soldiers seem to go on about this endlessly, beating their chests and bragging about their eagerness to fight. Internalizing his concern, Fleming feels just the opposite: He's already scared to death, and, since his fellow soldiers don't appear to be scared, he assumes that they are either stupid or that he lacks the courage his comrades possess.

Shortly after Fleming's company encounters the blood and death of battle, the Confederates counterattack, and Fleming runs away, hiding in the woods for most of the day. But later, he is accidentally wounded when another Union soldier hits him on the head with the butt of his gun. When finally reunited with his company, he is treated with respect, because the young man has apparently suffered a wound in battle: He has earned his "red badge of courage." As Crane's words are narrated over the scene, "[Henry] had performed his mistakes in the dark, so he was still a man."

Boys on the playing fields prepare themselves for their red badge by silently enduring scrapes and scratches and enduring the pain. Later, as men, they wear these badges proudly and silently and are respected by their peers for their willingness to stoically bleed manly blood while doing their appointed jobs. Fate has permitted Fleming to cross over and join this fraternity.

In a later battle, Fleming becomes angry at both the enemy and what he perceives as his unit's inept commanders. This anger changes him into a fire-breathing true believer, and he leads his company in battle, waving the Union flag and exhorting his comrades to follow him into the hail of Confederate bullets. Henry understands what is never articulated but universally understood about soldiers and fighting. He is in the army, which means that fighting the enemy is his appointed job. As discussed in earlier chapters, doing one's job of work is part of what transforms a boy into a man, and for a soldier, a man who is willing to risk danger and death. Men, Fleming learns, must persevere in doing their assigned job or risk losing their manly status. Courage, bravery, call it what you want, it's part and parcel of doing the job allotted to men who wear a uniform and carry a rifle. Fleming thought he had lost his manliness when he ran away, but fate, in the form of his red badge, dealt him a second chance and allowed him to keep his *andreia* and even to distinguish himself as a hero.

Similarly, in *Stop-Loss* (2008), SSgt. Brandon King (Ryan Phillippe) recognizes another former GI by his army green badge of courage, an army green American flag tattooed on his arm. The tattoo signifies that he, too, served and suffered in the army in Iraq and/or Afghanistan. There is no need to show each other their wounds or tell their individual stories: The recognition that these brothers-in-arms experienced the same horror was tacitly sufficient to cement their relationship as soldiers, like Fleming and his comrades, who had earned their manhood on the killing fields.

SOME MEN HAVE HAD ENOUGH

What happens when men, whose bravest act as a civilian might have been to stand up to a bully on a playground, must face a truly fearful enemy whose sole intention is to kill them? What happens to one's courage when the first shells fall and the man a few feet away dies horribly? Some can't take it, and, like Fleming at the outset of his adventures, they cut and run. Others who are not suited to permanent, Wayne-like stoicism endure the fear, blood, destruction, and uncertainty of it all for a time, and then, like Sgt. Eddie Porter (Herbert Rudley) in *A Walk in the Sun* (1945), they check out. They fall victim to combat fatigue and experience a psychological breakdown. Others, like Lt. Carl Abbott (Lee Philips) in *The Hunters* (1958), observe the courage of others and imitate it as best they can, acting bravely in combat, but afterward they continue to consider themselves cowards, because they were fearful when performing their duties. Yet others silently endure their fear, hiding their consternation in such platitudes as, "I'm just doing my job."

CONVERSION CONVENTION

If a warrior gives into this fear and commits an act of cowardice, the typical war film plot's "conversion convention" dictates what he must do by way of atonement: In these films, unlike Fleming, the coward is doomed to pay some sort of price for this offense (Donald, 1991). The most common expiative act follows this well-worn scenario: After the character realizes that he has sunk to unmanly, cowardly depths, he gathers up the strength to throw off his craven mantle and attempts some desperate heroic act, during which he is usually killed or at least seriously wounded.

For example, earlier, in discussing Pvt. Jerry Plunkett's (James Cagney) cowardice in *The Fighting 69th* (1940), we note that his lack of courage causes the deaths of some of his comrades. Jailed for his offenses prior to a court-martial, fate intervenes, allowing him to escape. Faced with a choice of flight and a lifetime as a fugitive versus returning to the trenches, Plunkett chooses the latter and makes his way back to the battle lines, where he dies, fighting bravely. Again the point is made: Even if a soldier is guilty of as grave an offense as "showing the white feather," there is still a manly option and a clear-cut formula for his redemption. In *The Tragedy of Julius Caesar* (2002), William Shakespeare's famous truism resonates down through the ages: "Cowards die many times before their death; the valiant never taste of death but once" (Act II, Scene 2).

SHELL SHOCK AND BATTLE FATIGUE

Some soldiers, like Porter, experience a psychological breakdown, curl up in a ball on the ground, and try to escape reality, but these brave men who crack up are treated charitably by most of their fellow soldiers, who realize that there—but for fortune—they might also lie. Wounded in the mind, the soul, or both, those who had previously earned their red badge of courage are not scorned like Plunkett.

Similarly, in the HBO miniseries *Band of Brothers* (2001), Lt. Buck Compton (Neal McDonough) watches as two of his closest friends are blown to bits when a shell lands in their foxhole, and another two comrades are severely wounded. Finally, Compton has seen too much and cares too much, and he succumbs to battle fatigue. This courageous, once-wounded, often-decorated officer must be removed from the line and sent to the rear for psychotherapy. As in the platoon's charitable assessment of their psychologically wounded sergeant in *A Walk in the Sun*, Sgt. Carwood Lipton's (Donnie Wahlberg) voice-over echoes his men's assessment of Compton's collapse: "No one thought any less of him for it."

But this isn't always the case. Some soldiers understand, while others see cases of battle fatigue as the coward's way out of the fighting—the unmanly alternative. Porter's and Buck's comrades' charitable assessments of their mentally incapacitated comrades were not universal, either in life or in the movie *Patton* (1970): There was Pvt. Paul G. Bennett, the famous "Soldier Who Gets Slapped," played in the movie by Tim Considine. The slapping scene in *Patton* is based on a true incident in which Gen. George Patton (George C. Scott) confronted Bennett while he was sitting dejectedly, seemingly unwounded, in an army hospital. Like Porter and Buck, Bennett suffered from battle fatigue. Patton has just visited and decorated a number of severely wounded men lying in the beds nearby Bennett. One of these soldiers, a severely wounded man, his head covered in bandages and breathing on oxygen, lies unconscious as the general pins a Purple Heart on his pillow. Overcome with emotion, Patton whispers something in the wounded man's ear and pats him on the top of his head. Then Patton rises, full of emotion, turns and spots Bennett, and interrogates the soldier:

> PATTON: What's the matter with you?
>
> BENNETT: Well, I . . . I guess I . . . I can't take it anymore.
>
> PATTON: What did you say?
>
> BENNETT: It's my nerves, sir. I . . . I just can't stand the shelling anymore.
>
> PATTON: (becoming enraged) Your *nerves*? Well, hell, you're nothing but a goddamned coward.

Bennett starts sniveling, and Patton retorts, "Shut up! [he slaps Bennett twice] I'm not going to have a man sitting here *crying* in front of these brave men who have been wounded in battle!" Bennett snivels some more, and Patton slaps him again, knocking the man's helmet away. Patton exclaims the following:

> *Shut up!* [to the doctors] Don't admit this yellow bastard. There's nothing wrong with him. I won't have a man who's just afraid to fight stinking up this place of honor! You will get him back up to the front. [to Bennett] You're going back to the front, boy. You may get shot, and you may get killed, but

> you're going back to the fighting. Either that or I'll stand you up before a firing squad. Why, I ought to shoot you right now, you . . .

The general pulls his pistol. At that, the doctors leap forward and hustle the soldier out of the tent. Patton continues, shouting angrily at the soldier's back:

> Goddamned bastard! Get him out of here! Take him back to the front! You hear me? You goddamned coward! [the general takes a deep breath as he exits before his next line] I won't have cowards in my army.

In Patton's mind, the badge of courage signifying the bond of manliness between soldiers had been broken, and the general simply could not stomach the presence of a man who had broken ranks—so to speak—with those who had done their jobs and earned their badges. Bennett's placement in the hospital tent next to those whose blood-soaked bandages attested to their courage was an affront Patton could not bear.

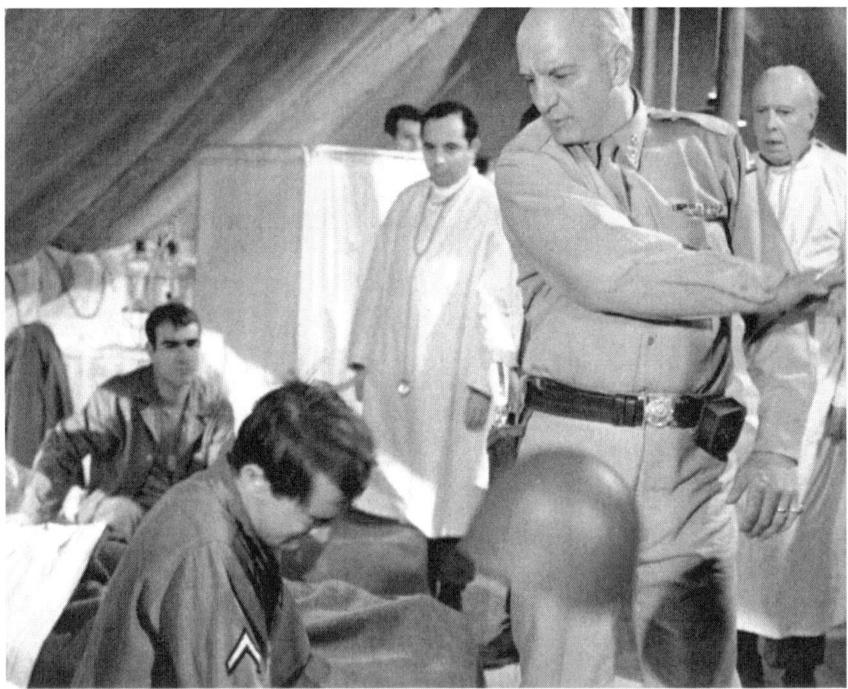

General Patton (George C. Scott) slaps soldier (Tim Considine). ***20th Century Fox / Photofest © 20th Century Fox***

THEY'RE HARDEST ON THEMSELVES

Although Lt. Abbott's situation in *The Hunters* seems atypical, it really isn't. Deciding whether you're measuring up to the manly ideal of courage is a personal thing that a soldier doesn't always share out loud. Abbott flies combat missions every day and endures the same risks as the rest of the pilots in his squadron, but because he is afraid every time he takes off, he's completely convinced that he's a coward. Abbott gets drunk every night because he cannot meet his high standards for courage. Like Henry Fleming in a war a century earlier, Abbott looks around and is convinced that no one in the squadron is as scared as he is. There is no chat with John Wayne that would convince Abbott that everyone is as afraid as he is.

As discussed in chapter 3, especially when Abbott compares himself to phlegmatic pilot Maj. Cleve "Iceman" Saville (Robert Mitchum), he brands himself a coward—this despite another pilot's assessment of him as the "bravest man in the squadron." Such wingmen as Lt. Corona (John Gabriel) consider Abbott the unit's bravest man because, despite his nearly incapacitating fear and average flying ability, and despite the fact that he can turn in his wings to the flight surgeon at any time and take a desk job, Abbott still willingly dons his flight gear, takes off, and flies into harm's way. That to Corona—and many other characters in war films—is a greater kind of courage.

EACH BRINGS HIS OWN BURDEN

Similarly, as mentioned in chapter 3, Capt. Paul Cabot Winston (Robert Duvall), in *Captain Newman, M.D.*, committed no acts of cowardice but still considers himself lacking. The officer has the added psychological burden of being a "Winston," growing up in an emotionless, blue-blooded family from whom much is expected. Raised by demanding parents on the false notion that anything short of perfection is unacceptable, Winston has condemned himself to a catatonic state rather than explain his lack of courage to his loved ones. Shot down during World War II in Nazi-held territory, he had found a cellar to hide in and sympathetic people to feed him and help him survive. Rather than try to escape to the Allied lines, which he judged was the only right and courageous thing to do, he holed up in the cellar for months until he was liberated during the Allied advance. For the average soldier, this might have been acceptable behavior, given the circumstances. He wished to avoid capture, so he hid. Perhaps hiding in this cellar was his way of escaping the reality of war and reducing his exposure to danger. But for a Winston, it was less than perfect behavior.

When he is later repatriated, Winston lapses into a catatonic state to once again go into hiding in a cellar of his own creation, this time to avoid his new shameful reality.

To silently endure fear, to rationalize it by a combination of a veteran's fatalistic attitude combined with a stoic, task-oriented approach ("I'm doing the job I was sent here to do") is often portrayed as the ultimate in manliness, and, therefore, courage. In *Saving Private Ryan* (1998), Capt. Miller (Tom Hanks) gets the shakes. His angst is not otherwise noticeable, but before and after moments of combat, his shaking hand becomes an outward and visible sign of an inward and personal panic. Besides having a heavy heart over the bloodshed and devastation in which he has engaged, the number of young men he's led to their deaths, and wishing there was something honorable and decent he could accomplish in the war, Miller is beginning to have doubts about both his survival and the welfare of his immortal soul. He hopes his current task—saving one soldier from the war—will become his act of redemption, earning himself and his men, as he puts it, the "right to go home."

Miller has long ago abandoned any sense that manliness demands such actions as doing one's job and displaying courage. A veteran of North Africa, Sicily, and Omaha Beach on D-Day, he is far beyond that, and with this current mission to find and save Pvt. Ryan, his cynicism rises to new heights. At first, he considers it only a FUBAR (fucked up beyond all recognition) assignment, as Pvt. Jackson calls it: "From my way of thinkin', sir, this entire mission is a serious misallocation of valuable military resources" (namely Miller's squad). But eventually, Miller and his father confessor, Sgt. Horvath (Tom Sizemore), come to look at their assignment not as a new way to distinguish themselves, act manly, or even do a job of work. Instead, they see this deed as perhaps their only chance in the war to do something besides kill people, an opportunity to a deed for which they can later be proud. Once they find Ryan, the young man refuses to leave his buddies shorthanded as they defend a bridge against a larger force of Germans. Miller and Horvath discuss the situation, and the sergeant agrees with Miller that their squad should stay and reinforce Ryan's outfit, both keeping the young man safe and doing their jobs:

> HORVATH: I don't know. Part of me thinks the kid's right. He asks what he's done to deserve this. He wants to stay here, fine. Let's leave him and go home. But then another part of me thinks, what if by some miracle we stay, then actually make it out of here. Someday we might look back on this and decide that saving Private Ryan was the one decent thing we were able to pull out of this whole God-awful, shitty mess. Like you said, captain, maybe we do that, we all earn the right to go home.

In their own estimation, Miller and Horvath have sinned: They have disobeyed God's law by killing so many human beings. Miller also feels guilt for the many men he has ordered to their deaths. They view this one act—saving Pvt. Ryan—as perhaps their only chance to square themselves with God.

Similarly, in *Tears of the Sun* (2003), Lt. A. K. Walters (Bruce Willis) carries the burden and guilt of the many missions in which he and his U.S. Navy SEALs team have killed a great many people. The team's current mission is to rescue an American missionary, Dr. Lena Kendricks (Monica Belluci) from danger and likely death when a bloody civil war breaks out in Nigeria. The team is dropped into a village soon to be overrun by rebels bent on genocide. They find the doctor, but she will not leave. She insists that the team also evacuate a group of villagers who will surely be killed by the rebels. But Walters's orders are to evacuate the doctor, "not indigenous personnel." Walters is sympathetic but knows that his commander won't agree to a mass evacuation. So he lies to the doctor and takes her and the villagers a few miles away to the pickup point where helicopters appear to evacuate the team and the doctor. After Kendricks thanks Walters for saving her life, Walters replies, "It wasn't about saving your life, it was about getting the job done, completing the mission. That's all."

Walters has used his job, his orders, and his mission to justify everything he has done—and didn't do—on his team's bloody missions, but he is now faced with the reality that these villagers—men, women, and children—will be brutally slaughtered if he doesn't forget about the job, his orders, and the orderly way he has dealt with the deaths he has caused. The helicopters have arrived, and Walters has finally come up against a no-win situation. He has been the good soldier, obeying orders and compromising his morality for the sake of doing his job. He finally decides to pack the helicopters with the weakest villagers, the ones who would hold up the rest, and sets out to lead and protect the rest of the party to safety in Cameroon.

This disobeying of the U.S. Navy SEALs team's mission orders is truly a different kind of courage, quite similar to Miller's and Horvath's disregard of their orders, to pull Pvt. Ryan out of combat and convey him safely home. The trouble is, Ryan won't leave his small band of buddies as they defend an important bridge and try to fight off a superior German force. So Miller and Horvath decide to stay, too. Walters decides to disregard his orders to stay in the jungle and protect the doctor and the villagers and escort them out of harm's way. Walters tells his men, "I broke my own rule . . . I started to give a fuck. I brought you guys along with me," so he asks them to speak freely about it. One says that it's not their war, but that the team has now redefined their own orders, and saving the villagers is their new mission. It becomes a matter of honor to these men to "get these people out . . . or die tryin'." One more introspective soldier believes that the team is doing the right thing for their sins, which he defines as all those other Navy SEAL missions in which they just did their narrowly defined jobs, obeyed orders, and left human suffering behind when they could have done something about it.

In the midst of war, to stop and think about what's right, and to have the courage of their convictions to do something about it, is another, perhaps higher form of courage. After successfully saving many of the villagers from pursuing rebels, some Navy SEAL team members die. But the theme of the movie is clear, as it ends with the following quote from Edmund Burke: "The only thing necessary for the triumph of evil is for good men to do nothing."

A film with quite similar themes of repentance and guilt for prior sins is *The Patriot* (2000). In the French and Indian War, South Carolina farmer Benjamin Martin (Mel Gibson) was a fierce warrior. But in the Battle of the Wilderness, in revenge for enemy atrocities, Martin and his men engaged in even worse slaughter. Although praised by friends and neighbors for his courage, Martin still suffers post-traumatic stress and guilt for his sins. Almost twenty years later, he speaks in the South Carolina Legislature against the War of Revolution, in part because of his great guilt, and also because he fears that such a war will bring punishment upon himself and his family for his youthful transgressions. When asked why he refuses to stand on his beliefs, since politically he stands with the principles of the revolution, Martin responds, "I'm a parent. I don't have the luxury of principles." Both at the start of the film and later, he explains his concern, saying, "I have long feared that my sins would return to visit me, and the cost is more than I can bear."

Although Martin served as a courageous soldier a generation earlier, other members of the legislature and even his oldest son, Gabriel (Heath Ledger), ironically accuse him of cowardice because he won't fight for his beliefs. Gabriel says to him, "Father, I thought you were a man of principle." Martin replies, "When you have a family of your own, perhaps you'll understand." Gabriel retorts, "When I have a family of my own, I won't hide behind them."

Despite Martin's intention to remain neutral in the war, death and destruction are forced upon him. First, Thomas (Gregory Smith), one of his sons, is murdered by a brutal British dragoon officer, and Gabriel, now a Colonial soldier, is taken away to be hanged. Martin, grieving for one son, cannot stand by while another is executed, so, with the help of his two youngest sons' sharpshooting and he himself armed with a pistol and an old Indian tomahawk, he single-handedly ambushes an entire squad of British soldiers and rescues Gabriel. Drenched in enemy blood, Martin stands, dazed, as his sons stare at him aghast, realizing that his sins have truly come back to haunt him.

Later, grieving for these newest sins, Martin is consoled by his sister-in-law, Charlotte, who reminds him, "You have done nothing for which you should be ashamed." But the courageous Martin, having finally realized the folly of his neutrality, replies, echoing Edmund Burke, "I have done nothing, and for that I am ashamed."

Then, both to repent for his inaction and exact revenge on the British for Thomas's murder, Martin joins the Colonial Army, is instantly commissioned a colonel, and is assigned the job of recruiting and leading a guerilla force to harass and confound British forces. Fighting like Indians rather than in the European style of battle of formal, frontal attack, Martin and his Colonial Militia open up a second front in the American South, preventing British general Charles Cornwallis (Tom Wilkinson) from disengaging in the South and moving his army North to surround and defeat the army of George Washington. Fighting cleverly and with great courage against a vastly superior army, Martin and his men eventually combine with the Colonial Army to defeat Cornwallis, forcing British surrender and the eventual victory of the Colonials over the British.

THE COURAGE TO BE RESPONSIBLE

The Iraq war film *The Lucky Ones* (2008) shows little combat footage, but courage and the challenge of doing the right thing is not found exclusively on the battlefield. Only a scene at the beginning depicts fighting in Iraq, and the scene shows only one of the three protagonists, a soldier named T. K. (Michael Pena). T. K. is wounded, so he rates a leave in the United States. In a New York airport, T. K. encounters fellow soldiers Colee (Rachel McAdams), also on leave, and Cheaver (Tim Robbins), a reservist who was called up, served in Iraq, and who now has separated from the army. Because all flights are grounded, the three set out together for Cheaver's home in St. Louis, where Cheaver will part company with the other two, who are headed for Las Vegas.

Like many soldiers who fought bravely in Iraq, they carry wounds, both psychological and physical. T. K. was wounded when shrapnel from an improvised explosive device (IED) pierced his leg, an injury that is temporarily rendering him impotent. Part of the story involves T. K.'s recovery from this injury. Colee is still bandaged and occasionally bleeding from a bullet wound in her leg, and she walks with a slight limp. Cheaver has a back problem as a result of an injury suffered when an outhouse (fortunately for him a new, empty one) fell off a forklift onto him. Cheaver considers this an ironic testament to the futility of the war.

Unfortunately, Cheaver's homecoming in St. Louis is not a happy one. His wife, whom he has not seen in almost two years, wants a divorce, and his son is desperate for money for college. His business failed while he was in Iraq, he can't help his son, and he feels lost and despondent. He is heartbroken about his wife and guilty that he has failed in his fatherly (read manly) responsibility to help his son get into college. While sorting things out, he decides to accompany his new friends to Las Vegas. He has concocted a plan to win his son's tuition at the gambling tables. Glad to get out of the army, he even advises T. K. to go AWOL to Canada rather than return to Iraq for a fourth tour.

Cheaver is not a fearful man, just a pragmatist who knows the odds are not good that T. K. will get through his next deployment without injury or death. But as the three travel across the country, Cheaver has time to think about things, and it becomes clear that the only way he can do the right thing for his son is to reenlist himself. There is a $20,000 bonus for enlistments, which happens to be the exact amount his son needs for college tuition. It will take great courage for Cheaver to go back to Iraq, but his life at home is over, and all that's left is his manly duty to his son and the implicit knowledge that if he should be killed in his next tour in Iraq, there will be another $100,000 coming to his son from his GI insurance. This is truly another, quite different kind of courage.

COURAGE DUE TO FATALISM

Most soldiers who appear to be courageous have found solace in some form of stoic calm, resigned to the fact that some power other than themselves controls their destiny. This is clearly shown in a theological sense in the civil war film *Gods and Generals* (2003). Most of the film centers on the rise to prominence of Confederate general Thomas "Stonewall" Jackson (Stephen Lang). At one point during a battle, one of the general's aides is perplexed by how Jackson can so calmly and courageously stand (or sit on his horse) in the thick of a battle, with artillery shells crashing around him and bullets whizzing by. His response is simple: He firmly believes that God had already set the day and time of his death and nothing can change that. This fatalistic view allows him to clear his mind of fear and appear courageous in battle, providing the troops he commands with an inspiring, courageous leader to rally around. Not concerned about injury and death, Jackson more calmly focuses on the job at hand.

Confirming this philosophy, later in this picture, during the battle of Fredericksburg, a Confederate cannon misfires and explodes near Gen. Robert E. Lee (Robert Duvall), casting Lee and his staff to the ground. Although the explosion kills some artillerymen, Lee emerges unscathed but dusty. As he brushes himself off, one of his aides asks if he is injured. Like Jackson, the unflappable Lee displays his own stoicism, saying, "No. It is not yet our time."

Gen. Jackson (Stephen Lang) in *Gods and Generals* appears unafraid in the midst of battle. *Warner Bros. / Photofest © Warner Bros. Pictures*

In *Band of Brothers*, God's choosing the time to die isn't a part of the fatalistic Lt. (later captain) Speirs's philosophy of war. A soldier, Blithe, confesses to Speirs that on D-Day, when he landed in France, rather than seek out his unit, the real reason he slept all day in a ditch was because he was scared. Speirs responds, saying the following:

> We're all scared. You hid in that ditch because you think there's still hope. But Blithe, the only hope you have is to accept the fact that you're already dead. And the sooner you accept that, the sooner you'll be able to function as a soldier is supposed to function. Without mercy. Without compassion. Without remorse. All war depends upon it.

A similar approach to the stoic treatment of death, thus fueling a different kind of courage by removing the constant fear of being killed, was articulated by famed combat film director Samuel Fuller in the World War II film *The Big Red One* (1980). The film centers around a gruff career NCO, appropriately cast with only the screen name the "Sergeant" (Lee Marvin). In this film, World War I veteran "Sarge" leads his "squad of wet noses," so called because of their youth and inexperience, from the debacle of the battle of the Kasserine Pass through D-Day to the very end of the war in Europe. Through it all, only four of the Sergeant's troops survive unscathed. Soldiers "up at Division," one soon-to-be-wounded replace-

The Big Red One*: Clockwise, from bottom left: Pvt. Zab (Robert Carradine), Pvt. Griff (Mark Hamill), Pvt. Johnson (Kelly Ward), Pvt. Vinci (Bobby Di Cicco), and, center, the Sergeant (Lee Marvin).** ***United Artists / Photofest © United Artists

ment troop tells them, call these four surviving soldiers the Sergeant's "Four Horsemen," referring to the Four Horsemen of the Apocalypse. As these four had survived so many brushes with death, another kind of nontheistic fatalism had set in. Although not specifically articulated regarding themselves, one of the four, Pvt. Zab (WWII veteran Fuller's personal voice in the film), refers to the constant flow of young replacements thusly, saying the following:

> By now we'd come to look at all replacements as dead men who temporarily had the use of the arms and legs. They came and went so fast and so regularly that sometimes we didn't even learn their names. Truth is, after a while, we sort of avoided gettin' to know them.

When one replacement asks Zab if the veteran thinks he will be wounded or killed, Zab simply asks him if he considers himself special. Throughout this film, Fuller maintains that no one is special. Some are simply lucky and will probably survive the war without a scratch, and some are not. To those soldiers who accept that they are likely to die before the war for them is over, it becomes much easier to do their duty courageously. As Lt. Miller in *Saving Private Ryan* might add, doing the job of war efficiently and courageously is a way to get them one step closer to going home.

WHY COURAGE?

Anais Nin wrote in her diary, "Life shrinks or expands in proportion to one's courage." But few characters in this book—perhaps Capt. Buzz Rickson in *The War Lover* (1961) and Cpl. Jack Rabinoff and Dick Ennis in *Anzio* (1968) and SSgt. William James in *The Hurt Locker* (2009) in the following chapter are exceptions—exhibit courage along with an eagerness for insinuating themselves into dangerous situations solely for the thrill-seeking goal of expanding their repertoire of exciting life experiences. Most soldiers possess a human survival instinct that restricts courageous actions only to when they are required, rather than to experience a rush of adrenaline. Many exhibit courage because the job requires it. Others act bravely out of a need to protect their comrades. Sometimes, when asked later why they committed a certain courageous deed, soldiers respond that they reacted instinctively in the heat of the moment, with little thought to the consequences. Or then again, as Thomas Fuller wrote, "Some have been thought brave because they were afraid to run away."

Perhaps real courage emanates from none of these things but rather from the greatest commandment: to love one's neighbor. As is portrayed in the story about a World War II Japanese labor camp, *To End All Wars* (2001), and as is written in the Bible in John 15:13, "Greater love has no one than this, that he lay down his life for his friends." *To End All Wars* tells the true story of a ragged band of British soldiers (and a sole American) who were forced to build a railway through the Burmese jungle under terrible conditions, with little food and medicine, routinely brutalized by their Japanese captors. At first, the Japanese see their prisoners as lowly, dishonored men, because these Allies were ordered to surrender. The Japanese *Bushido* code would dictate that a soldier should commit suicide rather than surrender, so the Japanese wrongly assume that their captives are cowards and lesser human beings. But, slowly in the coming months, these Allied soldiers learn to rise above the tendency among prisoners to care only for themselves, and they help and support each other. They read the Bible and demonstrate love for their fellow prisoners. They even seem to grow to tolerate their abusive captors, a virtue not lost on many—but not all—of the Japanese.

In one instance, upon returning from a work detail, a Japanese sergeant discovers that a shovel is missing. The savage Sgt. Ito threatens severe punishment for all the prisoners if the culprit does not identify himself, so the sole American prisoner, Lt. Reardon (Kiefer Sutherland), innocent of this offense, steps forward and claims that he stole the shovel. Ito takes another shovel and beats Reardon so severely that he is paralyzed from the waist down for the rest of the film. Only later does Ito discover that the soldier who counted the shovels was mistaken and that there were none missing. So Ito takes his shovel and beats the Japanese soldier an equal amount.

This incident creates great dissonance in Ito, a firm believer in the *Bushido* code. He can't understand the Christian charity and courage necessary for Reardon to accept such savage punishment to save his friends. He looks over a prisoner's Bible, looking for answers, but because he can't read English, all he discovers is a picture of the crucifixion of Christ. He fixates on this, but in the wrong way. Then, later, when of the prisoners, Maj. Campbell (Robert Carlyle), kills two Japanese guards while trying to escape, Ito decides to use crucifixion as a punishment. To Ito's utter amazement, a charitable and courageous soldier, Dusty Miller (Mark Strong), steps forward to insist on taking the place of his fellow prisoner who is sentenced to die. Frustrated and confused, Ito accepts Miller's request, spares Campbell, and crucifies Miller.

After the incident, the Japanese are all demoralized and confused. A few, like Ito, resent the Christians' love for one another, while other Japanese soldiers' admiration of the Allied soldiers grows. As Allied forces close in on Japanese-held Asian territories toward the end of the war, Japanese soldiers from a neighboring camp are wounded in a bombing raid. A truck full of wounded Japanese leave their post and drive to the prison camp for medical assistance, but Ito will not let them into the camp, disgusted with the soldiers for deserting their posts. But, as Ito stands by, dumbfounded, the prisoners take pity on the wounded Japanese and care for them. This kind of courage and love for one's neighbor he simply cannot understand.

The film ends with a quote from Shakespeare's *Henry V* (2002):

> For he today that sheds his blood with me shall be my brother; be he ne'er so vile, this day shall gentle his condition; and gentlemen in England now-a-bed shall think themselves accurs'd they were not here, and hold their manhoods cheap while any speaks that fought with us. (Act IV, Scene 3)

The next and final chapter delves yet again into men's psyches to ask perhaps the toughest question of all: Why do men fight in the first place?

6

Why Men Fight

Edward Dmytryk's 1968 film *Anzio* was produced during the Vietnam War. *Anzio* reminded audiences that similar to the disastrous American landing on this seaside Italian village, the United States had once again in Southeast Asia managed to ignore the lessons taught by history. The principal message of *Anzio* is conveyed through the quest of an Ernie Pyle-type war correspondent named Dick Ennis (Robert Mitchum) for the answer to an ultimate question. In this quest, Ennis repeatedly risks his life on the front lines, reporting the human stories of infantry troops placed in harm's way. What answer does Ennis seek? Why does he continue to endanger himself, an unarmed journalist, on the front lines? He wants to discover why men are willing to go to war. From Cpl. Jack Rabinoff (Peter Faulk), Ennis finally gets his answer:

> [Why?] It's got nothing to do with [defending] democracy. [It's] *because I like it*. I *want* this. A guy sells shoes for forty years, and I live more in *one day*. I see more, I feel more, I taste more, I think more. I *am* more. Do you understand? *I'm more.*

Soon after this, Rabinoff is killed by a German sniper's bullet, and Ennis suddenly finds himself at risk of becoming the sniper's next victim. In covering front line action with U.S. troops since they came ashore in North Africa, Ennis has never had to fire a shot. But suddenly, to defend himself, he is forced to pick up a dead man's rifle and engage in single combat against a clever German sniper. After a desperate duel, Ennis manages to maneuver into position and, with a great amount of luck, kills the sniper. Both disgusted with himself for stepping over his self-imposed line and becoming a combatant, and strangely stimulated by the kill, he begins to understand the excitement that Rabinoff felt. He also realizes that his own attraction to witnessing war from the front lines is more than just seeking an answer to his question. He, too, lives more, experiences more, and feels more in one day than he ever would back home, sitting at the city desk of his newspaper.

At the end of the picture, having found his grail and lived out the feelings described by Rabinoff, Ennis reports what he has learned about his quest to Maj. Gen. Jack Lesley (Arthur Kennedy), the commander of the Allied forces at Anzio:

> ENNIS: Men kill each other because *they like to.*
>
> LESLEY: Because they *like* to? And that's it?
>
> ENNIS: That's it. Plain and simple. They *love* to. Wars never solve anything. History teaches us that. But you face a man with a gun in your hands, you live more intensely that moment than any other moment in your life . . . because you're scared to death, and you've *got* to kill him.
>
> LESLEY: (disappointed) We kill each other because we like to. That's a helluva condemnation of mankind, Mr. Ennis.
>
> ENNIS: Yes, I'm afraid it is, general, but maybe if we recognize it and admit it to ourselves, we might learn to live with each other.
>
> LESLEY: We hope.

This ending, like similar tidy wrap-ups to *Platoon* (1986) and countless other war films, assumes that man is capable of learning from his mistakes, rather than—as we see over and over again in current events—destined to relive them. But U.S. conflicts since World War II have shown us that Ennis was right: War is not really what Carl von Clausewitz defined as the "continuation of [a country's foreign] policy with other means." It's much more elemental than that and much more endemic to testosterone-fueled males. It's a Jungian archetype dating back to the dawn of Homo sapiens: the heart-pounding thrill of the hunt, an inherited instinct to survive against an adversary, whether it's a dangerous animal or defending one's own territory from another human being. Finally, it's the elation when the objective is won.

Likewise, in *The Hurt Locker* (2009), a film about discord within a U.S. Army explosive ordinance disposal (EOD) squad deployed in Iraq, the lure of danger and excitement versus safety and caution is at the root of the conflict. After an improvised explosive device (IED) explodes, killing their squad leader, the squad's replacement leader arrives. This sergeant is quite different from the squad's by-the-book, safety-conscious former boss. Instead, SSgt. William James (Jeremy Renner) goes about his job in a completely different fashion. Instead of following safety protocols, James ignores most of them, doing his dangerous duty as one soldier calls it, "like a cowboy." Like Rabinoff in *Anzio*, James is a war lover, a thrill junkie seeking the adrenaline high of putting his life on the line.

ADVENTURE VERSUS SURVIVAL

Besides the dangers of war, the major conflict in *The Hurt Locker* centers on the difference between the attitudes of Sgt. J. T. Sanborn (Anthony Mackie), second-in-command, and SSgt. James. Sanborn sees no adventure or romance in war: Like many NCOs in Vietnam-era and later films, Sanborn only wants to complete the mission and bring his men safely back home after their tour of duty. He tries to find ways to do this dangerous job with the minimum of risk. Sanborn is as careful and safety conscious as James is reckless, which leads to many conflicts and even a few fistfights between the two NCOs. This is not to say that Sanborn is less manly or in any way cowardly: Sanborn is a hard-boiled, brave, and dedicated soldier ready to fight and do his duty. But Sanborn judges James to be so enamored with thrill seeking that his recklessness will sooner or later result in not just his death, but the deaths of other squad members. And the rest of the squad are "short-timers," soon to finish their tour of duty and return home. To complicate matters, Sanborn can't go over James's head to complain, because their

In *The Hurt Locker,* James (Jeremy Renner) stubbornly refuses to listen to subordinate Sanborn (Anthony Mackie). *Summit Entertainment / Photofest © Summit Entertainment*

battalion commander, the macho Col. Reed (David Morse), considers James's antics exciting and heroic.

Toward the end of the picture, another unsafe order by James finally results in a squad casualty, but the soldier survives. Shortly after this incident, the squad is rotated back home. James has a wife and two-year-old boy, and it is during a session with his son that we get an insight into why he fights. James remarks that at the age of two, his son loves everything around him, his Mama, his toys, his Daddy. But James remarks that as his son ages, the number of things he loves will decrease. Finally, James says—about himself—the number of things he loves may dwindle to just one: not his wife or his son, but in his case, the rush he gets when he tempts death by disarming bombs. As the film ends, James has abandoned his wife and son to volunteer for another tour in Iraq. Director Kathryn Bigelow still-frames James as he confidently walks down a dusty Iraq street, dressed in his EOD armor to disarm another IED, symbolizing a western sheriff at high noon walking confidently toward a gunfight with a six-gun on his hip.

WINNING

Regardless of why humans take up arms against a foe, the elixir achieved at the journey's end can be defined rather simply: winning. In war, as in hunting a dangerous animal, there is great risk. Since the dawn of man, this risk, this chance of dying, puts men, the designated hunters of this species, on high alert, brains racing, blood flow increasing, adrenaline and testosterone pumping. Besides survival, winning has meant food for the table and victory over natural elements. Ennis felt all these emotions when he dueled with the sniper and won. Athletes feel something similar to these primal urges when they defeat their opponents on the playing fields.

In the opening speech of the film *Patton*, the bellicose general encourages his men to fight and to taste the fruits of the winner, attributing what is an attribute of all human males exclusively to Americans:

> Men, all this stuff you've heard about America not wanting to fight, wanting to stay out of the war, is a lot of horse dung. Americans traditionally *love* to fight. All real Americans *love* the sting of battle. . . . Americans love a winner and will not tolerate a loser. . . . The Nazis are the enemy. Wade into them! Spill *their* blood! Shoot *them* in the belly. When you put your hand into a bunch of *goo* that a moment before was your friend's face, you'll know what to do.

Later in the film, Patton gushes forth with his personal love of combat and winning, symbolized by military might. As he gazes at a long column of his tanks and other vehicles making their way up a curvy mountain road on their way to conquering Palermo, he tells an aide, "Compared to war, all other forms of human endeavor shrink to insignificance." Later, after a fierce battle, surveying a battlefield in which his men and German soldiers lie dead, Patton remarks, "I love it. God help me, I *do* love it so. I love it more than my life."[1]

Another film character, a fictional war lover, appropriately named Col. Bill Kilgore (Robert Duvall), is equally passionate about the manly thrill of winning. After his U.S. Army Airborne forces in *Apocalypse Now* (1979) have won another engagement, he pauses wistfully and pronounces, "I love the smell of napalm in the morning. . . . Smells like . . . victory." He pauses again to reflect, his demeanor changes, and he suddenly becomes melancholy: "Someday this war's gonna end," he says. He pauses again, as if regretting he ever spoke the words out loud and then walks away, hoping to erase his statement from the air. Like Patton, Kilgore knows that these moments of combat and victory are transitory.

At the end of *Patton*, the war against Germany is won. The general has been relieved of his command because he insists that the United States should continue fighting, this time against their allies, the Soviets. As he walks off into the sunset, his voice-over says the following:

In one of the more memorable scenes of *Apocalypse Now*, Col. Kilgore (Robert Duvall) utters the famous line, "I love the smell of napalm in the morning. Smells like . . . victory." ***United Artists / Photofest © United Artists***

> For over a thousand years, Roman conquerors returning from the wars enjoyed the honor of a triumph—a tumultuous parade. In the procession came trumpeters and musicians and strange animals from the conquered territories, together with carts laden with treasure and captured armaments. The conqueror rode in a triumphal chariot, the dazed prisoners walking in chains before him. Sometimes his children, robed in white, stood with him in the chariot or rode the trace horses. A slave stood behind the conqueror, holding a golden crown, and whispering in his ear a warning . . . that all glory is fleeting.

"SEDUCED BY WORLD WAR II AND JOHN WAYNE MOVIES"

But in the movies, the romanticizing effect doesn't have to be fleeting, and in this lies great danger. It can sustain itself, creating its own momentum and perpetuating its own myths, inspiring, persuading, and seducing the next generation to become war lovers. In the article "Is That You, John Wayne? Is This Me? Myth and Meaning in American Representations of the Vietnam War" (2007), Simon Newman explains the following:

> These Hollywood creations not only informed how a generation recalled their fathers' war, but allowed young Americans to imagine themselves similarly engaged in such noble warfare. One recalled that he had been "seduced by World War II and John Wayne movies," while another had "flash images of John Wayne films, with me as the hero." As young boys, Ron Kovic and his friend Richie Castiglia saw *Sands of Iwo Jima* at their local cinema: "The Marine Corps hymn was playing in the background as we sat glued to our seats, humming the hymn together and watching Sergeant Stryker, played by John Wayne, charge up the hill and get killed just before he reached the top. And then they showed the men raising the flag on Iwo Jima with the Marines' hymn still playing, and Castiglia and I cried in our seats. I loved the song so much, and every time I heard it I would think of John Wayne and the brave men who raised the flag on Iwo Jima that day. Like Mickey Mantle and the fabulous New York Yankees, John Wayne in the *Sands of Iwo Jima* became one of my heroes."

IDEALISM VERSUS DISILLUSIONMENT

It's only human that boys look to men to find their role models. As mentioned earlier, in ancient times, heroic examples for boys were the men—the warriors—of the tribe. As providers of food and shelter and defenders of their families, male elders were what boys were supposed to become. In modern times, thanks to today's mass media, boys have a much larger palette to draw from to create who and what they wish to become.

In the Vietnam War film *The Deer Hunter* (1978), Michael (Robert De Niro) is drunk, celebrating the wedding of his friend, Steven (John Savage), but this doesn't keep him from going back to the bar for another cold one. There, at the end of the bar, Michael sees a welcome party crasher at any American Legion hall: a quiet man with a dark expression, dressed in the highly decorated uniform of the U.S. Army's elite Green Berets. Michael, Steven, and their friend Nick (Christopher Walken), see in the uniform and this soldier an idealized role model, the honored, elite fighter they hope to become. The young men immediately buy the soldier a drink and introduce themselves. Expecting comradeship, or perhaps even a mentor to tell them stories, the three tell the Green Beret that they, too, have requested U.S. Army Airborne service, and, by implication, their intention to follow him into the Green Berets. All the soldier says in response is, "Fuck it."

Although the disillusioned soldier is probably referring to the futility, waste, suffering, and death he witnessed while fighting the war in Vietnam, and not to them or their ambitions, the three young men take offense, especially Michael. They ask what it's like over there, and the soldier only replies again, "Fuck it." Michael, now quite peeved and very drunk, wonders if the Green Beret actually meant, "Fuck you." Michael has to be restrained by his friends from going down the bar after the Green Beret, but another friend, Axel (Chuck Aspegren), to lighten the moment, turns the incident into a joke. The Green Beret continues to drink in grim silence. There, practically on the eve of the three men's departures for the army, their myths and illusions of war and becoming warriors have been debunked by a single phrase.

The rest of the picture completes these young men's disillusionment. Nick dies, Steven returns home with no legs, Michael is clearly traumatized by his experiences in Vietnam, and all their friends and relations are clearly changed for the worse. At the end of this Oscar-winning picture, after Nick's funeral, with nothing but their grief to bind them together, they sit at a table in a bar and sadly sing, "God Bless America." Incapable of sorting things out, they fall back on all that they have left, blind patriotism, to reduce their anxieties and avoid the inevitable realization that what happened to them was a useless and unnecessary waste of three young lives. These three men didn't win, and the United States had lost, too. The last helicopter had already lifted off from the U.S. Embassy in Saigon, signaling America's most complete wartime defeat.

CHANNELED FANATICISM

As discussed in chapter 2, between armed conflicts, and oftentimes coinciding with America's smaller, less popular brushfire wars, American males participate in and cheer fanatically for athletes in sporting events. These events become alternative rites of passage that are close analogs to wars for a male population that requires these conflicts to provide them opportunities to perform manly acts. To ascend from boyhood to the society of men, young, impressionable lads are taught to adopt this same fanaticism. So, idolizing Mickey Mantle and John Wayne, boys model their behavior in the fashion of sports/celluloid heroes. These media models all had one thing in common: They won.

Even when Wayne's character died at the end of *Sands of Iwo Jima* (1949), Sgt. Stryker was a winner. He lived on in triumph because the young men he trained, who had assumed and perpetuated his persona and values, won the battle. They captured Mount Suribachi and planted the American flag at the top. From the earliest times, winning was the exhilarating payoff for all the blood, sweat, and death that armed conflict requires. Lucy Komisar (1976) characterizes this as the "masculine mystique," saying the following:

> The masculine mystique is based on toughness and domination, qualities that once may have been necessary in a time when men felled trees and slew wild animals. Now they are archaic and destructive values that have no legitimate place in our world, but continue to exist as idealized standards for some lofty state of "masculinity." The mystique has characterized many nations, but it is particularly dangerous in contemporary America because of our distinctively high levels of internal violence, our "Bonnie and Clyde" tendencies toward its glorification, our enormous capacities for mechanized warfare, and our virtual obsession with being Number One. (202)

To become successful as a warrior ("number one"), and thus measure up as a man, there is a terrible danger. In learning to be a disciplined, self-controlled Übermensch who keeps his feelings to himself and plays hurt, who never cries out and abhors any demonstration of weakness, much of the rest that life has to offer can easily be missed. Despite Patton's feelings to the contrary, perhaps there's virtue in compromise, perhaps even to the point of feeling satisfied about a fight lost but well fought. As feminine as it sounds, perhaps there's room for other than a complete and devastating victory in life, and especially in relationships. Consider Julie Drew's (2004) discussion of the rhetorical feminization of those who speak out against our current war:

> Much of this [crisis rhetoric that insists that war is the only way to insure public safety] is exacerbated, and arguably generated, by gendering the nation through public discourse in ways that make use of a cultural devaluation of those characteristics, actions, and reactions deemed feminine—such as diplomacy, negotiation, and compromise—and a hyper-valuation of the masculine characteristics of physical strength, punitive response, and violent aggression. (76)

But as shown earlier, the imperative in sport in America, and equally significant in its analog, war is the win. Chaim Shatan (1989) writes, "In the United States, winning is the central theme in the making of a boy's self-image. Boys learn early that 'any boy can win'" (127). Doesn't every sports stadium public address system have recorded on permanent audio disc storage the rock group Queen's ballad "We Are the Champions"? Consider some of the lyrics of this very telling song:

I've paid my dues—
Time after time—
I've done my sentence
But committed no crime—
And bad mistakes
I've made a few
I've had my share of sand kicked in my face—
But I've come through:

We are the champions—my friends
And we'll keep on fighting—till the end—
We are the champions—
We are the champions
No time for losers cause we are the champions—
of the world.
(www.lyricsfreak.com/q/queen/we+are+the+champions_20112595.html)

WINNING CAN BE DANGEROUS

Corporations teach their employees to revere Green Bay Packer coach Vince Lombardi's famous motto that "Winning isn't everything. It's the only thing." But the male fixation with winning has great dangers: Fear of showing weakness by backing down in a schoolyard fight can result in, at worst, a bloody nose, but American presidents Lyndon B. Johnson's and Richard Nixon's refusals to back down from the debacle of Vietnam—and be branded by history as a loser—killed 57,000 Americans and two to three million Vietnamese men, women, elderly, and children. And, in case readers believe that Vietnam was only an anomalous mistake made decades ago, fast-forward to the twenty-first century and see the United States embroiled in a Vietnam of a new president's creation, the needless U.S. intervention in Iraq. Unable to win and unwilling to admit defeat, President George W. Bush would not agree to leave until he won the war. After all, media cameras rolling, he landed on an aircraft carrier and declared victory. Winning must be irrefutable, no asterisks beside the "W" in the record books. On the day of this writing, another president at the helm, and despite

U.S. withdrawals, three more huge bombs went off in Baghdad, killing yet more Americans.

Also consider Joan Mellen's (1977) statement concerning film heroes she describes as "indomitable males":

> The stereotype of the self-controlled, invulnerable, stoical hero who justifies the image of unfeeling masculinity as a means of winning in a world that pounces on any sign of weakness. . . . Male heroes pontificate platitudes such as that invoked by an elderly John Wayne in *The Shootist*: "I won't be wronged, I won't be insulted, I won't be laid a hand on. I don't do these things to others, and I require the same of them." (5)

Winning has simply become so vital to our culture that the ultimate insult for a man is to be branded a loser. In *Heartbreak Ridge* (1986), Clint Eastwood's character, Gunnery Sgt. Tom Highway, evocative of John Wayne's Sgt. Stryker, buys into this nonsense. He has characterized his entire career's record in the U.S. Marine Corps as if it was simply a won-lost statistic on the sports page: When the film concludes, Highway is satisfied, finally ready to retire, because his personal war record (read sports won-lost record) had evened out at "1-1-1," one win (no matter how small—his marines' victory in Grenada), one loss (the war in Vietnam), and one tie (the stalemate in Korea). Eastwood's character feels that he is vindicated both as a marine and a man because he could finally chalk one up in the victory column. But might doesn't make right, and films that teach youngsters that there is any kind of righteousness in such tallies only perpetuate the value of war as a means of solving human problems. Vietnam veteran and author Tim O'Brien writes the following in *The Things They Carried* (1998):

> A true war story is never moral. It does not instruct, nor encourage virtue, nor suggest models of proper human behavior, nor restrain men from doing the things men have always done. If a story seems moral, do not believe it. If at the end of a war story you feel uplifted, or if you feel that some small bit of rectitude has been salvaged from the larger waste, then you have been made the victim of a very old and terrible lie. (68)

In *The Americanization of Emily* (1964), screenwriter Paddy Chayefsky penned a speech for Lt. Cmdr. Charley Madison (James Garner) to protest against the glorification of war. A creature of his times (World War II), Madison sarcastically brands pacifism as cowardly and immoral—but ultimately preferable to the grisly alternative. But his key point is that war is *not* virtuous, and as long as humans idealize war and its warriors, settling disputes in a peaceful manner is an impossibility:

In *The Americanization of Emily*, Madison (James Garner) explains to Emily (Julie Andrews) why he, a decorated veteran of the battle of Guadalcanal, refers to himself as a coward. *MGM / Photofest © MGM*

I'm not sentimental about war. I see nothing noble in widows. . . . War isn't hell at all. It's man at his best; the highest morality he's capable of. It's not war that's insane, you see. It's the morality of it. It's not greed or ambition that makes war, it's goodness. Wars are always fought for the best of reasons: for liberation or manifest destiny . . . always against tyranny and always in the interest of humanity. So far this war, we've managed to butcher some ten million humans in the interest of humanity. Next war it seems we'll have to destroy all of man in order to preserve his damn dignity. It's not war that's unnatural to us, it's virtue. As long as valor remains a virtue, we shall have soldiers. So, I preach cowardice. Through cowardice, we shall all be saved.

Perhaps the obsession with winning is the most serious and potentially dangerous of all the absurd notions that American war films and sports fixations inflict upon the psyches of our young boys. Unfortunately, this macho attitude is the most outmoded and least helpful value in a contemporary world in which the peoples of all nations must learn to adapt, change, and become more tolerant of so many kinds of racial, cultural, political, and religious diversity. If centuries-old governments and political philosophies can give way, if all the world is changing and adapting to everything from new values to new technology, perhaps the macho, uncommunicative, unemotional, pseudo-athletic misogynists America's national culture seems intent on perpetuating should also consider some fundamental alterations. After all, life's much more than a game.

NOTE

1. Patton is a perfect example of an individual one would diagnose as having a narcissistic personality disorder. As outlined in the American Psychiatric

Association's *Diagnostic and Statistical Manual of Mental Disorders* (1994), his character disorder exhibits a "pervasive pattern of grandiosity, need for admiration, and lack of empathy" (282). Patton is able to discount the human toll of war to the point to which he can say that he loves it, exemplifying his meeting the criteria for a narcissistic personality disorder. The narcissistic individual "reflects a grandiose sense of self-importance, requires excessive admiration, has a sense of entitlement, is interpersonally exploitative, is often envious of others, and shows arrogant haughty behaviors or attitudes" (American Psychiatric Association, 1994, 282). Patton further meets the criteria for narcissism by his being "preoccupied with fantasies of unlimited success and power." At the end of the film, as he walks his dog among the windmills into the sunset, his voice-over describes a Roman conqueror returning from war being lavishly honored with a parade of the treasures and prisoners from the conquered territories. Patton's delusional fantasy of what he saw as the glories of war is an extreme example of his egotistically absurd vanity.

Annotated Filmography

Note: On occasion, these plot synopses include spoilers.

***Action in the North Atlantic* (1943)**
DIRECTOR: Lloyd Bacon
SCREENPLAY: John Howard Lawson
STORY: Guy Gilpatric
CAST: Humphrey Bogart, Raymond Massey, Alan Hale, Ruth Gordon, Sam Levene
ACADEMY AWARD NOMINATIONS: Best Writing, Best Original Story
DVD: Warner Home Video
SUMMARY: This motion picture is a U.S. World War II propaganda film about the contributions of the men of the U.S. Merchant Marine in keeping the Allies, especially the Soviet Union, supplied with war material. The story follows one such crew and officers through convoys to England and Russia, engaging with Nazi submarines and attack aircraft.
FILM'S TREATMENT OF MASCULINITY: Courage in the face of a better-armed enemy is simply assumed for truly manly men. Fear is not an option.

***Air Force* (1943)**
DIRECTOR: Howard Hawks
SCREENPLAY: Leah Baird, Dudley Nichols, William Faulkner
CAST: John Ridgely, Gig Young, Harry Carey, Arthur Kennedy, John Garfield
ACADEMY AWARD WIN: Best editing

Academy Award Nominations: Best Original Screenplay, Best Cinematography (Black and White), Best Effects and Special Effects

DVD: Warner Home Video

Summary: This Oscar-winning classic U.S. World War II propaganda film details the adventures of a B-17 crew that arrives at Hickam Air Base right after the attack on Pearl Harbor. The aircrew hops from Hawaii to Wake Island and the Philippines, seemingly constantly pursued by the Japanese, and ends up dropping bombs on enemy ships in the Battle of the Coral Sea.

Film's Treatment of Masculinity: As with sports, part of manliness is the virtue of teamwork: In war, working for and sacrificing for the team is highly valued.

***Aliens* (1986)**

Director: James Cameron

Screenplay: James Cameron

Story: David Giler, Walter Hill

Cast: Sigourney Weaver, Michael Biehn, Paul Reiser, Bill Paxton, Lance Henrickson

Academy Award Wins: Best Visual Effects, Best Sound Effects Editing

Academy Award Nominations: Best Editing, Best Original Score, Best Art Direction/Set Decoration, Best Sound, Best Actress (Sigourney Weaver)

DVD: 20th Century Fox

Summary: This is an Oscar-winning science fiction film and a thinly veiled Vietnam War allegory that is also deeply critical of America's military–industrial complex. Futuristic colonial marines, arrogant and overconfident in their firepower, lose every encounter with powerful, intelligent, well-organized "bug" creatures. Nearly all the humans are killed, and only the heroine of the original film, *Alien*, Ellen Ripley, and a few others survive the encounter. The filmed scored a Best Actress Oscar nomination, a rarity for a science fiction/action motion picture.

Film's Treatment of Masculinity: Courage and bravado are expected from marines, but not when these traits are governed by hubris.

***American Guerilla in the Philippines* (1950)**

Director: Fritz Lang

Screenplay: Lamar Trotti, based on the novel by Ira Wolfert

Cast: Tyrone Power, Micheline Presle, Tom Ewell, Bob Patten, Tommy Cook, Jack Elam

DVD: Available for viewing online via Amazon Video on Demand

SUMMARY: This is the story of a U.S. Navy ensign stranded in the Philippines after the Japanese takeover of those islands during World War II. The officer helps organize Filipino resistance forces and fights a guerilla campaign against the Japanese until Gen. MacArthur and Allied troops return to retake the islands.

FILM'S TREATMENT OF MASCULINITY: The virtue of teamwork is again a salient manly theme. In this case, working as a team with both male and female guerillas of different races and nationalities is praised.

***The Americanization of Emily* (1964)**

DIRECTOR: Arthur Hiller

SCREENPLAY: Paddy Chayefsky, based on the novel by William Bradford Huie

CAST: James Garner, Julie Andrews, Melvyn Douglas, James Coburn, Keenan Wynn

DVD: Warner Home Video

SUMMARY: This is a comedy about a navy officer, an aide to an important admiral, who has a unique approach to his job in World War II: He wishes to avoid fighting at all costs while living the good life in London in the weeks prior to D-Day. He falls in love with a British woman who has a much more traditional view of war. During the D-Day invasion, the officer becomes an accidental hero and must find a way to come to grips with his beliefs.

FILM'S TREATMENT OF MASCULINITY: The terms *hero* and *coward* are irrelevant. The context explains and defines "what a man's gotta do."

***Anzio* (1968)**

DIRECTORS: Duilio Coletti, Edward Dmytryk

SCREENPLAY: H. A. L. Craig, based on the book by Wynford Vaughan-Thomas

CAST: Robert Mitchum, Peter Falk, Robert Ryan, Earl Holliman, Arthur Kennedy

DVD: Sony Pictures

SUMMARY: This film is both a historical treatment of the tragic circumstances surrounding the World War II invasion of Anzio and a combat reporter's search for truth. Following the U.S. Army from the beginning up until this invasion, the reporter continues risking his life on the battlefield to answer one question: Why do men fight? He finds not only his answer, but also the truth about himself and his own unspoken motives.

Film's Treatment of Masculinity: Some men are attracted to war like moths to flame, experiencing more, living more, feeling more in battle with their lives at risk than in any other time in their lives.

***Apocalypse Now* (1979)**

Director: Francis Ford Coppola

Screenplay: John Milius, Francis Ford Coppola, Michael Herr, based on the novella *Heart of Darkness* by Joseph Conrad

Cast: Martin Sheen, Marlon Brando, Robert Duvall, Frederic Forrest, Dennis Hopper

Academy Award Wins: Best Cinematography, Best Sound

Academy Award Nominations: Best Picture, Best Director (Francis Ford Coppola), Best Screenplay Adaptation

DVD: Lions Gate

Summary: Coppola's adaptation of Joseph Conrad's *Heart of Darkness*, set during the Vietnam War, received eight Academy Award nominations. A U.S. Army Special Forces assassin is ordered to venture upriver to Cambodia to "terminate with extreme prejudice" (kill) an insane American officer running amok throughout the countryside with local tribesmen, engaging in savage, unrestrained attacks; however, typical events in the war that the assassin experiences during his adventure create doubt that what his target is doing merits assassination.

Film's Treatment of Masculinity: Doing the things that are sometimes required of a soldier may be too much for a man to live with.

***Attack!* (1956)**

Director: Robert Aldrich

Screenplay: James Poe, based on the play by Norman Brooks

Cast: Jack Palance, Eddie Albert, Lee Marvin, Robert Strauss, Richard Jaeckel, Buddy Ebsen

DVD: MGM

Summary: This film is about a World War II U.S. National Guard infantry company commanded by a political appointee who is both grossly incompetent and cowardly. His mistakes and crucial hesitation in protecting his men cost many lives. One officer decides that the commander must pay for the deaths of these men with his own life.

Film's Treatment of Masculinity: There is no place in a fighting force for leaders without the courage and determination to lead.

***Away All Boats* (1956)**

Director: Joseph Pevney

Screenplay: Ted Sherdeman, based on the novel by Kenneth M. Dodson

CAST: Jeff Chandler, George Nader, Lex Barker, Richard Boone, Julie Adams

DVD: Good Times Video

SUMMARY: In this motion picture, a tough, demanding captain commands a new attack transport ship bound for the Pacific for the big push against Japan. In the meantime, there is an inexperienced crew and officers to train on the job, which the captain does with vigor and little subtlety. The crew is at first highly resentful, but they grow to respect the captain, and during the battle of Okinawa the hard work and training pays off.

FILM'S TREATMENT OF MASCULINITY: Manly military leaders are not paid to make friends: They must stand aloof and superior and give orders.

***Back to Bataan* (1945)**

DIRECTOR: Edward Dmytryk

SCREENPLAY: Ben Barzman, Richard H. Landau

STORY: Aeneas MacKenzie, William Gordon

CAST: John Wayne, Anthony Quinn, Beulah Bondi, Philip Ahn, Lawrence Tierney, Paul Fix

DVD: Warner Home Video

SUMMARY: In this film, a U.S. Army colonel leads a guerilla force of Filipino soldiers and civilians against the Japanese occupation. They rescue a Filipino officer—son of a famous Filipino military leader—from the Bataan Death March to assist them in their efforts and rally civilians to the cause. At first reluctant, the rescued officer witnesses the commitment of his people to the struggle and also becomes committed to the cause.

FILM'S TREATMENT OF MASCULINITY: There is no place in war for someone's personal wants and desires. A man must set this aside and do his job.

***Band of Brothers* (HBO miniseries, 2001)**

DIRECTORS: Phil Alden Robinson, Richard Loncraine, Mikael Salomon, David Nutter, Tom Hanks, David Leland, David Frankel, Tony To

SCREENPLAY: Tom Hanks, Erik Jendreson, E. Max Frye, Graham Yost, Bruce C. McKenna, Erik Bork, John Orloff

CAST: Damian Lewis, Donnie Wahlberg, Ron Livingston, Scott Grimes, Shane Taylor, Peter Youngblood Hills, Nicholas Aaron, Philip Barantini, Michael Cudlitz, Neal McDonough

DVD: HBO Home Video

SUMMARY: Based on Stephen Ambrose's history of Easy Company, 101st Airborne Division, and winner of Emmy Awards for Outstanding Miniseries and Outstanding Single Camera Sound Mixing for a

Miniseries or a Movie, this miniseries chronicles the gritty, realistic story of a group of average U.S. soldiers from paratrooper training in the United States, through their amazing experiences during D-Day, Operation Market Garden, the Battle of the Bulge, the capture of Hitler's Eagle's Nest, and the end of the war.

FILM'S TREATMENT OF MASCULINITY: Men become true brothers when they serve side by side in wars: Love of one's brother overcomes the horror of killing and provides a sense of nobility in the midst of all the slaughter.

***Bat-21* (1988)**

DIRECTOR: Peter Markle

SCREENPLAY: William C. Anderson, George Gordon, based on Anderson's book

CAST: Gene Hackman, Danny Glover, Jerry Reed, David Marshall Grant, Clayton Rohner

DVD: MGM

SUMMARY: Based on a true story of the Vietnam War, this picture details a senior officer's plane going down in Viet Cong-held territory. The officer is valuable because of his top secret knowledge, and the U.S. Air Force desperately wants to keep him from being captured. A U.S. Air Force forward air controller (FAC) pilot keeps in close contact with the officer, and they work out an escape route. After many mishaps, the officer and the now-downed FAC pilot are both rescued.

FILM'S TREATMENT OF MASCULINITY: Killing the enemy from the air can become scientific and impersonal, but "up close and personal" makes a man recalculate his occupation.

***Bataan* (1943)**

DIRECTOR: Tay Garnett

SCREENPLAY: Robert Hardy Andrews

CAST: Robert Taylor, George Murphy, Thomas Mitchell, Lloyd Nolan, Robert Walker, Desi Arnaz

DVD: MGM

SUMMARY: In this film, which picks up shortly after December 7, 1941, and the Japanese invasion of the Philippines, a collection of U.S. Army, U.S. Navy, and U.S. Army Air Corps volunteers holds a critical crossing against waves of attacking Japanese. Knowing they can't hold out for long, members of this brave squad of soldiers choose to engage in a delaying action, fighting to the last man so others have the time to escape the enemy.

FILM'S TREATMENT OF MASCULINITY: Doing one's duty is a man's job in war, and that may include sacrifices beyond the call of duty.

***Battleground* (1949)**
Director: William Wellman
Screenplay: Robert Pirosh
Cast: Van Johnson, John Hodiak, Ricardo Montalban, George Murphy, Marshall Thompson, James Whitmore
DVD: Warner Home Video
Summary: This is the Oscar-winning story of a squad of 101st Airborne soldiers in Bastogne during the Battle of the Bulge. Great characters and acting depict the hardships and everyday experiences of this exceptional group of paratroopers called the "Battling Bastards of Bastogne," who held off a German force of superior numbers and armament until units of the U.S. Army could arrive to relieve them.
Film's Treatment of Masculinity: Here we find the same masculine theme as *Band of Brothers* (2001): Men become brothers when they serve together in war.

***The Beast (of War)* (1988)**
Director: Kevin Reynolds
Screenplay: William Mastrosimone, based on Mastrosimone's play
Cast: George Dzundza, Jason Patric, Steven Bauer, Stephen Baldwin, Don Harvey
DVD: Sony Pictures
Summary: This is the story of a Soviet tank crew fighting against Mujahedeen rebels in Afghanistan. A tyrant of an NCO tank commander becomes more and more unhinged after he and his crew are separated from their squadron. Facing a mutiny, the sergeant abandons one of his tank crew in the desert, but later, both the rebels and the abandoned crewmember close in on the sergeant with revenge in mind.
Film's Treatment of Masculinity: Even though one man is in an authority position, his men should not blindly obey: War is hell, but there should still be a place for humanity.

***The Big Red One* (1980)**
Director: Samuel Fuller
Screenplay: Samuel Fuller
Cast: Lee Marvin, Mark Hamill, Robert Carradine, Bobby Di Cicco
DVD: Warner Home Video
Summary: This film tells the story of a sergeant, a veteran of World War I, and four soldiers of his squad and their adventures during World War II. Beginning with the disastrous Battle of the Kasserine Pass, these soldiers experience the war in Italy, the devastation of D-Day, an ironic firefight with the Germans in an insane asylum, and the liberation of a Nazi death camp at the end of the war.

Film's Treatment of Masculinity: Stoicism is a man's best ally in war: No amount of worry will change a soldier's fate.

***Biloxi Blues* (1988)**
Director: Mike Nichols
Screenplay: Neil Simon, based on Simon's play
Cast: Matthew Broderick, Christopher Walken, Matt Mulhern, Corey Parker, Casey Siemaszko
DVD: Universal Studios
Summary: A screenplay adaptation of Neil Simon's stage play, this is a sequel to Simon's *Brighton Beach Memoirs*. It follows the hero, Eugene, through U.S. Army basic training during World War II, as he and his friends try to survive their slightly insane drill sergeant. Eugene learns to understand and respect the many different kinds of young men in his company, who represent a cross-section of Americana.
Film's Treatment of Masculinity: There are great similarities between army basic training and a high school gym class, at least when it comes to a male pecking order.

***Birth of a Nation* (1915)**
Director: D. W. Griffith
Screenplay: Thomas F. Dixon, D. W. Griffith, Frank E. Woods, based on Dixon's novels *The Clansman* and *The Leopard's Spots*
Cast: Lillian Gish, Mae Marsh, Henry B. Walthall, Miriam Cooper, Wallace Reid
DVD: Kino Video
Summary: This is a classic D. W. Griffith epic of the American Civil War and the chaos wreaked by scallywags and carpetbaggers in the defeated South during the Reconstruction. The motion picture is famous for Griffith's revolutionary film techniques, but also infamous for Griffith's positive, heroic depiction of the Ku Klux Klan.
Film's Treatment of Masculinity: The role of honorable men in the postwar South was as protector and avenger.

***Black Hawk Down* (2001)**
Director: Ridley Scott
Screenplay: Ken Nolan, based on the book by Mark Bowden
Cast: Josh Hartnett, Ewan McGregor, Tom Sizemore, Eric Bana, William Fichtner, Sam Shepard
Academy Award Wins: Best Editing, Best Sound
DVD: Columbia Pictures
Summary: This film details the disastrous U.S. Army raid on Mogadishu, Somalia, in 1993, to capture top subordinates of Somali warlord

Muhammed Farah Aidid. The plot centers on one young U.S. Army Ranger NCO, as he and U.S. Army Special Forces troops engage in a running gun battle with hundreds of armed Aidid supporters. The film shows helicopter crashes and American casualties, including the event made famous by world news cameras when mobs dragged the dead body of a U.S. soldier through the streets of Mogadishu. The picture won dozens of awards.

Film's Treatment of Masculinity: When thrust into a leadership role, a man must set aside his self-doubt and concentrate on two things: doing his job and getting his men home safely.

***The Blue Max* (1966)**

Director: John Guillermin

Screenplay: Ben Barzman, based on the novel by Jack Hunter

Cast: George Peppard, James Mason, Ursula Andress, Jeremy Kemp, Karl Michael Vogler

DVD: 20th Century Fox

Summary: This film tells the World War I story of a common soldier who applies to be a combat aviator. He turns out to be an exceptional pilot, skillful in air combat, but the ranks of German combat aviation are reserved for aristocrats, and this commoner, despite his flying skill, is shunned by most of his comrades. Nonetheless, his success in the air leads to fame and glory and earns him the coveted Blue Max medal. But his torrid affair with the unstable wife of an aristocratic general eventually leads to his undoing and death.

Film's Treatment of Masculinity: In modern war, contrary to the outdated code of knightly chivalry, a man must be ruthless to survive and win.

***Bombardier!* (1943)**

Director: Richard Wallace

Screenplay: John Twist, Martin Rackin

Cast: Pat O'Brien, Randolph Scott, Anne Shirley, Eddie Albert, Robert Ryan

Academy Award Nomination: Best Special Effects

VHS: Warner Home Video

Summary: Beginning with standard World War II military training, all this changes into a propaganda film when bombardier trainees learn of the attack on Pearl Harbor. Now graduates, these flyers attack Japanese targets, and one bomber is shot down. The aircrew's Japanese captors are depicted as savage and murderous, torturing and killing most of the squad. But one escapes and sets fire to the Japanese compound to light the target for the bombardiers, who show off their training in an Oscar-nominated sequence of special effects destruction.

FILM'S TREATMENT OF MASCULINITY: In the face of a savage, cruel enemy, a man must be both brave and clever to succeed.

***The Boys in Company C* (1978)**

DIRECTOR: Sidney J. Furie

SCREENPLAY: Rick Natkin, Sidney J. Furie

CAST: Stan Shaw, Andrew Stevens, James Canning, Craig Wasson, James Whitmore Jr., R. Lee Ermey

DVD: Henstooth Video

SUMMARY: Anti-Vietnam War propaganda adorns this era story of a company of young men going through basic and advanced training, followed by a tour in Vietnam. In-country, these Americans learn that they can't trust their allies, the army of South Vietnam, and they become generally disdainful of the U.S. mission in Southeast Asia.

FILM'S TREATMENT OF MASCULINITY: Boys must learn to set aside childish things to become men, especially men at war. Along with this new maturity comes an understanding that shades of gray are part of human existence.

***The Bridge on the River Kwai* (1957)**

DIRECTOR: David Lean

SCREENPLAY: Carl Foreman, Michael Wilson, based on the novel *Le Pont de la Rivière Kwaï* by Pierre Boulle

CAST: William Holden, Alec Guinness, Jack Hawkins, Sessue Hayakawa, James Donald

ACADEMY AWARD WINS: Best Actor (Alec Guinness), Best Cinematography, Best Director (David Lean), Best Film Editing, Best Scoring, Best Picture, Best Screenplay Adaptation

ACADEMY AWARD NOMINATION: Best Supporting Actor (Sessue Hayakawa)

DVD: Columbia TriStar Motion Picture Group

SUMMARY: Winner of seven Oscars, this is the story of two battles of wills and personalities: the first, a British colonel stubbornly standing on principle against a Japanese colonel fanatically adhering to his code of Bushido; the other between an American slacker whose humanism and instinct to survive the war clashes with the duty he finds himself obliged to perform.

FILM'S TREATMENT OF MASCULINITY: There are times when men must stand on a point of honor, but they must guard against being too bullheaded.

***A Bridge Too Far* (1977)**
DIRECTOR: Richard Attenborough
SCREENPLAY: William Goldman, based on the book by Cornelius Ryan
CAST: Dirk Bogarde, James Caan, Michael Caine, Sean Connery, Edward Fox, Elliott Gould, Gene Hackman, Anthony Hopkins, Laurence Olivier, Ryan O'Neal, Robert Redford, Maximilian Schell
DVD: MGM
SUMMARY: This is Richard Attenborough's epic account during World War II of Field Marshall Montgomery's disastrous plan to "end the war by Christmas." An all-star cast dramatizes a factual account of Operation Market Garden, an attempt to drop thousands of Allied paratroopers into Holland and gain access to bridges across the Rhine River into Germany. A half-dozen key Allied blunders and the chance presence of two German panzer divisions in Holland foil the attempt.
FILM'S TREATMENT OF MASCULINITY: There is great nobility among men who fight on for an unwinnable objective.

***The Caine Mutiny* (1954)**
DIRECTOR: Edward Dmytryk
SCREENPLAY: Stanley Roberts, based on the novel by Herman Wouk
CAST: Humphrey Bogart, José Ferrer, Van Johnson, Fred MacMurray, Robert Francis, Tom Tully, E. G. Marshall
ACADEMY AWARD NOMINATIONS: Best Picture, Best Actor (Humphrey Bogart), Best Supporting Actor (Tom Tully), Best Screenplay, Best Film Editing, Best Scoring, Best Sound
DVD: Sony Pictures
SUMMARY: One of the first American films to deal with post-traumatic stress disorder, it's the story of the conflict between the officers and crew of a World War II mine tender and its mentally unbalanced captain, which eventually leads to a mutiny. During the court-martial and its aftermath, the officers of the USS *Caine* realize that their lack of support for their captain contributed both to his instability and the conditions that precipitated the mutiny.
FILM'S TREATMENT OF MASCULINITY: "The coward dies a thousand deaths; the brave man only once."

***Captain Newman, M.D.* (1963)**
DIRECTOR: David Miller
SCREENPLAY: Richard L. Breen, Henry Ephron, Phoebe Ephron, based on the novel by Leo Rosten
CAST: Gregory Peck, Tony Curtis, Angie Dickinson, Eddie Albert, Robert Duvall, Bobby Darin

DVD: Universal Studios

Summary: During World War II, psychiatric wards of U.S. military hospitals were filled with patients suffering from post-traumatic stress disorder (then called battle fatigue). In this film, extra beds in one such ward are filled with comical Italian prisoners of war. Through both comedic and dramatic incidents, the picture depicts life in this hospital, along with the medical staff's fears that if they cure and clear soldiers for return to active duty, they may also be sending them to their deaths.

Film's Treatment of Masculinity: There are times in war when even a brave man reaches his breaking point. For the man stricken with guilt about his shortcomings, the worst obstacle may be his own assessment of his failure to measure up.

***Casablanca* (1943)**

Director: Michael Curtiz

Screenplay: Julius J. Epstein, Philip G. Epstein, Howard Koch, based on the play *Everybody Comes to Rick's* by Joan Alison and Murray Burnett

Cast: Humphrey Bogart, Ingrid Bergman, Paul Henried, Claude Rains, Conrad Veidt, Peter Lorre, Sydney Greenstreet, Dooley Wilson

DVD: Warner Home Video

Summary: One of the greatest classic films and perhaps the best screenplay ever written, this story is set in unoccupied North Africa during World War II. Rick's Café is the setting for intrigue, black marketeering, and refugees trying to get exit visas to Lisbon and, perhaps, America. Rick meets up with two such refugees, one of whom, Ilsa, is his former lover. Against his usual neutral principles ("I stick my neck out for nobody"), Rick makes an exception and helps Ilsa and her freedom-fighting husband escape to Lisbon. As her husband Victor says to Rick, "Welcome back to the fight."

Film's Treatment of Masculinity: War requires that a man must set aside his personal feelings for the sake of a higher cause.

***Casualties of War* (1989)**

Director: Brian DePalma

Screenplay: David Rabe, based on the book by Daniel Lang

Cast: Michael J. Fox, Sean Penn, John C. Reilly, Don Harvey, John Leguizamo, Erik King

DVD: Sony Pictures

Summary: In one movie-long post-traumatic flashback, a tragic Vietnam War story unfolds, in which a long-range reconnaissance patrol kidnaps, rapes, and murders a young Vietnamese girl. One member of the patrol refuses to participate and tries to protect the girl, but he must do so at the risk of being murdered by his comrades. Eventually he turns them in, and the men are court-martialed and convicted.

Film's Treatment of Masculinity: Even in war, a man dare not abdicate his humanity: Soldiers must constantly evaluate situations to separate killing from criminality.

***Catch-22* (1970)**

Director: Mike Nichols

Screenplay: Buck Henry, based on the novel by Joseph Heller

Cast: Alan Arkin, Martin Balsam, Richard Benjamin, Art Garfunkel, Jack Gilford, Buck Henry, Bob Newhart, Anthony Perkins, Martin Sheen, Jon Voight, Orson Welles

DVD: Paramount Pictures

Summary: Buck Henry's screenplay from Joseph Heller's novel satirizes the military mentality and the military-industrial complex. This is the tale of a World War II bombardier who is desperate to be grounded and applies to the flight surgeon on the grounds that he should be grounded for medical reasons. As the screenplay puts it, "In order to be grounded, I've got to be crazy. And I must be crazy to keep flying. But if I ask to be grounded, that means I'm not crazy anymore, and I have to keep flying. . . . That's some catch, that Catch-22."

Film's Treatment of Masculinity: Doing one's manly duty is what soldiers are trained to do: To dare to question this is to question why one's country is really fighting, which they prefer you wouldn't do.

***China* (1943)**

Director: John Farrow

Screenplay: Frank Butler, based on the play by Archibald Forbes

Cast: Loretta Young, Alan Ladd, William Bendix, Philip Ahn, Richard Loo

VHS: Universal Studios

Summary: In pre–World War II China, an American oil profiteer changes from heel to freedom fighter when he meets a beautiful schoolteacher and witnesses Japanese atrocities against the Chinese people. He joins Chinese guerilla fighters and, with their help, ambushes and destroys a large Japanese Army convoy.

Film's Treatment of Masculinity: "No man is an island." True men cannot stand by while women and children are victimized. Like the knights of old, a man is expected to intervene.

***Coming Home* (1978)**

Director: Hal Ashby

Screenplay: Robert C. Jones, Waldo Salt

Story: Nancy C. Dowd
Cast: Jane Fonda, Jon Voight, Bruce Dern, Penelope Milford, Robert Carradine
Academy Award Wins: Best Actor (Jon Voight), Best Actress (Jane Fonda), Best Original Screenplay
Academy Award Nominations: Best Picture, Best Director (Hal Ashby), Best Supporting Actor (Bruce Dern), Best Supporting Actress (Penelope Milford), Best Film Editing
DVD: MGM
Summary: While her marine husband is fighting in Vietnam, a woman busies herself by volunteering in a veterans' hospital. She falls in love with a paraplegic veteran, and her whole life changes. Her husband comes home from his tour of duty, suffering from acute post-traumatic stress disorder. Realizing that he has lost his wife, and riddled with guilt for supposed atrocities he has committed in Vietnam, he commits suicide.
Film's Treatment of Masculinity: Most men go through great changes in war. Only the strong can survive it.

***Command Decision* (1948)**
Director: Sam Wood
Screenplay: William R. Laidlaw, George Froeschel, based on the play by William Wister Haines
Cast: Clark Gable, Walter Pidgeon, Van Johnson, Brian Donlevy, Charles Bickford, John Hodiak, Edward Arnold, Marshall Thompson
DVD: Warner Home Video
Summary: Army generals struggle with strategic necessity versus the huge cost in men's lives in this tale of commanders, politics, and decision making during wartime. In the end, a general makes the "right call," knowing it may cost him his command and his career.
Film's Treatment of Masculinity: As in *Twelve O'Clock High* (1949), a commanding officer's duty often means deciding to order men into battle and to their deaths. Manliness requires that these decisions be made.

***Courage under Fire* (1996)**
Director: Edward Zwick
Screenplay: Patrick Sheane Duncan
Cast: Denzel Washington, Meg Ryan, Lou Diamond Phillips, Michael Moriarty, Matt Damon
DVD: 20th Century Fox
Summary: Following the Iraq War, an army officer from the Pentagon investigates whether a female helicopter pilot should receive the Medal of Honor posthumously. But as he interviews various soldiers who

witnessed the event, he finds himself in a Rashomon-like situation: Every soldier tells a different story. Adding to this are the officer's own battles with post-traumatic stress disorder following a "friendly fire" incident during Desert Storm.

FILM'S TREATMENT OF MASCULINITY: Tragic mistakes and incidents in war often happen quickly, and only later does a man have time to consider his actions and decide how he will live with them.

***Crash Dive* (1943)**

DIRECTOR: Archie Mayo

SCREENPLAY: Jo Swerling

STORY: W. R. Burnett

CAST: Tyrone Power, Dana Andrews, Anne Baxter, James Gleason, Dame May Witty, Harry Morgan

ACADEMY AWARD WIN: Best Special Effects

DVD: 20th Century Fox

SUMMARY: A young PT boat skipper is reassigned to submarine duty and regrets it, but in between chasing the captain's girlfriend and experiencing new adventures in the silent service, the officer changes his mind about sub duty. In the end, all is forgiven about the love triangle, and the submariners engage in a secret mission to destroy a German supply base.

FILM'S TREATMENT OF MASCULINITY: In war, men must set aside their differences and do their duty, working together as a team.

***Crimson Tide* (1995)**

DIRECTOR: Tony Scott

SCREENPLAY: Michael Schiffer, Richard P. Henrick

CAST: Denzel Washington, Gene Hackman, Matt Craven, George Dzundza, Viggo Mortensen, James Gandolfini

ACADEMY AWARD NOMINATIONS: Best Film Editing, Best Sound, Best Sounds Effects Editing

DVD: Hollywood Pictures Home Entertainment

SUMMARY: This Oscar-nominated film depicts a conflict of wills between a submarine captain who's used to absolute, unthinking obedience from his crew and the sub's new executive officer. The conflict comes to a head when the sub receives an incomplete transmission ordering them to launch nuclear missiles.

FILM'S TREATMENT OF MASCULINITY: Even in war, humanity requires that one's clearly defined duty be reconsidered in light of unusual circumstances. Obstinate, robotic adherence to rules and procedures can cause tragedy for all.

***Cross of Iron* (1976)**

DIRECTOR: Sam Peckinpah

SCREENPLAY: Julius J. Epstein, James Hamilton, Walter Kelley, based on the novel *The Willing Flesh* by Willi Heinrich

CAST: James Coburn, Maximilian Schell, James Mason, David Warner

DVD: Henstooth Video

SUMMARY: In 1943, on the Russian front, an arrogant, aristocratic replacement officer reports for duty with a single goal: to earn Germany's Iron Cross, a medal awarded for valor. Unfortunately, he is not well suited for combat, and he spends most of his time hiding away in his bunker. But when he claims to have heroically led a counterattack against the Russians, an action that would lead to earning his Iron Cross, the officer comes into conflict with a sergeant who knows the truth and refuses to go along with him.

FILM'S TREATMENT OF MASCULINITY: To true fighting men, a badge of honor must be earned the hard way, with bullets and blood.

***Das Boot* (1981)**

DIRECTOR: Wolfgang Petersen

SCREENPLAY: Wolfgang Petersen, based on the novel by Lothar G. Buchheim

CAST: Jürgen Prochnow, Herbert Grönemeyer, Klaus Wennemann, Erwin Leder, Hubertus Bengsch

ACADEMY AWARD NOMINATIONS: Best Director (Wolfgang Petersen), Best Screenplay Adaptation, Best Editing, Best Cinematography, Best Sound Effects Editing, Best Sound

DVD: Sony Pictures

SUMMARY: This nearly four-hour-long saga uses a semidocumentary style to chronicle a mission on board a German submarine during World War II. Seen from the point of view of a military journalist on board a sub for the first time, the gritty, grueling everyday life of a submariner is shown as the crew narrowly avoids death in a daring raid near Gibraltar. Thinking that they had survived a close call, the crew limps the sub back to its home port, where it is bombed and sunk, and many of the squad are strafed and killed by an Allied air attack.

FILM'S TREATMENT OF MASCULINITY: Regardless of whose country is right in a war, fighting men must still do their duty and rely on each other to get back home safely (as ironic as that is in this particular film).

***The Deer Hunter* (1978)**

DIRECTOR: Michael Cimino

SCREENPLAY: Deric Washburn

STORY: Michael Cimino, Louis Garfinkle, based on the short story by Quinn Redeker

Cast: Robert De Niro, John Cazale, John Savage, Meryl Streep, Christopher Walken, George Dzundza

Academy Award Wins: Best Picture, Best Director (Michael Cimino), Best Supporting Actor (Christopher Walken), Best Film Editing, Best Sound

Academy Award Nominations: Best Leading Actor (Robert De Niro), Best Supporting Actress (Meryl Streep), Best Cinematography, Best Screenplay

DVD: MCA/Universal Home Video

Summary: This Oscar-winning film takes three young men from their hometown to the horrors of Vietnam and back again. The two survivors, one disabled, try as best they can to adjust to life after the war, to the loss of their deceased friend, and to the meaning of it all.

Film's Treatment of Masculinity: As in *Captain Newman, M.D.* (1963), good men can reach a breaking point in war, and it is no dishonor to suffer from post-traumatic stress disorder or survivor guilt.

***Destination Tokyo* (1943)**

Director: Delmer Daves

Screenplay: Delmer Daves, Albert Maltz, based on the story by Steve Fisher

Cast: Cary Grant, John Garfield, Alan Hale, John Ridgely, Dane Clark, Robert Hutton

DVD: Warner Home Video

Summary: This is the Oscar-nominated story of a World War II U.S. submarine on a mission to sneak into Tokyo harbor to obtain weather and other intelligence information to support the Doolittle bombing raid on Tokyo. The screenplay by Delmer Daves and Albert Maltz provides not-too-subtle propaganda against the enemy, the Japanese.

Film's Treatment of Masculinity: Young men grow up in war and learn lessons about manhood, honor, and bravery that they don't teach at the submarine academy.

***The D.I.* (1957)**

Director: Jack Webb

Screenplay: James Lee Barrett

Cast: Jack Webb, Don Dubbins, Lin McCarthy, Jackie Loughery, Monica Lewis, Virginia Gregg

DVD: Warner Archives

Summary: A tough-as-nails drill instructor has a problem: a foul-up recruit named Owens. He's convinced that Owens will make a good marine, but the young man can't seem to get out of his own way. Faced with a three-day deadline imposed by his company commander, the DI has to straighten up the young man or else.

Film's Treatment of Masculinity: To become a warrior, a transition must be made from boyhood to manhood.

***The Dirty Dozen* (1967)**

Director: Robert Aldrich

Screenplay: Nunnally Johnson, Lukas Heller, based on the novel by E. M. Nathanson

Cast: Lee Marvin, John Cassavetes, Charles Bronson, Jim Brown, George Kennedy, Telly Savalas, Donald Sutherland, Ernest Borgnine, Robert Ryan

Academy Award Win: Best Sound Effects

Academy Award Nominations: Best Supporting Actor (John Cassavetes), Best Film Editing, Best Sound

DVD: MGM

Summary: An insubordinate U.S. Army major is assigned the task of training and leading a group of bedraggled, rebellious convicts on a dangerous mission behind German lines right before D-Day.

Film's Treatment of Masculinity: There is a fine line separating killing from criminality. Men must learn the difference.

***Dr. Strangelove: Or How I Learned to Stop Worrying and Love the Bomb* (1964)**

Director: Stanley Kubrick

Screenplay: Stanley Kubrick, Terry Southern, Peter George, based on the novel *Red Alert* by Peter George

Cast: Peter Sellers (playing three characters), George C. Scott, Sterling Hayden, Slim Pickens, Keenan Wynn, James Earl Jones

Academy Award Nominations: Best Picture, Best Director (Stanley Kubrick), Best Actor (Peter Sellers), Best Screenplay Adaptation

DVD: Sony Pictures

Summary: During the Cold War, an insane general orders a B-52 wing to attack the Soviet Union with nuclear weapons. The president, his general staff, and the Russians all try to keep the unthinkable from happening, but their own hubris and stupidity cause them to fail. The film includes incredible performances by Peter Sellers, George C. Scott, and Sterling Hayden and is considered Stanley Kubrick's masterpiece.

Film's Treatment of Masculinity: Men must learn the difference between testosterone-fueled aggression and valid defense of one's own country and people.

***Eagle Squadron* (1942)**

Director: Arthur Lubin

Screenplay: Norman Reilly Raine
Story: C. S. Forester
Cast: Robert Stack, Diana Barrymore, Jon Hall, Eddie Albert, Nigel Bruce, John Loder
Summary: In this propaganda film designed to convince the American people that the United States should support their ally in the Battle of Britain, a headstrong young American pilot joins the Eagle Squadron, the contingent of U.S. flyers who enlisted in the Royal Air Force before their country declared war on Germany. Through his experiences, American audiences were shown Britain's desperate circumstances and their brave fight against the German onslaught.
Film's Treatment of Masculinity: Teamwork is essential if the enemy is to be defeated. A man must set aside his wants and desires for the greater good.

***Edge of Darkness* (1943)**
Director: Lewis Milestone
Screenplay: Robert Rossen, based on the novel by William Woods
Cast: Errol Flynn, Ann Sheridan, Walter Huston, Helmut Dantine, Judith Anderson, Ruth Gordon
DVD: Warner Home Video
Summary: This is a U.S. anti-Nazi propaganda film about the decision the people of a Norwegian fishing village had to make in the face of German occupation. They could either meekly and selfishly comply with their conquerors, as the German commander believes they will, or rise up as one to crush the invaders. The Nazis make the townspeople's decision easy by acting "normally," that is, mistreating and assaulting the villagers, goading them into collective action.
Film's Treatment of Masculinity: A man can only look the other way and serve his own interests for so long before a point is reached when he must act.

***84 Charlie Mopic* (1989)**
Director: Patrick Sheane Duncan
Screenplay: Patrick Sheane Duncan
Cast: Jonathan Emerson, Richard Brooks, Nicholas Cascone, Jason Tomlins, Christopher Burgard, Glenn Morshower, Byron Thames
VHS: Sony Pictures
Summary: Filmed in documentary style, entirely from the point of view of "Mopic," a combat cameraman, this gritty film documents an Army reconnaissance patrol during the Vietnam War. An Army PR camera team composed of an officer and a film cameraman accompanies a

squad of skilled but misfit soldiers on a dangerous mission. Tensions arise between the sergeant, "O.D.," responsible for the mission, and the officer, untrained and unsuited for "the bush." The patrol encounters a mostly invisible enemy and loses some of the men.

FILM'S TREATMENT OF MASCULINITY: A conflict between bloodied and skilled reconnaissance patrol "bush" veterans and the "F.N.G." officer and cameraman thrust upon them by headquarters becomes a metaphorical contrast between fully matured males and nonmen who have yet to earn their majority.

***The Enemy Below* (1957)**

DIRECTOR: Dick Powell

SCREENPLAY: Wendell Mayes, based on the novel by D. A. Rayner

CAST: Robert Mitchum, Curt Jurgens, David Hedison, Theodore Bikel, Russell Collins

ACADEMY AWARD WIN: Best Special Effects

DVD: 20th Century Fox

SUMMARY: This is the story of a classic World War II battle of wits between the skillful, crafty captains of a U.S. destroyer and a German submarine. The American captain is new to this ship and must earn the trust and respect of his crew. The German submarine captain is tired of war and unsympathetic to the Nazis but painfully determined to do his duty. Both vessels fight to a draw, as each ship destroys the other. But the surviving crews set aside their belligerence and help rescue their captains, who stay on board their vessels until the very end.

FILM'S TREATMENT OF MASCULINITY: Experienced, bloodied fighting men develop a stoic determinism about themselves and war. The best of them do their jobs as well as they can and try to act honorably, while harboring no illusions about the importance or meaning of it all.

***The Fighting Seabees* (1944)**

DIRECTOR: Edward Ludwig

SCREENPLAY: Borden Chase, Aeneas MacKenzie

CAST: John Wayne, Dennis O'Keefe, Susan Hayward, William Frawley, Paul Fix

DVD: Republic Pictures

SUMMARY: A World War II propaganda film, this story involves a construction company building installations in the Pacific for the U.S. Navy, faced with the difficulty of doing heavy construction while Japanese forces try to prevent them from doing so. In response, the navy creates Construction Battalions and recruits and trains these skilled workers to build and then fight to protect the installations they create. Through the experiences and mistakes made by one obnoxious contractor turned Seabee officer, the virtue of cooperation between nominal civilians and the military is preached.

FILM'S TREATMENT OF MASCULINITY: A fighting man must control his lust for personal revenge in war: This is immature, counterproductive, and not worthy of a true soldier.

***The Fighting 69th* (1940)**

DIRECTOR: William Keighley

SCREENPLAY: Norman Reilly Raine, Fred Niblo Jr., Dean Franklin

CAST: James Cagney, Pat O'Brien, George Brent, Jeffrey Lynn, Alan Hale, Frank McHugh, Dennis Morgan

DVD: Warner Home Video

SUMMARY: In this World War I story of the soldiers of this famous regiment, one man stands out: a brash, undisciplined egotist, seemingly spoiling for a fight and convinced he'll come home from the war draped in medals and commendations. But when the outfit finds itself in the trenches, the young trooper suddenly acts like a coward. Given a second chance, he does worse, causing some of his buddies to be killed. Finally, behind the lines, waiting for court-martial, he escapes, returns to the front, fights, and dies courageously.

FILM'S TREATMENT OF MASCULINITY: No man truly knows how he will act and react in battle: He can only try to overcome his fear and do his duty.

***Fixed Bayonets* (1951)**

DIRECTOR: Samuel Fuller

SCREENPLAY: Samuel Fuller, based on the novel by John Brophy

CAST: Richard Basehart, Gene Evans, Michael O'Shea, Richard Hylton, Craig Hill, Skip Homeier

DVD: 20th Century Fox

SUMMARY: Fighting the Korean War, Cpl. Denno is afraid of little, except the responsibility of command. An officer candidate school washout, Denno obeys orders but is unable to give them. His platoon is tasked with a rear guard action to delay the North Koreans so that his battalion can safely withdraw across a river, but as fate (and screenwriter Samuel Fuller) would have it, one by one, all of Denno's superior officers and sergeants are killed, leaving him the ranking man and charged with giving the orders. Denno faces his demons, makes some hard choices, and does the right thing, saving the battalion and most of his men.

FILM'S TREATMENT OF MASCULINITY: Fear takes many forms in war, including the concern that one's failure as a leader could cost lives. A man can only step up when called upon to lead and make the best decisions he can.

***Flags of Our Fathers* (2006)**
DIRECTOR: Clint Eastwood
SCREENPLAY: William Broyles Jr., Paul Haggis, based on the book by James Bradley, with Ron Powers
CAST: Ryan Phillippe, Jesse Bradford, Adam Beach, John Benjamin Hickey, John Slattery, Barry Pepper, Paul Walker
DVD: Dreamworks Video
SUMMARY: This story is based on the lives of three famous men, two marines and a navy corpsman. They are the three survivors of the six men who raised the U.S. flag over Mt. Suribachi on Iwo Jima immortalized in Joe Rosenthal's Pulitzer Prize-winning photograph. Pulled out of the fighting, exploited as heroes, and sent on war bond tours, two of the three have great difficulty dealing with their fame. Burdened with survivor guilt, whenever they were asked about the battle, all three credit their buddies who died on Iwo Jima.
FILM'S TREATMENT OF MASCULINITY: Out of both humility and survivor guilt, many men cannot wear the mantle of hero comfortably. Ultimately, all who fight and do their duty are heroes.

***Flyboys* (2006)**
DIRECTOR: Tony Bill
SCREENPLAY: Phil Sears, Blake T. Evans, David S. Ward
CAST: James Franco, Martin Henderson, Jean Reno, David Ellison, Jennifer Decker, Abdul Salis
DVD: MGM
SUMMARY: This is a fact-based story of a group of young Americans who join the French Air Force during World War I. Members of the Lafayette Escadrille, as the U.S. contingent of the French Air Force was called, learn to fly and fight against the Germans prior to the entrance of the United States into the war.
FILM'S TREATMENT OF MASCULINITY: Men choose to go to war for many different reasons, but when they all don the uniform, reasons don't matter. Combat is the same for all, and death is just as final.

***Flying Leathernecks* (1951)**
DIRECTOR: Nicholas Ray
SCREENPLAY: James Edward Grant
STORY: Kenneth Gamet
CAST: John Wayne, Robert Ryan, Don Taylor, J. C. Flippen, Janis Carter
DVD: Warner Home Video

Summary: A marine squadron commander proves his theory of close air support of ground forces while he tries to "toughen up" his executive officer, who is too close to his men to make sound, hard-nosed decisions. Typical for this kind of John Wayne 1950s war film (think *Sands of Iwo Jima*), finally, the subordinate adopts the mind-set and values of his superior and merits a promotion to squadron commander.

Film's Treatment of Masculinity: True leaders, and thus the manliest of men, must remain aloof and apparently unemotional, otherwise they cannot see their way clear to make the hard decisions that may lead to the deaths of their men.

***Flying Tigers* (1942)**

Director: David Miller

Screenplay: Kenneth Gamet, Barry Trivers

Cast: John Wayne, John Carroll, Anna Lee, Paul Kelly, Gordon Jones, Mae Clarke, Edmund MacDonald

Academy Award Nominations: Best Scoring of a Dramatic or Comedy Picture, Best Visual Effects, Best Sound

DVD: Republic Pictures

Summary: This film tells the story of a band of American mercenaries who, like the Lafayette Escadrille against the Germans in World War I, joined the Chinese Air Force to fight the Japanese prior to Pearl Harbor and the entrance of the United States into the war. The plot centers on a selfish, playboy pilot whose actions threaten good squadron discipline and even result in the death of a comrade. Finally, under the influence of John Wayne's character, the pilot realizes his mistakes and atones for his sins, flying a suicide mission.

Film's Treatment of Masculinity: Without teamwork, a military unit becomes chaotic. A man must set aside his petty wants and desires for the good of the unit.

***The Frogmen* (1951)**

Director: Lloyd Bacon

Screenplay: John Tucker Battle

Story: Oscar Millard

Cast: Richard Widmark, Dana Andrews, Gary Merrill, Jeffrey Hunter, Robert Wagner

Academy Award Nominatations: Best Motion Picture Story, Best Cinematography (Black and White)

DVD: 20th Century Fox

Summary: The new commander of a team of frogmen, called underwater demolition experts, who in World War II performed many watery tasks done today by the U.S. Navy SEALs, mourns the death of their commander. Enter the commander's replacement, an officer quite different from the laid-back, devil-may-care "skipper" his men grew to admire and care for. The new skipper manages the team "by the book," rubbing the men the wrong way. After a rough start, the commander earns his men's respect.

FILM'S TREATMENT OF MASCULINITY: Leadership by example can overcome many social differences when a new commander takes over a fighting unit. Men lead well when they themselves can demonstrate what they require of their men.

***From Here to Eternity* (1953)**

DIRECTOR: Fred Zinnemann

SCREENPLAY: Daniel Taradash, based on the novel by James Jones

CAST: Burt Lancaster, Montgomery Clift, Deborah Kerr, Donna Reed, Frank Sinatra, Ernest Borgnine

ACADEMY AWARD WINS: Best Picture, Best Director (Fred Zinnemann), Best Screenplay, Best Supporting Actor (Frank Sinatra), Best Supporting Actress (Donna Reed), Best Sound, Best Film Editing, Best Cinematography (Black and White)

ACADEMY AWARD NOMINATIONS: Best Leading Actor (Montgomery Clift), Best Leading Actor (Burt Lancaster), Best Leading Actress (Deborah Kerr), Best Costume Design, Best Scoring of a Dramatic or Comedy Picture

DVD: Sony Pictures

SUMMARY: This Oscar-winning adaptation of the National Book Award-winning James Jones novel tells the story of a group of people in and around Schofield Barracks in Hawaii in the months just prior to the attack on Pearl Harbor. One hardheaded soldier, an expert boxer, refuses easy duty and promotion because he refuses to fight anymore. Meanwhile, his first sergeant is having an affair with the neglected wife of his company commander, and a young GI ends up in the stockade, tortured by a sadistic jailer. No one wins.

FILM'S TREATMENT OF MASCULINITY: Without necessarily answering the question, the film asks when a man should stubbornly stand on his beliefs and when he should compromise.

***Full Metal Jacket* (1987)**

DIRECTOR: Stanley Kubrick

SCREENPLAY: Stanley Kubrick, Michael Herr, Gustav Hasford, based on the novel *The Short Timers* by Hasford

CAST: Matthew Modine, Adam Baldwin, Vincent D'Onofrio, R. Lee Ermey, Arliss Howard

ACADEMY AWARD NOMINATION: Best Adapted Screenplay

DVD: Warner Home Video

SUMMARY: This Oscar-nominated motion picture represents Stanley Kubrick's unique version of the adventures of the Vietnam generation in "their war." As with *Dr. Strangelove* (1964), Kubrick provides his typical sarcastic and critical views of the military and its leadership as he relates the adventures of a character nicknamed "Joker" and his friend, "Cowboy," from basic training to combat during the Tet Offensive of 1968.

FILM'S TREATMENT OF MASCULINITY: Regardless of the insanity of war and the equally insane nature of his leadership, a good, manly marine does his duty, fights, and perhaps dies a trained, lethal weapon of war.

***Gallipoli* (1981)**

DIRECTOR: Peter Weir

SCREENPLAY: Peter Weir, David Williamson, Ernest Raymond (uncredited)

CAST: Mel Gibson, Mark Lee, Harold Hopkins, Heath Harris, Robert Grubb

AWARDS: Nominated for 12 Australian Film Institute Awards; won 8, including best picture

DVD: Paramount Pictures

SUMMARY: At a track meet in the Australian outback, champion Archy Hamilton meets a runner almost as fast as he: Frank Dunne. The two join the Australian Army to fight in World War I. After training, these friends and their mates find themselves in the middle of one of the worst disasters of the war, the bloody Allied assault against the Turks at Gallipoli. Finally, their unit's survival boils down to whether one of these young men, assigned as dispatch runners, can get a message to their commander in time to prevent a needless slaughter of Australian soldiers.

FILM'S TREATMENT OF MASCULINITY: At one point in the picture, Archy overhears the "Jungle Book" story about growing up, becoming a man, and leaving his family. This and Archy's belief about courage—that man becomes a man when he steps up to defend his country when it's under attack—are the reasons he leaves his home, ranch, and family and volunteers for the Army.

***Gardens of Stone* (1987)**

DIRECTOR: Francis Ford Coppola

SCREENPLAY: Ronald Bass, based on the novel by Nicholas Proffitt

CAST: James Caan, James Earl Jones, Anjelica Huston, D. B. Sweeney, Dean Stockwell, Mary Stuart Masterson

DVD: Sony Pictures

SUMMARY: During the Vietnam War, two veteran U.S. Army sergeants take a young soldier—the son of an old Army buddy—under their wing to prepare him and his comrades to survive in the jungles of Vietnam. Survival is uppermost on the minds of these two veterans of multiple tours of duty in Vietnam, because they are members of the company known as the "Old Guard," tasked with guarding the tombs and burying soldiers at Arlington National Cemetery. Unfortunately, at this most deadly point of the war, business at the cemetery, which the men call the "Garden," is brisk.

FILM'S TREATMENT OF MASCULINITY: Such cemeteries as Arlington remind all men that death, although inevitable, is still death, and that in war, men and women still mourn.

***Gettysburg* (1993)**

DIRECTOR: Ronald F. Maxwell

SCREENPLAY: Ronald F. Maxwell, based on the novel by Michael Shaara

CAST: Tom Berenger, Jeff Daniels, Martin Sheen, Sam Elliot, Kevin Conway, C. Thomas Howell, Stephen Lang, Richard Jordan, Andrew Prine

DVD: Warner Home Video

SUMMARY: This file depicts the epic Civil War battle as seen from the perspectives of the many Confederate generals in service to Gen. Robert E. Lee and numerous Union officers, especially Brig. Gen. John Buford and Col. Joshua Lawrence Chamberlain. Featured are Buford's skillful and insightful stand on the first day, giving the Union Army a commanding position, Chamberlain's gallant defense of Little Round Top on the second day, and the decisive Union Victory after Gen. Pickett's charge on the third day.

FILM'S TREATMENT OF MASCULINITY: In history, men have fought for many reasons, but sometimes their motivations are nobler. Such satisfaction is especially motivating to the soldier.

***G.I. Jane* (1997)**

DIRECTOR: Ridley Scott

SCREENPLAY: David Twohy and Danielle Alexandra

CAST: Demi Moore, Viggo Mortensen, Anne Bancroft, Jason Beghe, James Caviezel

DVD: Walt Disney Video

SUMMARY: A U.S. senator with a feminist political agenda manages to place a female officer in Navy SEAL training, which has heretofore been reserved only for males. The officer, Jordan O'Neill, must overcome male prejudice as well as herself to succeed in this rigorous form of training. Later, on an actual mission, O'Neill distinguishes herself, rescuing the SEAL who has been her chief critic throughout training.

FILM'S TREATMENT OF MASCULINITY: One of main reasons SEAL trainer Master Chief Urgayle is prejudiced against Lt. O'Neill is because he fears that in a life-or-death situation, a woman can't pull her own weight, and that men could die because of it. His prejudice stems from the macho ethic of the SEALs, that only manly men are cut out—mentally and physically—to do the physically and mentally demanding work of a SEAL.

***Glory* (1989)**

DIRECTOR: Edward Zwick

SCREENPLAY: Kevin Jarre

CAST: Matthew Broderick, Denzel Washington, Morgan Freeman, Andre Braugher, Cary Elwes

ACADEMY AWARDS: Best Actor in a Supporting Role (Washington), Best Cinematography, Best Sound

ACADEMY AWARD NOMINATIONS: Best Film Editing, Best Art Direction-Set Decoration

DVD: Columbia/Tristar/Sony Pictures

SUMMARY: Based on the memoirs of Col. Robert Shaw, this Civil War film dramatizes the story of the Union's first all-African American regiment, the Massachusetts 54th. Col. Shaw, a bloodied veteran of the battle of Antietam, leads his men through their training, overcoming white Army prejudice, a death sentence levied by the Confederacy on all black soldiers, and the Union Army's refusal to allow the 54th to fight in a real battle. Finally the 54th gets its chance, and the men distinguish themselves in battle. The film ends in the bloody battle for Fort Wagner, South Carolina, as Shaw and half his regiment lose their lives in a gallant assault, proving conclusively their worth as soldiers and men.

FILM'S TREATMENT OF MASCULINITY: Cpl. Thomas Searles is an educated black man raised in the effete, overly polite, literary society of Boston. Faced with the rigors of Army basic training and bullied by both his racist drill sergeant and a black soldier, Pvt. Trip, Searles can't take it. Searles's story in this film is about coming to grips with requirements of manhood not found in his philosophy books.

***God Is My Co-Pilot* (1945)**

DIRECTOR: Robert Florey

SCREENPLAY: Peter Milne, Abem Finkel, based on the book by Robert L. Scott Jr.

CAST: Dennis Morgan, Dane Clark, Raymond Massey, Alan Hale, John Ridgely, Richard Loo

DVD: Warner Archives

SUMMARY: Based on his novelized memoirs of World War II, Robert L. Scott tells his tale as a U.S. Air Corps officer who persuades Gen. Claire Chennault, commander of China's Flying Tigers (see film synopsis above for the movie of the same name) to allow him to fly and fight alongside Chennault's squadron. Scott learns the successful aerial tactics of the Tigers and, in the end, shoots down the fictional Japanese ace known as "Tokyo Joe."

FILM'S TREATMENT OF MASCULINITY: Men can defeat other men in war for many reasons. Brute strength and force of numbers do not always prevail if one's opponent is cleverer.

***Gods and Generals* (2003)**

DIRECTOR: Ronald F. Maxwell

SCREENPLAY: Ronald F. Maxwell, based on the novel by Jeff Shaara

CAST: Jeff Daniels, Stephen Lang, Robert Duvall, Kevin Conway, C. Thomas Howell, Mira Sorvino

DVD: Warner Home Video

SUMMARY: The prequel to *Gettysburg* (1993) (see synopsis above) but released ten years later, this is the second installment in Ronald F. Maxwell's adaptation of Jeff Shaara's Civil War novel of the same name. There was to be a third installment, but plans for the production have been shelved indefinitely. This film begins with then-Col. Robert E. Lee turning down command of the Union Army at the outset of the war, but it primarily concerns the rise to power and fame of Gen. Thomas "Stonewall" Jackson, as he commands Confederate troops in the battles of Manassas, Fredericksburg, and later Chancellorsville, where he was mortally wounded.

FILM'S TREATMENT OF MASCULINITY: A man can act more bravely in battle if he adopts a stoic, deterministic view of his mortality. Realizing he can't know God's will about the time and place of his demise, a man can free his mind to more calmly do his duty.

***Go for Broke!* (1951)**

DIRECTOR: Robert Pirosh

SCREENPLAY: Robert Pirosh

CAST: Van Johnson, Lane Nakano, George Miki, Akira Fukunaga, Ken Okamoto

ACADEMY AWARD NOMINATION: Best Screenplay

DVD: Various distributors

Summary: This motion picture tells the story of the highly decorated World War II 442nd Regimental Combat Team, composed of Japanese American volunteers who chose to fight for their adopted country rather than sit out the war in internment camps. From the point of view of a prejudiced Caucasian officer from Texas, these Japanese soldiers could not possibly be as good as the white Americans. But as the officer witnesses the skill, pluck, and bravery of the men, his opinion radically changes. Finally, the officer comes to the conclusion that the men of the 442nd are better soldiers than he is.

Film's Treatment of Masculinity: The best officer learns to evaluate his men without prejudice, relying instead on his men's bravery, intelligence, and strength of character.

***Gone with the Wind* (1939)**

Directors: Victor Fleming (uncredited: George Cukor, Sam Wood)

Screenplay: Sidney Howard (uncredited: Oliver H. P. Garrett, Ben Hecht, Jo Swerling, John Van Druten), based on the novel by Margaret Mitchell

Cast: Clark Gable, Vivien Leigh, Leslie Howard, Olivia de Havilland, Thomas Mitchell, Hattie McDaniel

Academy Award Wins: Best Picture, Best Director (Victor Fleming), Best Actress (Vivien Leigh), Best Supporting Actress (Hattie McDaniel), Best Screenplay, Best Film Editing, Best Cinematography, Best Art Direction

Academy Award Nominations: Best Leading Actor (Clark Gable), Best Supporting Actress (Olivia de Havilland), Best Special Effects, Best Original Score, Best Sound

DVD: Warner Home Video

Summary: This classic adaptation of the Margaret Mitchell novel follows heroine Scarlett O'Hara through the Civil War, as she relentlessly and selfishly pursues the man of her dreams, Ashley Wilkes, who's married to her cousin, Melanie. Scarlett is persuaded to marry the dashing Rhett Butler, but she can't get Wilkes out of her mind. Finally, she decides that Butler is the one for her, but by then, Butler has had enough and speaks his classic exit line, "Frankly, my dear, I don't give a damn."

Film's Treatment of Masculinity: What a man, or a woman, for that matter, wants and truly needs in life is often contradictory. A man must learn the difference to be able to judge wisely.

***The Green Berets* (1968)**

Directors: Ray Kellogg, John Wayne (uncredited: Mervyn LeRoy)

SCREENPLAY: James Lee Barrett, based on the novel by Robin Moore
CAST: John Wayne, David Janssen, Jim Hutton, Aldo Ray, Bruce Cabot, Jack Soo, George Takei
DVD: Warner Home Video
SUMMARY: Perhaps the worst of the few pro-Vietnam War propaganda films, this obvious defense of an indefensible Vietnam policy centers on the men of the U.S. Army's Special Forces on missions to defend a firebase and kidnap a North Vietnamese general. The movie ends spectacularly, as one sarcastic review puts it: "The sun slowly sets into the East."
FILM'S TREATMENT OF MASCULINITY: Well-trained man can overcome obstacles through teamwork and dedication.

***Guadalcanal Diary* (1943)**
DIRECTOR: Lewis Seiler
SCREENPLAY: Lamar Trotti, Jerome Cady, based on the book by Richard Tregaskis
CAST: Preston Foster, Lloyd Nolan, William Bendix, Richard Conte, Anthony Quinn, Richard Jaeckel, Lionel Stander
DVD: 20th Century Fox
SUMMARY: Based on American war correspondent Richard Tregaskis's fact-based book, this film follows a marine company on the campaign to take the island of Guadalcanal, the first major Allied land offensive against the Japanese in World War II. Concentrating on the men's personal experiences and interactions, the marines mature into combat veterans as they face combat with a fierce and treacherous enemy.
FILM'S TREATMENT OF MASCULINITY: Manly maturity comes quickly under fire; discipline, remembering one's training, and following orders can make the difference between victory and death.

***Gung Ho!* (1943)**
DIRECTOR: Ray Enright
SCREENPLAY: Lucien Hubbard, Joseph Hoffman
STORY: W. S. LeFrancois
CAST: Randolph Scott, Alan Curtis, Noah Beery Jr., J. Carrol Naish, Sam Levene, Robert Mitchum
DVD: Various distributors
SUMMARY: Based on the true story of Carlson's U.S. Marine Raiders, this film recounts the recruitment of a special battalion of U.S. Marines whose mission is to approach Japanese-held islands by stealth and wipe out their garrisons. Like *Guadalcanal Diary* (1943), the motion picture includes scenes of intensive training, followed by a danger-

ous submarine journey and the marines' famous assault on Makin Island.

FILM'S TREATMENT OF MASCULINITY: Men have no choice but to mature quickly when their lives are at stake on the battlefield.

***The Guns of Navarone* (1961)**

DIRECTOR: J. Lee Thompson

SCREENPLAY: Carl Foreman, based on the novel by Alistair MacLean

CAST: Gregory Peck, David Niven, Anthony Quinn, Stanley Baker, Anthony Quayle, James Darren, Irene Papas

ACADEMY AWARD WIN: Best Special Effects

ACADEMY AWARD NOMINATIONS: Best Picture, Best Director (J. Lee Thompson), Best Screenplay, Best Film Editing, Best Scoring of a Dramatic or Comedy Picture, Best Sound, Best Screenplay Adaptation

DVD: Sony Pictures

SUMMARY: Based on Alistair MacLean's novel, this high adventure involves a British commando team and Greek partisans tasked with taking out a pair of massive cannons threatening the evacuation of 2,000 British troops from Kiros, an Aegean island. Built into the side of a mountain and highly fortified, the target becomes even more difficult to destroy when a traitor tips off the Germans to their every move. Finally, the traitor is discovered and dispatched and the objective destroyed.

FILM'S TREATMENT OF MASCULINITY: When does a warrior act too ruthlessly? Should he abandon humanistic values entirely?

***A Guy Named Joe* (1943)**

DIRECTOR: Victor Fleming

SCREENPLAY: Dalton Trumbo, Frederick Hazlett Brennan

STORY: Chandler Sprague, David Boehm

CAST: Spencer Tracy, Irene Dunne, Van Johnson, Ward Bond, James Gleason, Lionel Barrymore

VHS: MGM

SUMMARY: This is a fantasy film about a World War II bomber pilot killed near the beginning of the film who returns as a spirit mentor (read guardian angel) of a newly commissioned P-38 pilot. Under the "angel's" guidance, the new pilot advances in flying and combat skills and becomes an ace. Complicating matters is the fact that the young aviator begins romancing his own angel's girlfriend.

FILM'S TREATMENT OF MASCULINITY: A man must set aside his wants and needs for the good of the mission.

***Hamburger Hill* (1987)**
DIRECTOR: John Irvin
SCREENPLAY: James Carabatsos
CAST: Steven Weber, Dylan McDermott, Courtney B. Vance, Don Cheadle, Michael Boatman, Anthony Barrile
DVD: Lions Gate
SUMMARY: This is the bloody but truthful recreation of the 1969 battle for a nameless hill in the A Shau Valley of Vietnam between soldiers of the U.S. 101st Airborne and North Vietnamese soldiers, told mostly through the characters of one 101st squad. Between assaults on the hill, the Americans reveal the thoughts of the young soldiers of the Vietnam era. This film conveys their feelings of camaraderie, awkwardly mixed with the conflicts between their various personal backgrounds and force-blended American cultures, especially between the "brothers" of the company (the Black soldiers) and the rest of the men. Eventually, these differences blend into a brotherhood-in-arms.
FILM'S TREATMENT OF MASCULINITY: Young men must mature under fire, set aside their cultural differences, and learn to care for each other.

***Hanover Street* (1979)**
DIRECTOR: Peter Hyams
SCREENPLAY: Peter Hyams
CAST: Harrison Ford, Lesley-Anne Down, Christopher Plummer, Richard Masur, Patsy Kensit
DVD: Sony Pictures
SUMMARY: Romance and action blend awkwardly with an interesting discussion of how circumstance creates heroes in this film about a World War II-era illicit romance between a U.S. bomber pilot and a married British woman. The plot becomes complicated when the pilot realizes that as his plane is shot down over occupied France, the British spy with whom he has parachuted to safety is his lover's husband.
FILM'S TREATMENT OF MASCULINITY: A fighting man's worth is best measured by his deeds, and all deeds in support of the mission should be equally valued. "He also serves who stands and waits."

***Heartbreak Ridge* (1986)**
DIRECTOR: Clint Eastwood
SCREENPLAY: James Carabatsos
CAST: Clint Eastwood, Marsha Mason, Everett McGill, Mario Van Peebles, Moses Gunn
DVD: Warner Home Video

SUMMARY: Eastwood's gunnery sergeant, Tom Highway, a Medal of Honor winner, nonetheless feels like a failure as a U.S. Marine, mainly because of his sportslike "won-lost record" in wars during his career. A veteran of Korea (a tie) and Vietnam (a loss), Highway wishes to even his record at 1–1–1 before he retires. He shapes up a platoon of misfits and leads them to "victory" during the U.S. invasion of Grenada. Then he's ready to retire and patch up his romance with his long-suffering ex-wife.

FILM'S TREATMENT OF MASCULINITY: Whether the war concludes to his satisfaction, what should be important to a fighting man is the service itself.

***Hearts of the World* (1918)**

DIRECTOR: D. W. Griffith

SCREENPLAY: D. W. Griffith

CAST: Lillian Gish, Dorothy Gish, Mary Gish, Ben Alexander, Robert Harron, Erich von Stroheim, Noël Coward

VHS: Lions Gate

SUMMARY: This is the story of the people of a French village suddenly and brutally occupied by the Germans during World War I. To create his propaganda film, D. W. Griffith uses his usual melodrama, such as a hero preventing Erich von Stroheim's "beast of Berlin" from raping Lillian Gish, and a climactic race against time to the rescue, as he portrays the Germans as monsters finally driven off as the French Army retakes the town.

FILM'S TREATMENT OF MASCULINITY: A soldier's—like a knight's—greatest duty is to defend the helpless against evil men.

***The Horse Soldiers* (1959)**

DIRECTOR: John Ford

SCREENPLAY: John Lee Mahin and Martin Rackin

CAST: John Wayne, William Holden, Constance Towers, Judson Pratt, Hoot Gibson

DVD: MGM/UA Video

SUMMARY: Based on a true story (minus the love interest), during the Civil War, a battalion of Union Cavalry behind enemy lines drives through the South, destroying Confederate railroad assets. Along the way there are conflicts between the humanistic chief medical officer of the unit and its tough, no-nonsense commander. Complicating matters, they must transport a Confederate woman with them because she found out the battalion's plans and would reveal them to the Confederates if she could. The commander is job- and mission-objective oriented and could shoot her as a spy, but his sense of chivalry forbids it. Besides, she is attractive to the commander, and vice versa.

FILM'S TREATMENT OF MASCULINITY: When a man becomes a commander in war, he must balance the job he must do—his duty—with the requirements of his more feminine side, his obligations to humanity. Where, along the continuum of his choices, he sets the fulcrum for this balance describes his character and his manliness.

***The Hunters* (1958)**

DIRECTOR: Dick Powell

SCREENPLAY: Wendell Mayes, based on the novel by James Salter

CAST: Robert Mitchum, Robert Wagner, Richard Egan, Mai Britt, Lee Phillips

DVD: 20th Century Fox

SUMMARY: A study of the reality and true meaning of courage, this Korean War story follows a veteran fighter pilot after he joins a squadron flying F-86s against the enemy. On leave in Japan, the veteran meets and falls in love with the wife of another pilot, who is out of her favor because he is fighting off the fear he feels between missions with alcohol. After the pilot is shot down, the veteran's true sense of honor requires him to rescue his romantic rival, reuniting him with his wife.

FILM'S TREATMENT OF MASCULINITY: In battle, fear is not the same as cowardice: It's how a man handles his fear that counts. A pilot who fights and does his duty in spite of his fears may be the "bravest man in the squadron."

***The Hurt Locker* (2009)**

DIRECTOR: Kathryn Bigelow

SCREENPLAY: Mark Boal

CAST: Jeremy Renner, Anthony Mackie, Brian Geraghty, Guy Pearce, Ralph Fiennes, David Morse

ACADEMY AWARD WINS: Best Picture, Best Screenplay, Best Editing, Best Director (Kathryn Bigelow, the first bestowed upon a woman)

DVD: Summit Entertainment

SUMMARY: While trying to survive the deadly job of explosive ordinance disposal in Iraq, and with only a month to go on their tour, this explosive ordinance disposal unit loses its leader to an improvised explosive device. Quite different in temperament from the careful, by-the-book sergeant he is replacing, the unit's new leader seems to believe that he is charmed and cannot be killed, and thus he takes chances that upset the rest of the team. His devil-may-care attitude leads to many conflicts as the men do their duty but try to avoid going home in body bags.

FILM'S TREATMENT OF MASCULINITY: Some men are attracted to danger just for the thrill of it, but such men should never endanger their comrades-in-arms to experience it.

***In Harm's Way* (1965)**

DIRECTOR: Otto Preminger

SCREENPLAY: Wendell Mayes, based on the novel by James Bassett

CAST: John Wayne, Kirk Douglas, Patricia Neal, Tom Tryon, Brandon De Wilde, Paula Prentiss

ACADEMY AWARD NOMINATION: Best Cinematography (Black and White)

DVD: Paramount Pictures

SUMMARY: Directly following the Japanese attack on Pearl Harbor, a cruiser commander takes the initiative, throws away the "book," and pursues the enemy, but his ship is torpedoed. He loses his command and is relegated to a staff job but distinguishes himself and is forgiven. Promoted to rear admiral, he heads up a task force in a crucial part of the war in the Pacific. There, he must fight not only the Japanese, but avoid interference from another admiral, an inept dandy who tries to jump in and take all the credit.

FILM'S TREATMENT OF MASCULINITY: The best men accept both criticism and praise with the same demeanor. The most effective fighting men do not become bitter over failure: Instead, they double their efforts to overcome it.

***Jarhead* (2005)**

DIRECTOR: Sam Mendes

SCREENPLAY: William Broyles Jr., based on the book by Anthony Swofford

CAST: Jake Gyllenhaal, Peter Sarsgaard, Jamie Foxx, Lucas Black, Chris Cooper, Dennis Haysbert

DVD: Universal Studios

SUMMARY: An adaptation of marine Anthony Swofford's best seller, this classic war film plot begins—a la *Full Metal Jacket* (1987)—as marines are insulted and brutalized by their drill instructor in basic training. Swofford becomes a sniper and is deployed to Iraq to fight in the first Gulf War. In the deserts of Kuwait, as they impatiently wait and train for combat against Saddam Hussein's forces, the men revert to typical frat house behavior with typical sophomoric results. Finally ordered into action, the men encounter death and destruction, but after the fact. Eager to finally get into the action, Swofford and his spotter are dispatched to do a snipers' job but at the last second are ordered to stand down. Then, suddenly, the "war" is over, and after all he has experienced, Swofford never gets the chance to fire a shot in combat.

FILM'S TREATMENT OF MASCULINITY: Many young, inexperienced fighting men yearn for combat to prove themselves. Only afterward do most clearly understand what Gen. Dwight D. Eisenhower once said: "I hate war as only a soldier who has lived it can, only as one who has seen its brutality, its futility, its stupidity."

***Kelly's Heroes* (1970)**

DIRECTOR: Brian G. Hutton

SCREENPLAY: Troy Kennedy-Martin

CAST: Clint Eastwood, Telly Savalas, Don Rickles, Carroll O'Connor, Donald Sutherland, Gavin MacLeod, Stuart Margolin, Harry Dean Stanton

DVD: Warner Home Video

SUMMARY: As much of a "big caper" picture as it is a Vietnam era satire on the military, this film tells the story of a pick-up squad of tired, disillusioned soldiers who desert their World War II duties and run off to capture millions in gold bullion behind German lines. War genre antihero performances by the cynical Clint Eastwood as their leader, Don Rickles as the crooked supply sergeant financier of the expedition, Donald Sutherland as a beatnik (too early in history to be a hippie) tank commander, and Carroll O'Connor spoofing a Patton-like general who thinks the illicit operation is for real and roots for their success like a football fan.

FILM'S TREATMENT OF MASCULINITY: Some fighting men reach the limit of their selfless devotion to the cause and put themselves first.

***Knute Rockne, All American* (1940)**

DIRECTORS: Lloyd Bacon and William K. Howard (uncredited)

SCREENPLAY: Robert Buckner

CAST: Pat O'Brien, Ronald Reagan, Donald Crisp, Albert Bassermann

DVD: Warner Home Video

SUMMARY: This film is essentially the biography of the famous Notre Dame football coach who died in a tragic plane crash while still at the height of his coaching prowess. Among his achievements were revolutionary uses of the forward pass and, during the days of his famous "Four Horsemen" backfield, of impossible-to-defend backfield shifts. The film is also remembered for Ronald Reagan's portrayal of famous halfback/quarterback/punter George Gipp, nicknamed "the Gipper." Gipp's untimely death (of a streptococcal throat infection) caused Rockne, famous for motivational speeches to his players, to urge his men to "Win this one for the Gipper." Later in Reagan's political career, he would retain the nickname "The Gipper."

FILM'S TREATMENT OF MASCULINITY: In his famous motivational speeches to his players, Rockne reinforced the importance of manly hard work and teamwork. These virtues were seen as defining a man, whose job—as Rockne explained—was to do his job of work and to sacrifice himself for the sake of the team.

***Lawrence of Arabia* (1962)**

DIRECTOR: David Lean

SCREENPLAY: Robert Bolt, Michael Wilson, based on the writings of T. E. Lawrence

CAST: Peter O'Toole, Omar Sharif, Alec Guinness, Anthony Quinn, Jack Hawkins, José Ferrer, Anthony Quayle, Claude Rains

ACADEMY AWARD WINS: Best Picture, Best Director (David Lean), Best Art Decoration and Set Decoration (Color), Best Cinematography, Best Film Editing, Best Sound, Best Score

ACADEMY AWARD NOMINATIONS: Best Leading Actor (Peter O'Toole), Best Supporting Actor (Omar Sharif), Best Screenplay Adaptation

DVD: Columbia TriStar Motion Picture Group

SUMMARY: Based on the exploits of T. E. Lawrence, this Oscar winner tells the story of a British intelligence officer who is ordered to "consult" with the Arab army in their fight against the Turks during World War I. Lawrence is soon given command of this Arab army and recruits other Arabs to fight a successful guerilla war for two years, eventually contributing to the fall of the Ottoman Empire. But in the end, when the establishment of an independent Arab state is within their grasp, and despite Lawrence's best efforts to broker an alliance, the Arabs' own intertribal hatreds and prejudices prevent them from organizing, and they succumb to European colonial powers.

FILM'S TREATMENT OF MASCULINITY: Men must avoid becoming too addicted to the thrill of the fight, because such delusions can defeat a man as readily as the enemy.

***The Longest Day* (1962)**

DIRECTORS: Ken Annakin, Andrew Marton, Bernhard Wicki

SCREENPLAY: Cornelius Ryan, Romain Gary, James Jones, David Pursall, Jack Seddon, based on the book by Cornelius Ryan

CAST: Eddie Albert, Paul Anka, Richard Burton, Red Buttons, Sean Connery, Henry Fonda, Jeffrey Hunter, Peter Lawford, Roddy McDowall, Robert Mitchum, Edmund O'Brien, Robert Ryan, George Segal, Rod Steiger, Richard Todd, Tom Tryon, Robert Wagner, John Wayne

Academy Award Wins: Best Cinematography, Best Special Effects
Academy Award Nomination: Best Picture
DVD: 20th Century Fox
Summary: This film tells the story of D-Day, the Normandy invasion that paved the way to Allied victory in Europe during World War II. It retells this story through the experiences of many participants, both German and Allied, from their commanders to common soldiers.
Film's Treatment of Masculinity: This film is comprised of many different stories, but all of them have one thing in common: Ordinary men are capable of extraordinary deeds in pursuit of a great cause.

***The Lucky Ones* (2008)**
Director: Neil Burger
Screenplay: Neil Burger, Dirk Whittenborn
Cast: Rachel McAdams, Tim Robbins, Michael Peña, Anne Corley, John Diehl, John Heard
DVD: Lions Gate
Summary: This is the story of three soldiers who have recovered from wounds suffered during the Iraq War. They become friends on the trip back to the United States and end up stranded in a New York airport. They decide to rent a car and travel across the United States together. In this character study, we experience their suffering from post-traumatic stress disorder and some of the typical problems experienced by returning soldiers. Finally, although at the outset it was not planned, all three decide to return to Iraq for another tour.
Film's Treatment of Masculinity: In spite of wounds—mental and physical—suffered in war, many soldiers are drawn back to it, not always understanding why.

***Marine Raiders* (1944)**
Director: Harold Schuster
Screenplay: Warren Duff, Martin Rackin
Cast: Pat O'Brien, Robert Ryan, Ruth Hussey, Frank McHugh, Barton MacLane, Martha Vickers
VHS: Warner Home Video
Summary: This is the World War II story of two U.S. Marine officers whose close friendship is strained when one falls in love and wishes to get married. But later, all personal conflict is set aside as the two friends combine to assault a Japanese-held island.
Film's Treatment of Masculinity: The manly code dictates that these marines set aside personal wants for the good of the mission.

***M*A*S*H* (1970)**

DIRECTOR: Robert Altman

SCREENPLAY: Ring Lardner Jr., based on the novel by Richard Hooker (H. Richard Hornberger)

CAST: Donald Sutherland, Elliott Gould, Tom Skerritt, Sally Kellerman, Robert Duvall, Roger Bowen, Gary Burghoff

ACADEMY AWARD WIN: Best Screenplay Adaptation

ACADEMY AWARD NOMINATIONS: Best Picture, Best Supporting Actress (Sally Kellerman), Best Director (Robert Altman), Best Film Editing

DVD: 20th Century Fox

SUMMARY: Black comedy is featured in this Vietnam War allegory about a group of medical personnel serving together in a mobile army surgical hospital located in Korea during the Korean War. As per the television series that followed, Hawkeye and Trapper keep things light as they persecute head nurse Houlihan and holier-than-thou surgeon Frank Burns. Nominated for five Academy Awards, it lost in both categories to *Patton*; however, the film did win one Oscar.

FILM'S TREATMENT OF MASCULINITY: To avoid succumbing to the madness that surrounds them, men and women alike turn to humor, practical jokes, and each other.

***M*A*S*H* (Television series, 1972–1983)**

DIRECTORS: Gene Reynolds, Larry Gelbart

TELEPLAYS: Gene Reynolds, Larry Gelbart, Alan Alda

CAST: Alan Alda, Wayne Rogers, Mike Farrell, Loretta Swit, McLean Stevenson, Harry Morgan, Larry Linville, Gary Burghoff, Jamie Farr, William Christopher, David Ogden Stiers

DVD: 20th Century Fox

SUMMARY: This series carried the same plot as Robert Altman's movie version, but with more of an emphasis on character, especially Hawkeye's. The long-running series won fourteen Emmys and a Peabody Award.

FILM'S TREATMENT OF MASCULINITY: The same as the film version, with more emphasis on relying on friendships to get them through the horrors they witness daily.

***Memphis Belle* (1990)**

DIRECTOR: Michael Caton-Jones

SCREENPLAY: Monte Merrick

CAST: Matthew Modine, Eric Stoats, Tate Donovan, D. B. Sweeney, Billy Zane, Sean Astin, Harry Connick Jr., David Strathairn, John Lithgow

DVD: Warner Home Video

SUMMARY: This is a highly fictionalized World War II story of the last bombing mission of the B-17 bomber named the *Memphis Belle*. The crew of this bomber will be the first to complete their twenty-five missions and rotate home, but first they must carry out a mission to bomb Bremen, a target full of danger due to its defenses, which include heavy antiaircraft fire and German fighters.

FILM'S TREATMENT OF MASCULINITY: Young men must grow up quickly if they are to survive in the midst of war.

***Men of the Fighting Lady* (1954)**

DIRECTOR: Andrew Marton

SCREENPLAY: Art Cohn, based on stories by James Michener and Harry A. Burns

CAST: Van Johnson, Walter Pidgeon, Louis Calhern, Dewey Martin, Keenan Wynn, Frank Lovejoy

VHS: MGM

SUMMARY: Based on two *Saturday Evening Post* stories by James A. Michener, this film chronicles the adventures of carrier-based aircrews bombing targets and doing combat with enemy fighters during the Korean War. Included are tales of an insistent commander who schedules many repeated sorties to take out one important target, a bridge that seems to withstand bombing, and a story of a pilot guiding a wounded, blinded buddy's plane to a safe landing on board the aircraft carrier.

FILM'S TREATMENT OF MASCULINITY: The principal responsibilities of the warrior amount to doing one's duty and protecting one's comrades.

***Merrill's Marauders* (1962)**

DIRECTOR: Samuel Fuller

SCREENPLAY: Milton Sperling, Samuel Fuller, based on the book by Charlton Ogburn Jr.

CAST: Jeff Chandler, Ty Hardin, Peter Brown, Andrew Duggan, Will Hutchins, Claude Akins

DVD: Warner Home Video

SUMMARY: Based on the World War II story of Brig. Gen. Frank Merrill's exploits, this motion picture details Merrill's unit's trek behind enemy lines through jungles and across mountains in Burma to attack key Japanese positions. Fighting exhaustion and disease and stopping from time to time to fight battles against the enemy, the story focuses on the human cost of heroics.

FILM'S TREATMENT OF MASCULINITY: If a leader leads by example, inspiring loyalty and admiration, men can do and endure more than they think they possibly can.

***Mission Accomplished* (1943)**
Director: Uncredited (Office of War Information)
DVD: Not available
Summary: This is a documentary short film about the first high-altitude B-17 bombing raids into Germany during World War II.
Film's Treatment of Masculinity: Wars are won only through the bravery and determination of U.S. aircrews.

***Mister Roberts* (1955)**
Directors: John Ford, Mervyn LeRoy, Joshua Logan
Screenplay: Frank S. Nugent, Mervyn LeRoy, based on the novel by Thomas Heggen and the play by Thomas Heggen and Joshua Logan
Cast: Henry Fonda, James Cagney, William Powell, Jack Lemmon, Ward Bond, Betsey Palmer, Nick Adams
Academy Award Win: Best Supporting Actor (Jack Lemmon)
Academy Award Nominations: Best Picture, Best Sound
DVD: Warner Home Video
Summary: This is an Oscar-winning comedy about life aboard a U.S. Navy supply ship in the South Pacific during World War II. The plot centers on the first officer, who does battle with a selfish, abusive captain; the elements; the crew's boredom; and malaise, while yearning for a chance aboard a destroyer to actually fight the enemy.
Film's Treatment of Masculinity: Leadership is not about personal gain: No one respects such a man. Leaders in war must be fair but demanding and lead by example.

***The Naked and the Dead* (1958)**
Director: Raoul Walsh
Screenplay: Denis Sanders, Terry Sanders, based on the novel by Norman Mailer
Cast: Aldo Ray, Cliff Robertson, Raymond Massey, William Campbell, Richard Jaeckel, Joey Bishop
VHS: United Home Video
Summary: On an island in the Pacific during World War II, a selfish, elitist general's campaign to overcome Japanese resistance bogs down. The general sees to it that he and his officers have the best quarters, food, and conditions, but he ignores the needs of the enlisted men under his command. To him, such men are pawns to sacrifice for his success. His aide, a young officer, protests, standing up for the men, which gets him fired from his safe and cushy job as general's aide and shoved back onto the front lines. There he comes into conflict with a sergeant whose attitude, although different, is every bit as cynical and cruel as the general.

Film's Treatment of Masculinity: Only leaders who lead by example earn the respect of their men.

***Navy SEALs* (1990)**

Director: Lewis Teague

Screenplay: Chuck Pfarrer, Gary Goldman

Cast: Michael Biehn, Charlie Sheen, Rick Rossovich, Bill Paxton, Dennis Haysbert, Joanne Whalley

DVD: MGM

Summary: In this film, elite navy commandos conduct combat and rescue operations in the Middle East. The plot centers on recovering or destroying a cache of Stinger missiles that have come into the possession of a group of terrorists. Along the way, U.S. Navy SEAL culture is shown to be one part skill, bravery, and sacrifice, and an equal part fraternity hijinks.

Film's Treatment of Masculinity: Seeking the thrill of battle can cause other men to die. A good soldier, much less a good officer, cannot be that selfish.

***1941* (1979)**

Director: Steven Spielberg

Screenplay: Robert Zemeckis, Bob Gale, John Milius

Cast: Dan Akroyd, John Belushi, John Candy, Robert Stack, Ned Beatty, Tim Matheson, Nancy Allen, Treat Williams, Toshiro Mifune, Christopher Lee

Academy Award Nominations: Best Sound, Best Visual Effects, Best Cinematography

DVD: Universal Studios

Summary: This Oscar-nominated large-cast comedy centers on the fears of Southern Californians a week after Pearl Harbor that the West Coast was about to be invaded. The only slim truth in all this hysteria is that a Japanese submarine is indeed offshore but has simply lost its compass and is scouring the California coast for signs of Hollywood. The captain, played for laughs by the stone-faced Toshiro Mifune, plans a Samurai-like attack on the film capital. He manages to count coup only by torpedoing a ferris wheel. The rest is slapstick, including a crazy fighter pilot zooming down Sunset Boulevard, a fight scene between servicemen and zoot-suiters, and an attempt by a young army officer to seduce a comely young woman in mid-flight.

Film's Treatment of Masculinity: Men in war must remain thoughtful and calm or irrational decisions follow.

***One Minute to Zero* (1952)**

Director: Tay Garnett

Screenplay: William W. Haines, Milton Krims and Andrew Solt (uncredited)

Cast: Robert Mitchum, Ann Blyth, Richard Egan, William Talman, Charles McGraw

VHS: Warner Home Video

Summary: The on-again, off-again romance of American Army colonel Steve Jankowski and United Nations humanitarian worker Linda Day with the Korean War as a backdrop. The two are attracted to each other, but when Jankowski is forced—for good military reasons—to call in an artillery strike that kills and injures Korean civilians along with enemy, the romance is off. Later in the picture they make up.

Film's Treatment of Masculinity: Along with the other rigors of command, manliness sometimes requires that men set aside sentimentality and even their humanity to make hard decisions.

***Operation Dumbo Drop* (1995)**

Director: Simon Wincer

Screenplay: Gene Quintano, Jim Kouf

Story: James Morris

Cast: Danny Glover, Ray Liotta, Dennis Leary, Doug E. Dough, Corin Nemic, James Hong

DVD: Walt Disney Video

Summary: Somewhere along the Ho Chi Minh Trail, in reprisal for assisting the Americans, the North Vietnamese Army forces kill an elephant revered by local villagers. To insure their continued cooperation and to win their hearts and minds, U.S. soldiers find another elephant and try to deliver it to the village. But packing a pachyderm into an airplane and getting it there is much easier said than done.

Film's Treatment of Masculinity: Loyalty and dedication separate leaders from followers. Also, in pursuit of mission goals, no task is beneath a good soldier.

***Operation Pacific* (1951)**

Director: George Waggner

Screenplay: George Waggner

Cast: John Wayne, Patricia Neal, Ward Bond, Scott Forbes, Philip Carey, Martin Milner

DVD: Warner Home Video

Summary: This is an all-too-pat World War II story about "Duke," a submarine executive officer who assumes command after his captain is killed in combat. While in port, Duke discovers and pursues his ex-wife, a nurse, who coincidentally is dating a navy flyer who just happens to be the younger brother of the late captain. All things sort themselves out when back in the Pacific—again coincidentally—Duke's sub is assigned to rescue this same flyer when he is shot down in combat.

FILM'S TREATMENT OF MASCULINITY: When in command, a good leader cannot always do what is popular among the men. The man in charge must, as President Abraham Lincoln once said, not plan on "pleasing all the people all the time."

***Paths of Glory* (1957)**

DIRECTOR: Stanley Kubrick

SCREENPLAY: Stanley Kubrick, Calder Willingham, Jim Thompson

CAST: Kirk Douglas, George Macready, Adolphe Menjou, Ralph Meeker, Timothy Carey, Joe Turkel, Wayne Morris

DVD: MGM/UA Home Video

SUMMARY: In World War I, in the midst of the worst of trench warfare, an incompetent and ambitious French Gen. Mireau sees a chance for advancement by ordering Col. Dax's regiment to attack an impregnable German position called the Anthill. When the first few companies are slaughtered, the remainder of the regiment refuses to get out of their trenches. Furious, Gen. Mireau orders three representative soldiers from the regiment to be tried, convicted, and executed for cowardice. Dax, a lawyer in civilian life, ably defends the men, but the verdict is predetermined and the men are shot by firing squad. But during the trial, Dax discovers facts that ultimately will cause Gen. Mireau's own court-martial.

FILM'S TREATMENT OF MASCULINITY: The mentally unbalanced and incompetent Gen. Mireau blames his men's failure on cowardice instead of his poor leadership. This film demonstrates how that even at the senior officer level, a man's failure to do his job effectively can cause someone of low character to blame people other than himself.

***The Patriot* (2000)**

DIRECTOR: Roland Emmerich

SCREENPLAY: Robert Rodat

CAST: Mel Gibson, Heath Ledger, Jason Isaacs, Chris Cooper, Tom Wilkinson, Adam Baldwin, Joely Richardson, Rene Auberjonois, Donal Logue

ACADEMY AWARD NOMINATIONS: Best Score, Best Sound, Best Cinematography

DVD: Sony Pictures

Summary: This Oscar-nominated story combines many real occurrences and people into a tale about a South Carolina farmer who, although famous for his exploits during the French and Indian War, wants nothing to do with the Revolutionary War. But his nightmares—and, he says, his sins—come home to plague him as a ruthless British officer murders one of his sons and condemns another to hang. The farmer takes up arms again, rescues his son, and joins the war. He commands a unit of irregulars who fight a guerilla war against the British, effectively preventing them from moving North to battle George Washington. Finally, under his leadership, these South Carolina militiamen and the Continental Army defeat the enemy in a stand-up battle, contributing to the defeat of Britain and the independence of the colonies.

Film's Treatment of Masculinity: Long after a war has ended, what a man did and how he conducted himself remains to haunt him.

***Patton* (1970)**

Director: Franklin J. Schaffner

Screenplay: Edmund H. North, Francis Ford Coppola, based on the books *Patton: Ordeal and Triumph* by Ladislas Farago and *A Soldier's Story* by Omar Bradley

Cast: George C. Scott, Karl Malden, Stephen Young, Michael Strong, Frank Latimore, James Edwards, Lawrence Dobkin, Karl Michael Vogler, Tim Considine

Academy Award Wins: Best Picture, Best Director (Franklin J. Schaffner), Best Leading Actor (George C. Scott), Best Set Direction, Best Film Editing, Best Sound, Best Screenplay

Academy Award Nominations: Best Special Effects, Best Original Score, Best Cinematography

DVD: 20th Century Fox

Summary: This Oscar-winning film chronicles the World War II exploits of the famous U.S. Army commander. Defeating Rommell's Africa Corps, Patton's leadership turns the tide of the war in North Africa. Commanding U.S. forces in the Allied invasion of Sicily, he selfishly competes with British Field Marshall Montgomery to lead the first Allied army into Messina. Later, Patton's public statements and harsh treatment of a shell-shocked soldier get him relieved of his command; however, after D-Day, Gen. Omar Bradley gives Patton another chance, and he and the Third Army strike out boldly and successfully against the Germans, including relieving U.S. forces during the Battle of the Bulge. Later, at war's end, Patton's intemperate remarks and distrust of Russian allies cannot survive the peace, and as the film ends, so, effectively, does Patton's career. The film does not depict the fact that soon thereafter the general dies in a car accident.

Film's Treatment of Masculinity: A fighting man—much less a general officer—can become addicted to war, affecting his judgment and putting his men in danger.

***Pearl Harbor* (2001)**

Director: Michael Bay

Screenplay: Randall Wallace

Cast: Ben Affleck, Josh Hartnett, Kate Beckinsale, Cuba Gooding Jr., Alec Baldwin, Jon Voight, Tom Sizemore, Jennifer Garner

DVD: Touchstone

Summary: Set against the backdrop of the Japanese attack on Pearl Harbor, this storyline creates a fierce love triangle among two fighter pilots and an army nurse. The two pilots distinguish themselves by getting their fighter planes airborne and shooting down a half dozen Japanese. Throwing history to the four winds (since only volunteer pilots from the 17th Bomb Group flew the raid), the plot next places these two fighter pilots in the cockpits of two of the sixteen B-25 bombers launched from the carrier USS *Hornet* in the Doolittle Raid to strike back against the Japanese homeland. One of the two is killed, and the surviving pilot marries the nurse.

Film's Treatment of Masculinity: War creates great friendships, and takes them away as well. How a man deals with such tragedy can define him.

***Platoon* (1986)**

Director: Oliver Stone

Screenplay: Oliver Stone

Cast: Charlie Sheen, Willem Dafoe, Tom Berenger, Forest Whitaker, John C. McGinley, Kevin Dillon

Academy Award Wins: Best Picture, Best Director (Oliver Stone), Best Film Editing, Best Sound

Academy Award Nominations: Best Supporting Actor (Willem Dafoe), Best Supporting Actor (Tom Berenger), Best Screenplay, Best Cinematography

DVD: MGM

Summary: Nominated for eight Academy Awards and winner of four Oscars, this motion picture proves the adage that in Vietnam, one wouldn't believe what a nineteen-year-old American boy is capable of. Chris, a young, naïve infantry replacement, joins a platoon fighting the enemy in the jungles of Vietnam, trying to stay alive long enough to learn how to survive. He gets no help from one brutal sergeant, Barnes, but he is befriended and assisted by another veteran sergeant, Elias, and later by some of the troops. After a My Lai-type incident involving the murders of Vietnamese villagers, a feud between the two sergeants divides the platoon's loyalties. Later, Barnes murders Elias, and Chris discovers the crime. During a climactic battle, to silence Chris, Barnes attempts to kill him, but an air attack foils his plans. Chris later shoots Barnes and—because he has been wounded in two battles—Chris is airlifted to safety and sent home.

FILM'S TREATMENT OF MASCULINITY: The things that soldiers do in war remain with them long after the killing is over. Then, somehow, they must find constructive ways to deal with it.

***Platoon Leader* (1988)**

DIRECTOR: Aaron Norris

SCREENPLAY: Andrew Deutsch, Rick Marx, David L. Walker, Peter Welbeck, based on the book by James R. McDonough

CAST: Michael Dudikoff, Robert F. Lyons, Michael DeLorenzo, Rick Fitts, Jesse Dabson

VHS: Starz/Anchor Bay Entertainment

SUMMARY: Capitalizing on the popularity of the film *Platoon* (1986), this action film accurately depicts what would happen when a naive West Point graduate arrives in Vietnam. As a "FNG just in from the world," Lt. Knight's education and training does him no good, and he receives no more respect from the men than any newly arrived enlisted man. Fortunately, Knight has a wise sergeant to show him the ropes. After a few false starts, Knight becomes both experienced as a commander and sufficiently cynical about the outcome of the war, but it's his war, and even after being wounded, he chooses to return to his firebase to do his duty.

FILM'S TREATMENT OF MASCULINITY: There is a great fraternity of men in war. Placing their lives in each other's hands, a manly love passes between such men that is as strong and defines their characters.

***Pork Chop Hill* (1959)**

DIRECTOR: Lewis Milestone

SCREENPLAY: James R. Webb, based on the book by S. L. A. Marshall

CAST: Gregory Peck, Harry Guardino, Rip Torn, George Peppard, Woody Strode, Norman Fell, Robert Blake

DVD: MGM

SUMMARY: This film tells the frustrating account of an army company tasked with attacking and holding a worthless hill while Allied and North Korean officials bicker at the peace table. The gritty story pits men's lives against negotiators' games over a meaningless objective.

The result is a generalized allegory about war in which soldiers do their duty and die while politicians move them like pawns around their chessboards.

Film's Treatment of Masculinity: Men must develop a fatalistic attitude about their chances to survive war, replacing their concerns with a dedication to duty, even if the mission is meaningless.

***The Purple Heart* (1944)**

Director: Lewis Milestone

Screenplay: Jerome Cady

Story: Darryl F. Zanuck

Cast: Dana Andrews, Richard Conte, Farley Granger, Kevin O'Shea, Sam Levene, Richard Loo

DVD: 20th Century Fox

Summary: This film is a fictionalized account (for World War II U.S. propaganda purposes) of the true kangaroo court trial of an aircrew from the Doolittle Raid. Because the Japanese didn't know that these flyers came from the carrier USS *Hornet* and not from any land base, the honor of the U.S. Army versus the Japanese Navy was at stake. Tortured for information about the location of their home base, the flyers endure and say nothing. Regardless of the manipulated "facts" of the trial, these men have only two choices: "confess" to bombing a hospital and civilians instead of their assigned military targets and divulge where their "secret" base was, or keep their secret and their honor and be executed.

Film's Treatment of Masculinity: True men faced with a choice between death or dishonor must always choose the former. "A coward dies a thousand deaths, but the valiant taste death but once."

***The Red Badge of Courage* (1951)**

Director: John Huston

Screenplay: John Huston, Albert Band, based on the novel by Stephen Crane

Cast: Audie Murphy, Bill Mauldin, Douglas Dick, Royal Dano, John Dierkes, Arthur Hunnicutt

DVD: Warner Home Video

Summary: This is the well-written story of a Union soldier, called the "Youth," who doubts if he has the courage to fight as he and his comrades prepare for their first battle. Although he doesn't run away the first time he faces the enemy, he does the next time and is accidentally wounded by another fleeing soldier. Returning to his unit, the Youth has earned respect because he appears to have been wounded in battle. Feeling the need to play the part and buoyed by his newfound status, the next time his company faces the enemy, he becomes a hero, leading the men to victory on the battlefield.

FILM'S TREATMENT OF MASCULINITY: Even if a man raises the white feather, he still can redeem himself and demonstrate courage another day in another battle.

***A Rumor of War* (1980)**

DIRECTOR: Richard T. Heffron

SCREENPLAY: John Sacret Young, based on the book by Philip Caputo

CAST: Brad Davis, Keith Carradine, Brian Dennehy, Michael O'Keefe, Richard Bradford, Lane Smith

VHS: Anchor Bay Entertainment

SUMMARY: This is a made-for-television movie (nominated for an Emmy) based on the autobiographical novel by former marine Philip Caputo. A young officer comes of age, is tutored by a fatherly sergeant, and finally comes to grips with the ambiguities and the utter folly of the Vietnam War.

FILM'S TREATMENT OF MASCULINITY: A young man—especially a leader—must mature quickly in war: Emotional, immature decisions cost men their lives.

***Run Silent, Run Deep* (1958)**

DIRECTOR: Robert Wise

SCREENPLAY: John Gay, based on the novel by Edward L. Beach

CAST: Clark Gable, Burt Lancaster, Jack Warden, Brad Dexter, Don Rickles

DVD: MGM

SUMMARY: During World War II, a U.S. submarine captain, Cmdr. Richardson, loses his ship to a Japanese destroyer and vows revenge. He convinces the admiral in charge to give him another sub, even if it means that this sub's executive officer, popular with the men and ready to assume command, is passed over. Without the support of either his exec or his men, Richardson has a difficult time training the crew for the particularly difficult "bow shot" attack with which he plans to sink the destroyer. The two eventually set aside their differences and complete the mission, as they discover that it wasn't just a Japanese destroyer that sank Richardson's sub, but a destroyer and a submarine working in concert.

FILM'S TREATMENT OF MASCULINITY: In war, a leader's obsession with revenge or personal closure can, like Capt. Ahab's quest, lead to tragedy for him and his men.

***Sahara* (1943)**

DIRECTOR: Zoltan Korda

SCREENPLAY: Zoltan Korda, John Howard Lawson, James O'Hanlon
STORY: Philip MacDonald
CAST: Humphrey Bogart, Bruce Bennett, J. Carrol Naish, Lloyd Bridges, Rex Ingram, Dan Duryea
ACADEMY AWARD NOMINATIONS: Best Supporting Actor (J. Carrol Naish), Best Sound, Best Cinematography (Black and White)
DVD: Sony Pictures
SUMMARY: This is a wartime propaganda film that shows how the Allies can set aside minor cultural differences to work together to defeat the swinish Nazis. A U.S. tank commander collects a band of British, French, and Australians in the Libyan Desert. Along the way, they encounter and befriend a sociable Italian soldier and a mean-as-a-snake Nazi pilot, each playing roles intended to create stereotypes for the propaganda scenario. They defend the only water in the desert for hundreds of miles to prevent access by a German infantry battalion. In the process, the small Allied force is reduced by sniper fire to only a few men. Nonetheless, demonstrating the moral superiority of the Allies, hundreds of parched Germans surrender to these few survivors.
FILM'S TREATMENT OF MASCULINITY: A soldier's lot often includes the need to sacrifice to achieve the objective. Quoting Spock in *Star Trek II*, "The needs of the many outweigh the needs of the few."

***The Sand Pebbles* (1966)**
DIRECTOR: Robert Wise
SCREENPLAY: Robert Anderson, based on the novel by Richard McKenna
CAST: Steve McQueen, Richard Attenborough, Richard Crenna, Candice Bergen, Mako, Simon Oakland, Gavin MacLeod
ACADEMY AWARD NOMINATIONS: Best Picture, Best Leading Actor (Steve McQueen), Best Supporting Actor (Mako), Best Art Direction (Color), Best Film Editing, Best Sound, Best Original Score, Best Cinematography (Color)
DVD: 20th Century Fox
SUMMARY: U.S. Navy chief engineer Jake Holman joins the gunboat USS *San Pablo* (called the *Sand Pebbles*) patrolling the Yangtze River in 1926. The Chinese loathe the U.S. presence, there only to protect national interests, and the Chinese civilian employees aboard the ship despise their new chief engineer only marginally less. Conflicts between these foreigners and the Chinese lead to a ferocious battle and a mission to rescue U.S. missionaries upriver.
FILM'S TREATMENT OF MASCULINITY: A professional soldier's mantra is, as Alfred, Lord Tennyson wrote, "Ours is not to reason why; ours is but to do and die."

***Sands of Iwo Jima* (1949)**
DIRECTOR: Alan Dwan
SCREENPLAY: Harry Brown, James Edward Grant
CAST: John Wayne, John Agar, Forrest Tucker, James Brown, Wally Cassell, Richard Webb, Arthur Franz
ACADEMY AWARD NOMINATIONS: Best Leading Actor (John Wayne), Best Film Editing, Best Sound, Best Screen Story
DVD: Republic Pictures
SUMMARY: There is no more fierce squad leader in the World War II-era marines than John Stryker, as the men he browbeats and trains incessantly will attest, especially Pvt. Conway. Conway, a humanist, is at first against everything Stryker stands for and often comes into conflict with his leader. But the value of Stryker's brand of soldiering pays off for the men when he leads them into combat, first at Tarawa, and later up the slopes of Mt. Suribachi on Iwo Jima. There, in the shadow of the men who raised that famous flag, a sniper shoots and kills Stryker. Inspired by Stryker's leadership, Conway begins channeling his sergeant and leads the squad to the top.
FILM'S TREATMENT OF MASCULINITY: There is a natural conflict between a soldier's code and that of the humanist's. But in the heat of battle, humanism can play no part. "Lock and load."

***Saving Private Ryan* (1998)**
DIRECTOR: Steven Spielberg
SCREENPLAY: Robert Rodat
CAST: Tom Hanks, Tom Sizemore, Jeremy Davies, Edward Burns, Barry Pepper, Adam Goldberg, Giovanni Ribisi, Vin Diesel, Matt Damon, Paul Giamatti, Ted Danson
ACADEMY AWARD WINS: Best Director (Steven Spielberg), Best Film Editing, Best Sound, Best Sound Effects Editing, Best Cinematography
ACADEMY AWARD NOMINATIONS: Best Picture, Best Leading Actor (Tom Hanks), Best Original Screenplay, Best Art Direction, Best Original Score, Best Makeup
DVD: Dreamworks Video
SUMMARY: This Oscar-winning story describes the trek taken by a squad of survivors of D-Day, led by Capt. Miller, to find and remove a single soldier, Pvt. Ryan, from harm's way. Ryan's three brothers had just been killed in action, and their mother received word of their deaths on the same day. Gen. George C. Marshall wishes to spare Mrs. Ryan another death notice. This idea doesn't sit well with Capt. Miller's men, who have just waded through their comrades' blood on Omaha Beach. They consider the "entire mission [to be] a serious misallocation of valuable military resources." When the squad finally

finds Ryan, the young private won't leave his buddies shorthanded, because they must stay and defend a bridge against the Germans. Miller's squad ends up joining Ryan.

FILM'S TREATMENT OF MASCULINITY: In this case, the needs of the one outweigh the needs of the many. Why? Orders. A man obeys them, no matter how FUBAR they might seem. As Alfred, Lord Tennyson wrote, "Ours is not to reason why; ours is but to do and die."

***Serenity* (2005)**

DIRECTOR: Joss Whedon

SCREENPLAY: Joss Whedon

CAST: Nathan Fillion, Gina Torres, Summer Glau, Adam Baldwin, Alad Tudyk, Chiwetel Elijofor

DVD: Universal Studios

SUMMARY: In this continuation of the short-lived but excellent television series into a feature film, a group of space war veterans, merely intent on some intergalactic smuggling, ends up in the middle of the Alliance hunt for a teenager who knows too much. Capt. Mal Reynolds refuses to hand the girl over to a fascist Alliance he despises anyway (he and a few other crew were on the losing side of the war that put the Alliance in power). Trying to avoid both savage mutants known as the Reavers and an Alliance hit man out to kill them and all their friends, Reynolds decides to "misbehave" and manages to broadcast the girl's terrible secret to the entire galaxy.

FILM'S TREATMENT OF MASCULINITY: There is a time when a man throws out the book and even common sense and just "misbehaves," when a just cause requires such extraordinary action.

***The Sergeant* (1968)**

DIRECTOR: John Flynn

SCREENPLAY: Dennis Murphy, based on his novel

CAST: Rod Steiger, John Phillip Law, Frank Latimore, Elliott Sullivan, Ludmila Mikaël

DVD: Warner Archive

SUMMARY: In one of the first American film treatments of gays in the military and long before the days of "Don't Ask, Don't Tell," Rod Steiger plays MSgt. Albert Callan, a war hero/first sergeant of a U.S. Army company stationed in post–World War II France. A deeply closeted homosexual, Callan struggles to hide his secret, but both his self-loathing and desire are heightened when he encounters a young, handsome new replacement, Pvt. Swanson. Callan, more and more conflicted, camouflages his self-contempt by hatefully mistreating Swanson. Eventually, the secret comes out, and as the film ends, Callan realizes he is ruined.

FILM'S TREATMENT OF MASCULINITY: The mission is what is important, and a man doesn't put his needs or wants before it.

***Sergeant York* (1941)**

DIRECTOR: Howard Hawks

SCREENPLAY: Abem Finkel, Harry Chandlee, Howard Koch, John Huston

CAST: Gary Cooper, Walter Brennan, Joan Leslie, George Tobias, Margaret Wycherly, Stanley Ridges, Ward Bond, Noah Beery Jr.

ACADEMY AWARD WINS: Best Leading Actor (Gary Cooper), Best Film Editing

ACADEMY AWARD NOMINATIONS: Best Picture, Best Director (Howard Hawks), Best Supporting Actor (Walter Brennan), Best Supporting Actress (Margaret Wycherly), Best Original Screenplay, Best Sound, Best Scoring of a Dramatic Picture, Best Art Direction (Black and White), Best Cinematography (Black and White)

DVD: Warner Home Video

SUMMARY: This Oscar-winning film dramatizes the true story of Alvin York, a poor farmer who was drafted to serve in the U.S. Army during World War I. After initially claiming to be a pacifist and a conscientious objector, York not only shoots and kills German soldiers, but in one engagement, kills twenty-five of them and captures a great many more. For his heroism, the unassuming NCO receives the Medal of Honor.

FILM'S TREATMENT OF MASCULINITY: There is a huge differentiation between manly courage, duty, and the commandment "Thou shalt not kill."

***She Wore a Yellow Ribbon* (1949)**

DIRECTOR: John Ford

SCREENPLAY: Frank S. Nugent, Laurence Stallings

STORY: James Warner Bellah

CAST: John Wayne, John Agar, Ben Johnson, Harry Carey Jr., Victor McLaglen, Joanne Dru, Mildred Natwick

ACADEMY AWARD WIN: Best Cinematography (Color)

DVD: Warner Home Video

SUMMARY: This Oscar-winning film tells the story of U.S. Cavalry captain Nathan Brittles as he leads one last patrol to avoid war between the whites and the Cheyennes and Arapahos, who break out from the reservation after the defeat of Gen. George Armstrong Custer. Meanwhile, Brittles must assure that the two young lieutenants who will soon replace him are properly seasoned. This becomes problematic, as these two young men fall over themselves competing for the hand of a beautiful young lady, the niece of the fort's commanding officer. Using his experience and relationship with one of the Indian chiefs, Brittles tries a parlay to stop the war, but young, ambitious warriors prevail at the council fires. Finally, Brittles returns with his men to raid the village and chase off all the horses. Without mounts, the Indians cannot win, so they have no choice but to walk back to the reservation in disgrace. Promoted to lieutenant colonel and given a new assignment as chief of scouts, Brittles postpones his retirement indefinitely.

FILM'S TREATMENT OF MASCULINITY: Bravery, lifelong dedication, and love of the service make such men models for the rest.

***The Siege of Firebase Gloria* (1989)**

DIRECTOR: Brian Trenchard-Smith

SCREENPLAY: William L. Nagle, Tony Johnston

CAST: Wings Hauser, R. Lee Ermey, Robert Arevalo, Mark Neely, Gary Hershberger, Margi Gerard, Richard Kuhlman

VHS: Delta Library

SUMMARY: A marine long-range reconnaissance patrol in Vietnam, let by tough, wily Sgt. Maj. Hafner, discovers signs of a huge enemy mobilization that will shortly become the Tet Offensive, but Hafner can't convince anyone in Saigon to believe him. The sergeant and his patrol come upon a firebase desperately in need of reorganization, led by an officer called the "Ghost" who spends his time lying naked in his bunker getting high all day long. Soon the "Ghost" has an "accident," and Hafner is in operational command, just in time, as the Viet Cong are about to attack in force. Hafner and his troops, with the help of attack helicopters and air strikes from above, hold back the superior force of Viet Cong.

FILM'S TREATMENT OF MASCULINITY: In war, discipline, toughness, and experience can overcome tremendous odds.

***Sink the Bismarck!* (1960)**

DIRECTOR: Lewis Gilbert

SCREENPLAY: Edmund H. North, based on the book by C. S. Forester

CAST: Kenneth More, Dana Wynter, Carl Möhner, Laurence Naismith, Geoffrey Keen, Karel Stepanek, Michael Hordern

DVD: 20th Century Fox

SUMMARY: Based on the true World War II story of the British Navy's all-out campaign to sink the most powerful battleship afloat in the Atlantic, the *Bismarck*. Much of this story is told from the point of view of officers at British Naval Headquarters in London, especially Capt. Shepherd, the director of operations. After the *Bismarck* sinks the HMS *Hood*, the best ship in the British fleet, Shepherd convinces the admirals to bring in air power. They summon the aircraft carrier the *Arc Royal*, whose air attacks cripple the *Bismarck*, damaging the huge battleship's ability to steer. Then the rest of Britain's surface fleet closes in and sinks her.

Film's Treatment of Masculinity: It's not always the dashing line officers who win wars: Those who plan and create the strategy are equally responsible for victory.

***Ski Troop Attack* (1960)**

Director: Roger Corman

Screenplay: Charles B. Griffith

Cast: Michael Forest, Frank Wolff, Wally Campo, Richard Sinatra, James Hoffman

DVD: Various distributors

Summary: In the winter of 1944, a U.S. Army reconnaissance patrol is behind enemy lines on skis. They discover an important railroad bridge that must be destroyed, but the young lieutenant in charge must first deal with a cynical sergeant before he can complete his mission.

Film's Treatment of Masculinity: Leadership in the face of defiant subordinates demands unusual toughness and an unwillingness to compromise the mission.

***Stalag 17* (1953)**

Director: Billy Wilder

Screenplay: Billy Wilder, Edwin Blum, based on the play by Donald Bevan and Edmund Trzcinski

Cast: William Holden, Otto Preminger, Peter Graves, Sig Ruman, Don Taylor, Robert Strauss, Harvey Lembeck, Neville Brand

Academy Award Win: Best Leading Actor (William Holden)

Academy Award Nominations: Best Director (Billy Wilder), Best Supporting Actor (Robert Strauss)

DVD: Paramount

Summary: In every prisoner of war camp, there's a "scrounger," a black marketeering soldier who can get you anything you want, usually for a price. Sgt. Sefton is the scrounger of Stalag 17. Not popular with the men because he's all business and no charity, Sefton is barely tolerated. But all goes well for Sefton until men from the barracks are shot while trying to escape. The prisoners assume that since Sefton trades with the Germans, as well as the prisoners, he's the traitor. After the men put him out of business and beat him badly, Sefton discovers that the true traitor is another prisoner, a spy planted in the barracks by the Germans. Appropriately, the men arrange for this spy to be "shot while trying to escape."

Film's Treatment of Masculinity: Forgetting that fighting men are a brotherhood and becoming a lone wolf puts everyone at risk.

***Star Trek II: The Wrath of Khan* (1982)**
DIRECTOR: Nicholas Meyer
SCREENPLAY: Jack B. Sowards, Harve Bennett
CAST: William Shatner, Leonard Nimoy, DeForest Kelley, James Doohan, Walter Koenig, George Takei, Nichelle Nichols, Ricardo Montalban
DVD: Paramount Pictures
SUMMARY: Adm. James T. Kirk is with Spock, who is now captain of the *Starship Enterprise*, surrounded by Starfleet Academy cadets on a training mission. Meanwhile, Khan, an old nemesis of Kirk's, has escaped from the planet where Kirk marooned him many years ago. Khan and his followers capture a device called Genesis that can be used either to turn solid rock planets into tropical paradises or destroy all existing life on a planet. Kirk sets out to retrieve this device from Khan or destroy it. Defeated and dying, Khan sets Genesis to explode. Spock sacrifices his life by exposing himself to deadly radiation to reengage the *Enterprise*'s engines and affect an escape from the explosion caused by Genesis.
FILM'S TREATMENT OF MASCULINITY: Men should never feel sorry for themselves for aging. Instead, men should look at maturity as a time to reinvent themselves and seek new challenges. Also, this film reminds men that the ultimate act, sacrificing one's self for his friends, is the ultimate act of manly virtue.

***The Steel Helmet* (1951)**
DIRECTOR: Samuel Fuller
SCREENPLAY: Samuel Fuller
CAST: Gene Evans, Robert Hutton, Steve Brodie, James Edwards, Richard Loo, Sid Melton, Richard Monahan, William Chun
DVD: Criterion
SUMMARY: A prisoner left by the North Koreans for dead with a bullet hole in his helmet, Sgt. Zack has a headache. But he's tied up. An orphaned Korean boy happens along and unties him. The hard-bitten, cynical Zack now has a companion, whether he wants one or not. They hook up with an army squad led by an inexperienced lieutenant. The squad is tasked with occupying a Buddhist temple located strategically on high ground. Unfortunately, the North Koreans also want the temple, and a terrible battle ensues. During the fighting, the boy is killed when a sniper mistakes him for a soldier. Zach, who has grown to care for the boy, is so angry he kills a North Korean prisoner, for which the lieutenant tells him he faces a court-martial. But in the final battle, the lieutenant and others are killed, and Zach, once again a survivor, and just a few others remain.

Film's Treatment of Masculinity: Men at war cannot close themselves off from their comrades. Missions are accomplished because men cooperate with one another, respect one another, and look out for one another.

***Stop-Loss* (2008)**

Director: Kimberly Peirce

Screenplay: Mark Richard, Kimberly Peirce

Cast: Ryan Philippe, Abbie Cornish, Channing Tatum, Joseph Gordon-Levitt, Rob Brown, Victor Rasuk, Terry Quay, Timothy Olyphant

DVD: Paramount Pictures

Summary: Brandon King, a war hero, and his army buddies return to their small Texas hometown following their tours of duty in Iraq and get a parade. Brandon is looking forward to getting on with his life and forgetting everything that happened in the Middle East. Haunted by civilian deaths and his own buddies' deaths in combat, he sees some of his comrades succumb to post-traumatic stress disorder. Then, against his will, the army uses their "stop-loss" program (read a nondraft draft for veterans) to order him back into uniform and to deploy once again to Iraq. At first, he decides to head for Washington to get help from a friendly senator, but he changes course a few more times and ends up back at home, resigned to his fate as cannon fodder once again.

Film's Treatment of Masculinity: Honor demands that a soldier maintains his, even when the army goes back on theirs.

***The Story of G.I. Joe* (1945)**

Director: William Wellman

Screenplay: Leopold Atlas, Guy Endore, Philip Stevenson, based on the writings of Ernie Pyle

Cast: Burgess Meredith, Robert Mitchum, Freddie Steele, Wally Cassell, Jimmy Lloyd

Academy Award Nominations: Best Screenplay, Best Supporting Actor (Robert Mitchum), Best Original Song, Best Scoring of a Dramatic or Comedy Picture

DVD: Image Entertainment

Summary: This Oscar-nominated film is a tribute to both Pulitzer Prize-winning war correspondent Ernie Pyle and the infantry soldiers he wrote about. Pyle followed the same company through their battles in North Africa and then rejoined them in Italy as they fought at San Vittorio and Monte Casino. The picture shows how even the most imposing soldiers can suffer combat fatigue, how lonely command of a company can be, and how very human and fragile men are, even when they must be at their toughest.

FILM'S TREATMENT OF MASCULINITY: Men at war become closer than at any other time or during any other circumstance. The needs of many outweigh the needs of a few or one.

***The Sullivans* (1944)**

DIRECTOR: Lloyd Bacon

SCREENPLAY: Mary C. McCall Jr.

STORY: Edward Doherty, Jules Schermer

CAST: Anne Baxter, Thomas Mitchell, Selena Royle, Ward Bond, Bobby Driscoll, Edward Ryan, John Campbell, James Cardwell, John Alvin, George Offerman

ACADEMY AWARD NOMINATION: Best Original Story

DVD: VCI Video

SUMMARY: This Oscar-nominated film and U.S. wartime propaganda film, loosely based on true events, chronicles the lives of the five Sullivan brothers, the U.S. Navy's greatest single-family loss during World War II. All died serving aboard the light cruiser USS *Juneau*; however, in reality, some of the brothers, along with much of the crew of the *Juneau*, probably died in the water, waiting for rescue planes and ships that didn't arrive for two days after the ship sank. The film puts a more dramatic, heroic ending on it: Four of the brothers drown when they go back down below decks to rescue one brother trapped there.

FILM'S TREATMENT OF MASCULINITY: True men are willing to sacrifice all for the sake of a brother.

***Take the High Ground* (1953)**

DIRECTOR: Richard Brooks

SCREENPLAY: Millard Kaufman

CAST: Richard Widmark, Karl Malden, Elaine Stewart, Carleton Carpenter, Russ Tamblyn, Jerome Courtland, Steve Forrest, Robert Arthur

ACADEMY AWARD NOMINATION: Best Screenplay

SUMMARY: This Oscar-nominated work is the usual GI-issue basic training movie, circa 1953. A tough-as-nails drill instructor, Ryan, who wishes he was back fighting in Korea, and his friend, Holt, another sergeant, are assigned a new group of recruits. Stuck with training duty, Ryan decides if he's going to be stuck with the job, he's going to train the men hard and prepare them well for combat. There is a love triangle between the two drill instructors and a woman in town, and, as in every basic training film, there is an obligatory underachiever recruit who requires special attention from Ryan. Eventually, neither drill instructor gets the woman, and they finish their job of training their platoon, ready to start the same day with a new gaggle of raw recruits.

Film's Treatment of Masculinity: Part of the responsibility of the seasoned fighting man is to train new troops to survive in battle.

***Target Tokyo* (1945)**

Director: Uncredited (U.S. Army Air Forces First Motion Picture Unit)

Cast: Narrated by Ronald Reagan

DVD or VHS: Unavailable

Summary: This is a documentary short about the first B-29 Superfortress bombing raid on Tokyo by the U.S. Army Air Corps. The film follows flyers from the United States to the island of Saipan in the Northern Mariana Islands, to their successful bombing raid on the Nakajima aircraft plant outside Tokyo.

Film's Treatment of Masculinity: Men working together to achieve important goals win wars.

***Task Force* (1949)**

Director: Delmer Daves

Screenplay: Delmer Daves

Cast: Gary Cooper, Jane Wyatt, Walter Brennan, Wayne Morris, Bruce Bennett, Julie London, Jack Holt, John Ridgely

DVD: Warner Archives

Summary: From the uncertain and dangerous outset flying planes off the first U.S. aircraft carrier, the USS *Langley*, Jonathan Scott, a naval aviator, spends the next twenty-seven years promoting the idea of naval aviation to a mostly hostile crowd of admirals and politicians who are stuck on the belief that naval power begins and ends with battleships. Finally, after the Japanese sink so many battleships at Pearl Harbor with air power, the naysayers are ready to listen, and Scott helps guide the navy into the future.

Film's Treatment of Masculinity: Sometimes a man who knows he's right must endure great adversity to achieve his goal. But an important goal requires patience and perseverance.

***Tears of the Sun* (2003)**

Director: Antoine Fuqua

Screenplay: Alex Lasker, Patrick Cirillo

Cast: Bruce Willis, Monica Bellucci, Cole Hauser, Eamonn Walker, Johnny Messner, Charles Ingram, Tom Skerritt

DVD: Sony Pictures

Summary: In the middle of a bloody Nigerian civil war, a group of U.S. Navy SEALs must choose between following orders to evacuate only one white woman, a Doctors without Borders physician, versus disobediently protecting a village full of people slated for extermination by rebels. The men choose humanity instead of obeying higher authority and, at the cost of some of their lives, protect and escort everyone to safety.

Film's Treatment of Masculinity: Sometimes a man is conscience bound to disobey orders, especially a man who regrets not disobeying a few orders in the past.

They Were Expendable **(1945)**

Director: John Ford

Screenplay: Frank Wead, based on the book by William L. White

Cast: Robert Montgomery, John Wayne, Donna Reed, Ward Bond, Marshall Thompson, Leon Ames

DVD: Warner Home Video

Summary: Based on a true story, at the outset of World War II, PT boats had not yet been used in combat, and, at first, the navy, barely holding onto the Philippines, had no use for them. But Lt. Brickley and Lt. Ryan continue to hope that they will get their chance on a PT boat, and finally they do. Sinking an amazing amount of enemy tonnage, the small, fast, and effective PTs help delay the Japanese takeover of the islands. Finally Brickley, Ryan, and a few other PT officers are ordered to Australia and then back to the United States to teach others PT boat tactics.

Film's Treatment of Masculinity: As Samuel Milton wrote, "They also serve who only stand and wait."

The Thin Red Line **(1998)**

Director: Terrence Malick

Screenplay: Terrence Malick, based on the novel by James Jones

Cast: James Caviezel, Sean Penn, Adrien Brody, Ben Chaplin, Nick Nolte, Elias Koteas, John Cusack, Woody Harrelson, George Clooney

DVD: Criterion

Summary: Terrence Malick's artful, highly visual, Oscar-nominated adaptation of the James Jones novel begins following one soldier in particular, Pvt. Witt, as his army company takes over for the marines to clear Japanese off the island of Guadalcanal during World War II. Malick eventually explores other soldiers' stories, but we first learn that Witt is not really a fighter and that he sometimes gets in the mood to go AWOL just to smell the roses. His company commander is in conflict with their ambitious battalion commanding officer, more concerned with taking the high ground than conserving the lives of his men. Finally, they take the Japanese position, but Witt ends up in the wrong place at the wrong time and is killed.

ACADEMY AWARD NOMINATIONS: Best Picture, Best Director (Terrence Malick), Best Screenplay Adaptation, Best Film Editing, Best Sound, Best Original Score, Best Cinematography

FILM'S TREATMENT OF MASCULINITY: There are circumstances when leaders must disobey orders and ignore the mission for the good of their men.

***Thirty Seconds over Tokyo* (1944)**

DIRECTOR: Mervyn LeRoy

SCREENPLAY: Dalton Trumbo, based on the book by Ted W. Lawson and Robert Considine

CAST: Van Johnson, Phyllis Thaxter, Robert Walker, Tim Murdock, Don DeFore, Herbert Gunn, Robert Mitchum, Spencer Tracy

DVD: Warner Home Video

SUMMARY: From pilot Ted W. Lawson's book, this is the factual story of the Doolittle Raid, the daring bombing mission on the Japanese mainland in retaliation for Pearl Harbor. Told through the eyes of Lawson, who commanded the B-25 "The Ruptured Duck," the story follows these flyers as they train for the mission, conduct the raid, crash land in China, and are rescued by brave Chinese allies who prevent them from falling into the hands of the Japanese.

FILM'S TREATMENT OF MASCULINITY: Men who do their duty and care for each other are the greatest heroes of our time.

***This Land Is Mine* (1943)**

DIRECTOR: Jean Renoir

SCREENPLAY: Dudley Nichols

CAST: Charles Laughton, Maureen O'Hara, George Sanders, Walter Slezak, Kent Smith

VHS: Warner Home Video

SUMMARY: Mamby-pamby Albert Lory is afraid of his own shadow, and while the Germans occupy his French town during World War II, he avoids trouble and involvement in the Resistance. But when the Germans apprehend and kill his mentor and father figure for publishing an underground newspaper, Lory grows a backbone. He speaks out against the Germans, sealing his fate. But before he is arrested, he passes on the *French Declaration of the Rights of Man* to his students.

FILM'S TREATMENT OF MASCULINITY: It is never too late for a man to set aside his fears and show courage in the face of the enemy.

***To End All Wars* (2001)**
Director: David L. Cunningham
Screenplay: Brian Godawa, based on the book by Ernest Gordon
Cast: Robert Carlyle, Kiefer Sutherland, Ciarán McMenamin, Mark Strong, Yugo Saso, Sakae Kimura
DVD: 20th Century Fox
Summary: This is a factual World War II story of Allied prisoners of war who suffer brutal treatment by the Japanese as they are forced to build a railroad through the Burmese jungle. Little by little, the character and charity of these mostly Scottish POWs gains the grudging respect of their captors. Finally, after the prisoners study the Bible, most manage to forgive their enemies.
Film's Treatment of Masculinity: Sometimes it takes greater courage to forgive and forego vengeance than to strike out against a savage enemy.

***Top Gun* (1986)**
Director: Tony Scott
Screenplay: Jim Cash, Jack Epps Jr.
Cast: Tom Cruise, Kelly McGillis, Val Kilmer, Anthony Edwards, Tom Skerritt, Meg Ryan
Academy Award Win: Best Original Song
Academy Award Nominations: Best Film Editing, Best Sound Effects Editing, Best Sound
DVD: Paramount Pictures
Summary: Suffering from an advanced case of testosterone poisoning, a group of navy aviators train and compete at Miramar Naval Air Station at the Top Gun Naval Flying School. The best pilot in his class, nicknamed "Maverick," whose pilot father crashed in Vietnam under suspicious circumstances, has more to prove than the rest. Maverick's erratic yet excellent flying record at the school and his chance to win the Top Gun trophy suffer a setback when "Goose," his "rear" (electronic warfare officer who sits in the seat behind the pilot) is killed in an accident. After graduation, once again flying off an aircraft carrier in the Indian Ocean, Maverick manages to put aside his grief over Goose's loss, distinguishing himself in actual aerial combat.
Film's Treatment of Masculinity: A fighting man must mature to achieve his goals.

***Tribes* (1970)**
Director: Joseph Sargent
Screenplay: Tracy Keenan Wynn, Marvin Schwartz

Cast: Darren McGavin, Earl Holliman, Jan-Michael Vincent, John Gruber, Danny Goldman

VHS: Fox Home Entertainment

Summary: Winner of three Emmys, including Outstanding Writing Achievement in Drama, this made-for-television movie pits a marine drill instructor against a hippie drafted into the U.S. Marine Corps during the Vietnam War. Disgusted with the idea of draftees in his beloved Corps, the drill instructor is even more appalled by the hippie and his Zen Buddhism. But, little by little, the hippie's gentle ways win over most of the company, and even the drill instructor begins to appreciate the personal calm and sense of oneness that result.

Film's Treatment of Masculinity: A smart leader should never be so rigid that he can't learn new ways.

***Twelve O'Clock High* (1949)**

Director: Henry King

Screenplay: Sy Bartlett, Beirne Lay Jr., based on their novel

Cast: Gregory Peck, Hugh Marlowe, Gary Merrill, Millard Mitchell, Dean Jagger

Academy Award Wins: Best Supporting Actor (Dean Jagger), Best Sound

Academy Award Nominations: Best Picture, Best Leading Actor (Gregory Peck)

DVD: 20th Century Fox

Summary: As the air war over Germany in World War II yields heavier losses, a "hard luck" bomber group gets a change in command as a new, tough-as-nails commander is given the job of shaping up the group. He replaces a commander who made the mistake of getting too close to his men, preventing him from making hard decisions. At first at odds with the men of the group, the general eventually wins them over. But he, too, learns to care too much, and it leads him to a mental breakdown.

Film's Treatment of Masculinity: A commanding officer's duty often means deciding to order men into battle and to their deaths. Manliness requires that these decisions be made.

***U-571* (2000)**

Director: Jonathan Mostow

Screenplay: Jonathan Mostow, Sam Montgomery, David Ayer

Cast: Matthew McConaughey, Bill Paxton, Harvey Keitel, Jon Bon Jovi, David Keith

DVD: Universal Studios

Summary: This is the historically inaccurate and wildly unbelievable World War II story of U.S. submariners who capture a heavily damaged German U-boat but somehow manage to sink another U-boat and German destroyer. This enables them to bring back a German cipher machine and all of its codes without letting the Germans find out that they did it. These submariners also manage to do all this with a highly inexperienced officer in charge, who at one point nearly avoids shooting a crew member to avert a mutiny.

FILM'S TREATMENT OF MASCULINITY: An officer, even one who is secretly unsure of himself, must sound like a leader to his men, or he earns no respect.

***Up Periscope* (1959)**

DIRECTOR: Gordon Douglas

SCREENPLAY: Richard H. Landau, based on the novel by Robb White

CAST: James Garner, Edmond O'Brien, Andra Martin, Alan Hale Jr., Edd Byrnes

DVD: Warner Home Video

SUMMARY: During World War II, a navy lieutenant in training to become a frogman is surprised to learn that the woman he's in love with has been investigating him to see if he's right for a top-secret assignment, an assignment that turns out to be quite risky: A submarine will convey him to a Japanese-held island, where he must sneak ashore, infiltrate the enemy camp, and photograph secret codes.

FILM'S TREATMENT OF MASCULINITY: Good training, daringness, and courage are required to achieve victory.

***Vietnam War Story* ("The Pass") (HBO miniseries, 1987)**

DIRECTOR: Kevin Hooks

SCREENPLAY: Patrick Sheane Duncan, Ronald Rubin

CAST: Tony Becker, Merritt Butrick, Hetty Edwards, Bill Nunn, Wendell Pierce

DVD: HBO Home Video

SUMMARY: This is a HBO miniseries episode that takes place in a sleazy bar/brothel in Vietnam. A REMF misrepresents himself as a combat soldier as he and two combat soldiers spend an evening getting drunk, fighting, making up, and eventually singing songs. Unfortunately, the bar is frequented by Americans during the day and the Viet Cong at night. The soldiers don't obey the curfew and have to lie low when the Viet Cong arrive. Later, while trying to sneak out, they awaken the drunken enemy, and the REMF is killed.

FILM'S TREATMENT OF MASCULINITY: Many young men yearn for battle but are not assigned to fight. But they should never represent themselves as warriors. It's dishonest, and those who have been bloodied in battle deeply resent it.

***Von Ryan's Express* (1965)**
Director: Mark Robson
Screenplay: Wendell Mayes, based on the novel by David Westheimer
Cast: Frank Sinatra, Trevor Howard, Raffaella Carrà, Sergio Fantoni, Brad Dexter, Edward Mulhare, Adolfo Celi, James Brolin
DVD: 20th Century Fox
Summary: Col. Joseph Ryan, a newly arrived senior POW in an Italian prison camp during World War II, is much more of a humanist than his second in command, a British officer. When Italy surrenders to the Allies and the Italian guards desert their posts, the freed prisoners want to kill Col. Battaglia, the Italian commander, who beat and starved the former POW senior officer. Ryan says no and simply confines Battaglia. Unfortunately, as the prisoners try to escape to friendly territory, Battaglia leads a force of Germans to recapture the prisoners. Put on board a train headed for a stalag in Germany, Ryan and his men overcome the guards and take it over, rerouting the train once more to friendly territory.
Film's Treatment of Masculinity: In military leadership, rigidity and an unwillingness to compromise cost lives.

***Wake Island* (1942)**
Director: John Farrow
Screenplay: W. R. Burnett, Frank Butler
Cast: Brian Donlevy, Macdonald Carey, Robert Preston, William Bendix, Albert Dekker
Academy Award Nominations: Best Picture, Best Director (John Farrow), Best Supporting Actor (William Bendix), Best Original Screenplay
DVD: Universal Studios
Summary: An inspirational propaganda film for Americans during the early days of World War II, this is the story of the brave marine garrison on Wake Island in November of 1941. Greatly outnumbered and out-gunned, the marines hold off a Japanese invasion force for days and even sink a heavy cruiser before they are finally overrun.
Film's Treatment of Masculinity: Bravery in defense of a lost cause is even greater than assisting in a winning effort.

***A Walk in the Sun* (1945)**
Director: Lewis Milestone
Screenplay: Robert Rossen, based on the novel by Harry Brown
Cast: Dana Andrews, Richard Conte, Sterling Holloway, George Tyne, John Ireland, Lloyd Bridges, Norman Lloyd, Herbert Rudley, Huntz Hall

DVD: VCI Entertainment

SUMMARY: Based on the Harry Brown novel, a U.S. Army platoon lands on shore, joining the Allied 1943 invasion of Italy. After the deaths of its commander and top sergeant, the highest-ranked NCO takes over, leading his men inland toward a strategically located farmhouse, their objective for the day. But the sergeant has seen too many battles, and the stress of leadership overcomes him. Another sergeant steps up, takes command, and leads the platoon to completing their objective.

FILM'S TREATMENT OF MASCULINITY: No man is invincible; everyone has a breaking point. That doesn't make him a lesser soldier or a lesser man. He's just wounded another way.

***The War Lover* (1961)**

DIRECTOR: Philip Leacock

Screenplay: Howard Koch, based on the novel by John Hersey

CAST: Steve McQueen, Robert Wagner, Shirley Anne Field, Gary Cockrell, Michael Crawford

DVD: Sony Pictures

SUMMARY: Buzz Rickson is a great pilot, who, despite taking chances while on World War II bombing missions over Germany, always brings his plane—and his admiring aircrew—back alive. But his exceptional flying ability is all Buzz has going for him. His egotism and abrasive personality assure that his only friends are the loose women he relentlessly pursues when he's off duty. He even tries to seduce his own copilot's girlfriend. Eventually, Buzz's luck runs out, and, returning from a mission, his bomber is too badly shot up to return to base. He orders all the crew to bail out and then tries his luck once more, but this time he goes down with his ship.

FILM'S TREATMENT OF MASCULINITY: True masculinity is chivalrous and kind, reserving the macho element for his battles with the enemy.

***We Were Soldiers* (2002)**

DIRECTOR: Randall Wallace

SCREENPLAY: Randall Wallace, based on the book *We Were Soldiers Once . . . and Young* by Harold G. Moore and Joseph L. Galloway

CAST: Mel Gibson, Barry Pepper, Sam Elliott, Madeleine Stowe, Greg Kinnear, Chris Klein

DVD: Paramount Pictures

SUMMARY: This Vietnam War story, based on books by Harold G. Moore and Joseph L. Galloway, tells the story of the first major engagement between the North Vietnamese Army and the newly formed U.S. Army Air Cavalry. From time to time, the film cuts away to the home front, as the commander's wife and other officer's wives deal with comforting those whose husbands have been killed. Outnumbered five to one in a sector that became known as the "Valley of Death," the forces of the U.S. Army Air Cavalry—thanks to their cerebral commander's strategy and tactics and the great spirit of his men—overcome the enemy.

FILM'S TREATMENT OF MASCULINITY: A fighting man's worth is measured by both his brains and brawn. Smart planning and using one's experience wins battles.

***The Wild Bunch* (1969)**

DIRECTOR: Sam Peckinpah

SCREENPLAY: Walon Green, Sam Peckinpah, Roy N. Sickner

CAST: William Holden, Ernest Borgnine, Robert Ryan, Edmond O'Brien, Warren Oates, Ben Johnson, Jaime Sánchez, Strother Martin

ACADEMY AWARD NOMINATIONS: Best Screenplay, Best Original Score

DVD: Warner Home Video

SUMMARY: This anti-Western, Sam Peckinpah's most artistic and influential visual ballet of death, tells the tale of outlaws who have outlived their time. Shortly before World War I, the bunch, led by Pike Bishop, try for one last score, a bank robbery, but mercenaries paid to pursue and kill them were tipped off in advance. This leads to a bloodbath at the bank, in which a dozen townspeople are caught in the crossfire. Escaping to Mexico, the group decides to steal guns for an evil general whose army has occupied the town of Agua Verde. But the youngest member of the bunch angers the general when he shoots his former fiancé, who has become the general's mistress. The clan of outlaws won't stand for the general's torture of the young man, and, in a bloody finale, they battle the entire army to the last man.

FILM'S TREATMENT OF MASCULINITY: True men are loyal to the members of their unit, and they support them to the end.

***Windtalkers* (2002)**

DIRECTOR: John Woo

SCREENPLAY: John Rice, Joe Batteer

CAST: Nicolas Cage, Adam Beach, Peter Stormare, Roger Willie, Noah Emmerich, Mark Ruffalo, Christian Slater

DVD: MGM

SUMMARY: Decorated U.S. Marine Joe Enders suffers from hearing loss, as well as post-traumatic shock, after his stubborn refusal to disobey orders causes the death of his entire squad in the Allied campaign to take Guadalcanal during World War II. He fakes a hearing test so he can return to duty, presumably to atone for surviving. Enders's next assignment is to protect another marine, a Native American "windtalker," who uses a coded version of the Navajo language to communicate during combat via radio to avoid the Japanese intercepting their messages. Still in pain over the orders that caused his men to die the last time, Enders is conflicted by his new orders, which include killing his marine windtalker, rather than let him be captured and tortured for the code. This time, although at the cost of his life, Enders refuses to do his duty, sparing his windtalker's life when it looks like the Japanese are closing in.

FILM'S TREATMENT OF MASCULINITY: Sometimes a leader is honor bound to not blindly obey orders. Then he lives with the consequences.

***A Wing and a Prayer* (1944)**

DIRECTOR: Henry Hathaway

SCREENPLAY: Jerome Cady

CAST: Don Ameche, Dana Andrews, William Eythe, Charles Bickford, Sir Cedric Hardwicke, Richard Jaeckel

ACADEMY AWARD NOMINATION: Best Original Screenplay

DVD: 20th Century Fox

SUMMARY: A World War II U.S. aircraft carrier has an unusual set of orders: Steam all over the Pacific and allow itself to be spotted by the Japanese, but avoid a fight at all costs. This tactic was designed to convince the Japanese that the United States had carriers all over the Pacific, but that the United States was not as spoiling for a fight as the carrier's crew was. But regardless of the crew's dislike of their mission, orders are orders, and while the rest of the fleet was recovering from Pearl Harbor and preparing for what was to be the Battle of Midway, it was this carrier's job to confuse the enemy.

FILM'S TREATMENT OF MASCULINITY: Sometimes orders, no matter how difficult, must be followed if the mission is to succeed.

***Wings* (1927)**

DIRECTOR: William Wellman

SCREENPLAY: Hope Loring, Louis D. Lighton

STORY: John Monk Saunders

CAST: Buddy Rogers, Richard Arlen, Clara Bow, Jobyna Ralston, Gary Cooper, Roscoe Karns

ACADEMY AWARD WINS: Best Picture, Best Effects

VHS: Paramount Pictures

SUMMARY: This Oscar-winning film tells the story of two young Americans who leave their love lives behind in pursuit of glory in the skies as World War I fighter pilots. Unwilling to let her beau run away to war without her, Mary (Bow) signs up to be a nurse and follows her man to the front lines. The melodramatic story confirms that war is hell, air battles are final, and that in spite of goodness, not every hero comes home.

FILM'S TREATMENT OF MASCULINITY: It's not unmasculine to love a comrade-in-arms.

***Winning Your Wings* (1942)**

DIRECTOR: John Huston

SCREENPLAY: Owen Crump

CAST: James Stewart, Jean Ames, Leah Baird, Don DeFore, Charles Drake

ACADEMY AWARD NOMINATION: Best Documentary

DVD: Warner Home Video (as an extra on Larceny, Inc.)

SUMMARY: This is an Oscar-nominated recruiting film for flying officers in the U.S. Army Air Force during World War II.

FILM'S TREATMENT OF MASCULINITY: Young men seeking adventure should become flyers.

Bibliography

Adler, Max. "Tired of Being the Short Hitter?" *Golf Digest* (November 2010), 67.

American Heritage Dictionary, 4th ed. New York: Delta, 2001.

American Psychiatric Association. *Diagnostic and Statistical Manual of Mental Disorders*, 4th ed. Washington, D.C.: APA Press, 1994.

Azar, Beth. "Science Watch: A Case for Angry Men and Happy Women." *Monitor on Psychology*, 38, 4 (April 2007), 18.

Balswick, Jack O., and Charles W Peek. "The Inexpressive Male: A Tragedy of American Society." In Deborah S. David and Robert Brannon (eds.), *The Forty-Nine Per Cent Majority: The Male Sex Role*. New York: Random House, 1976.

Bandura, A. *Social Learning Theory*. New York: General Learning Press, 1977.

Barcus, F. E. *Images of Life on Children's Television*. New York: Praeger, 1983.

Basinger, Jeanine. *The World War II Combat Film: Anatomy of a Genre*. New York: Columbia University Press, 1986.

Black, Donald. *Bad Boys, Bad Men: Confronting Antisocial Personality Disorder*. New York: Oxford University Press, 1999.

Bourne, Edmund J. *The Anxiety and Phobia Workbook*. Oakland, CA: New Harbinger Publishers, 2005.

Boxwell, David. "Howard Hawks." Accessed September 12, 2010, from www.sensesofcinema.com/contents/directors/02/hawks.html.

Brothers, Barbara Jo. *The Abuse of Men: Trauma Begets Trauma*. New York: Haworth Press, 2001.

Carlin, George. *Braindroppings*. New York: Hyperion, 1997.

Carpenter, Ronald H. "America's Tragic Metaphor: Our Twentieth-Century Combatants as Frontiersmen." *Quarterly Journal of Speech* 9 (1990), 1–22.

Coleman, Penny. *Flashback: Post-Traumatic Stress Disorder, Suicide, and the Lessons of War*. Boston: Beacon Press, 2007.

Cooper, James F. *The Last of the Mohicans*. New York: Charles Scribner's Sons, 1919.

Creedon, Pam. The Super Bowl and War: Theater for the Masculine Myth in Democracy. An unpublished paper presented to the Sports Interest Division, International Association of Mass Communication Research, Port Alegre, Brazil, 2004.

David, Deborah S., and Robert Brannon, eds. *The Forty-Nine Per Cent Majority: The Male Sex Role*. New York: Random House, 1976.

Doherty, Thomas. *Projections of War: Hollywood, American Culture, and World War II*. New York: Columbia University Press, 1993.

Donald, Ralph R. "Conversion as Persuasive Convention in American War Films." In Paul Loukides and Linda Fuller (eds.), *Beyond the Stars II: Plot Convention in American Popular Film*. Bowling Green, OH: Bowling Green University Popular Press, 1991.

Drew, Julie. "Identity Crisis: Gender, Public Discourse, and 9/11." *Women and Language* 27, 2 (2004), 71.

Easthope, Anthony. *What a Man's Gotta Do: The Masculine Myth in Popular Culture*. New York: Routledge, Chapman and Hall, 1990.

Ebert, Michael, Peter T. Loosen, and Barry Nurcombe. *Current Diagnosis and Treatment in Psychiatry*. New York: McGraw-Hill, 2000.

Farrell, Warren. "The Politics of Vulnerability." In Deborah S. David and Robert Brannon (eds.), *The Forty-Nine Per Cent Majority: The Male Sex Role*. New York: Random House, 1976.

Fasteau, Marc F. "Vietnam and the Cult of Toughness in Foreign Policy." In Deborah S. David and Robert Brannon (eds.), *The Forty-Nine Per Cent Majority: The Male Sex Role*. New York: Random House, 1976.

Fejes, Fred. "Images of Men in Media Research." *Critical Studies in Mass Communication* (June 1989), 215–21.

Fiddick, Thomas. "Beyond the Domino Theory: Vietnam and Metaphors of Sport." *Journal of American Culture* 12 (1989), 79–88.

Frayser, Suzanne G. *Varieties of Sexual Experience: An Anthropological Perspective on Human Sexuality*. New Haven, CT: HRAF Press, 1985.

Groth, Nicholas A. *Men Who Rape: The Psychology of the Offender*. Cambridge, MA: DeCapo Press, 2001.

Hacker, Helen. "The New Burdens of Masculinity." *Marriage and Family Living* 19 (1957), 231.

Hartley, Ruth E. "Sex-Role Pressures and the Socialization of the Male Child." In Deborah S. David and Robert Brannon (eds.), *The Forty-Nine Per Cent Majority: The Male Sex Role*. New York: Random House, 1976.

Hendin, H., and A. P. Haas. "Suicide and Guilt as Manifestation of PTSD in Vietnam Combat Veterans." *American Journal of Psychiatry* 148 (1991), 586–91.

Hoch, Paul. "School for Sexism." In D. F. Sabo Jr. and Ross Runfola (eds.), *Jock: Sports and Male Identity*. Englewood Cliffs, N.J.: Prentice-Hall, 1980.

Internet Movie Database. "Mark Fleetwood." Accessed September 12, 2010, from www.imdb.com/title/tt0063585/plotsummary.

Jeffords, Susan. *The Remasculinization of America: Gender and the Vietnam War*. Bloomington: Indiana University Press, 1989.

Jenkins, Dan. *You Gotta Play Hurt*. New York: Simon & Schuster, 1991.

Jung, Carl. *Analytical Psychology: Its Theory and Practice*. New York: Random House, 1968.

Kimmel, Michael S. *Changing Men: New Directions in Research on Men and Masculinity*. Newbury Park, CA: Sage, 1987.

Kipling, Rudyard. *Rewards and Fairies*. New York: Doubleday, 1914.

Komisar, Lucy. "Violence and the Masculine Mystique." In Deborah S. David and Robert Brannon (eds.), *The Forty-Nine Percent Majority: The Male Sex Role*. New York: Random House, 1976.

Kübler-Ross, Elisabeth. *On Death and Dying*. New York: Macmillan, 1969.

Leed, Eric J. "Violence, Death, and Masculinity." *Vietnam Generation* 1 (1989), 168–89.

LyricsFreak. Accessed September 12, 2010, www.lyricsfreak.com/q/queen/we+are+the+champions_20112595.html.

Mahler, Margaret S., Fred Pine, and Anni Bergman. *The Psychological Birth of the Human Infant*. New York: Basic Books, 1975.

Matsakis, Aphrodite. *Back from the Front: Combat, Trauma, Love, and the Family*. Baltimore, MD: Sidran Institute Press, 2007.

McBride, Joseph. *Hawks on Hawks*. Berkeley: University of California Press, 1982.

Mellen, Joan. *Big Bad Wolves: Masculinity and the American Film*. New York: Pantheon, 1977.

Miller, Alice Duer. "Why We Oppose Votes for Men." In Deborah S. David and Robert Brannon (eds.), *The Forty-Nine Percent Majority: The Male Sex Role*. New York: Random House, 1976.

Newman, Simon. "Is That You, John Wayne? Is This Me? Myth and Meaning in American Representations of the Vietnam War." *American Studies Online*, March 27, 2007. Accessed September 12, 2010, from www.americansc.org.uk/Online/Newman.htm.

Nietzsche, Friedrich. *Thus Spake Zarathustra*, trans. Thomas Cannon. Mineola, N.Y.: Dover Publications, 1999.

O'Brien, Tim. *The Things They Carried*. New York: Broadway Books, 1998.

Parkinson, Frank. *Post-Traumatic Stress Disorder/Prevention*. Cambridge MA: DeCapo Press, 2000.

Person, Ethel S., Arnold M. Cooper, and Glen O. Gabbard. *American Psychiatric Publishing Textbook of Psychoanalysis*. Washington, DC, and London: American Psychiatric Publishing, 2005.

Peter, Laurence J., and Raymond Hull. *The Peter Principle*. New York: Bantam Books, 1970.

Pudovkin, Vsevolod Illarionovich. *Film Technique and Film Acting: The Cinema Writings of V. I. Pudovkin*. London: Vision, 1954.

Quotations Page. "Thomas Fuller." Accessed September 12, 2010, from www.quotationspage.com/quotes/Thomas_Fuller/.

Richards, Davis. *Identity and the Case for Gay Rights: Race, Gender, and Religion as Analogies*. Chicago: University of Chicago Press, 1999.

Roy, Michael J. *Approaches to the Diagnosis and Treatment of Posttraumatic Stress*. Lancaster, U.K.: IOS Press, 2006.

Sabo, Donald F., and Ross Runfola, eds. *Jock: Sports and Male Identity*. Englewood Cliffs, N.J.: Prentice-Hall, 1980.

Scaer, Robert. *The Trauma Spectrum: Hidden Words and Human Resiliency*. New York: W. W. Norton and Co., 2005.

Schickel, Richard. "The Burden of Heroes." *Time* (October 23, 2006), 81.

Schultz, William T. *Handbook of Psychobiography*. New York: Oxford University Press, 2005.

Shakespeare, William. *Henry V*. New York: Oxford University Press. 2002.

———. *The Tragedy of Julius Caesar*. New York: Oxford University Press, 2002.

Shatan, Chaim F. "Happiness Is a Warm Gun: Militarized Mourning and Ceremonial Vengeance." *Vietnam Generation* 1 (1989), 127–51.

Smith, Julian. *Looking Away: Hollywood and Vietnam*. New York: Scribner, 1975.

Smith, Lorrie. "Back against the Wall: Anti-Feminist Backlash in Vietnam War Literature." *Vietnam Generation* 1 (1989), 127–519.

Smith, M. K. "Bruce W. Tuckman: Forming, Storming, Norming, and Performing in Groups." *Encyclopedia of Informal Education*, 2005. Accessed September 19, 2010, from www.infed.org/thinkers/tuckman.htm.

Stouffer, Samuel A. "Masculinity and the Role of the Combat Soldier." In Deborah S. David and Robert Brannon (eds.), *The Forty-Nine Per Cent Majority: The Male Sex Role*. New York: Random House, 1976.

Tennyson, Alfred, Lord. "The Charge of the Light Brigade." *London Examiner* (December 9, 1854).

Tiger, Lionel. *Men in Groups*. New York: Random House, 1970.

Top-Flite. Accessed September 19, 2010, from www.theballstogoforit.com/base.html.

U.S. Department of the Army. *U.S. Army Combat Stress Control Handbook*. Guilford, CT: Lyons Press, 2003.

Van Gennep, Arnold. *The Rites Of Passage*. Chicago: University of Chicago Press, 1960.

Von Clausewitz, Carl. *On War*. New York: Oxford University Press, 2007.

Weiner, Hilary R. "Group-Level and Individual-Level Mediators of the Relationship between Soldier Satisfaction with Social Support and Performance Motivation." *Military Psychology* 2, 1 (1990), 21–32.

Wise, E. Tayloe. *Eleven Bravo: A Skytrooper Memoir of War in Vietnam*. Jefferson, N.C.: McFarland, 2004.

Index

Note: Page numbers in italics refer to photographs.

About the Authors

Ralph Donald is professor of mass communications at Southern Illinois University, Edwardsville. He has taught broadcasting, journalism, and film at the college level for thirty-six years. Professional credits include jobs as a newspaper reporter and copy editor, a radio and television news producer, TV station production manager, and a writer-producer-director of commercials and documentaries on film and video. Dr. Donald's research and publications include gender-related research in film and television, film and television propaganda, motion picture history, American studies, and pedagogical and curriculum issues in mass communications.

Clinical psychologist **Karen MacDonald** has been in private practice for twenty-six years. Besides counseling returning veterans suffering from post-traumatic stress disorder, Dr. MacDonald provides clinical psychological services to children, adolescents, and adults and conducts family therapy and group psychotherapy. Much of her focus has been in the areas of attention deficit disorder with hyperactivity, marital and conflict resolution, sexual trauma issues, and depression in children and adults. She has performed psychological evaluations for Missouri's Division of Family Services, attorneys, Head Start and school systems, Social Security Disability, and County Medical Assessment eligibility.

Dr. MacDonald and Dr. Donald (yes, the similar names often lead to confusion), who reside in Edwardsville, IL, are delighted (most of the time, anyway) to have eight children and eleven grandchildren.